Practice *Planners*®

W9-ANZ-469

Arthur E. Jongsma, Jr., Series Editor

Helping therapists help their clients . . .

Practice *Planners*

Second Edition

THE COMPLETE ADULT
PSYCHOTHERAPY
Treatment Planner

A new, fully revised edition of the bestselling *The Complete Psychotherapy Treatment Planner*, this invaluable resource features:

• Treatment plan components for 39 behaviorally based problems—including five completely new problem sets

• A step-by-step guide to writing treatment plans

• Over 900 additional prewritten treatment goals, objectives, and interventions

• Handy workbook format with space to record your own treatment plan options

• Over 100,000 *Practice Planners* sold

Arthur E. Jongsma, Jr., and L. Mark Peterson

Practice *Planners*

Arthur E. Jongsma, Jr., Series Editor

Brief Therapy
HOMEWORK
PLANNER

• Contains 62 ready-to-copy homework assignments that can be used to facilitate brief individual therapy

• Homework assignments and exercises are keyed to over 39 behaviorally-based presenting problems from *The Complete Psychotherapy Treatment Planner*

• Assignments may be quickly customized using the enclosed disk

• Over 100,000 *Practice Planners* sold

Gary M. Schultheis

Practice *Planners*®

The Clinical
DOCUMENTATION
SOURCEBOOK

Second Edition

A Comprehensive Collection of Mental Health Practice Forms, Handouts, and Records

FEATURES

• Contains ready-to-use forms for managing the mental health treatment process

• Covers every stage of the treatment process

• Includes customizable forms on disk

• Over 100,000 *Practice Planners* sold

Donald E. Wiger

Practice *Planners*

Arthur E. Jongsma, Jr., Series Editor

The Adult Psychotherapy
PROGRESS NOTES PLANNER

This time-saving resource:

• Contains Progress Notes components for 39 behaviorally based problems

• Covers the period of possible codes to fit many clinical/set suggested in the best-selling *Complete Adult Psychotherapy Treatment Planner, 2nd Edition*

• Includes 1,500 consistent the statement and patient responses or categories

• Provides a handy workbook format with space to record your own progress note options

• Over 150,000 *Practice Planners* sold

Arthur E. Jongsma, Jr.

WILEY

TheraScribe®

The Treatment Planning and Clinical Record Management System for Mental Health Professionals.

Spend More Time on Patients— Not Paperwork

TheraScribe®—the latest version of our popular treatment planning, patient record-keeping software. Facilitates intake/assessment reporting, progress monitoring, and outcomes analysis. Supports group treatment and multiprovider treatment teams. Compatible with our full array of **PracticePlanners**® libraries, including our *Treatment Planner* software versions.

- This bestselling, easy-to-use Windows®-based software allows you to generate fully customized psychotherapy treatment plans that meet the requirements of all major accrediting agencies and most third-party payers.

- In just minutes, this user-friendly program's on-screen help enables you to create customized treatment plans.

- Praised in the *National Psychologist* and *Medical Software Reviews,* this innovative software simplifies and streamlines record-keeping.

- Available for a single user, or in a network version, this comprehensive software package suits the needs of all practices—both large and small.

Treatment Planner Upgrade to TheraScribe®

The behavioral definitions, goals, objectives, and interventions from this *Treatment Planner* can be imported into TheraScribe®. For purchase and pricing information, please send in the coupon below or call 1-866-888-5158 or e-mail us at planners@wiley.com.

For more information about **TheraScribe**® or the Upgrade to this *Treatment Planner,* fill in this coupon and mail it to: R. Crucitt, John Wiley & Sons, Inc., 7222 Commerce Center Dr., Ste. 240, Colorado Springs, CO 80919 or e-mail us at planners@wiley.com.

❑ Please send me information on **TheraScribe**®

❑ Please send me information on the *Treatment Planner* Upgrade to **TheraScribe**®
Name of *Treatment Planner* _____

❑ Please send me information on the network version of **TheraScribe**®

Name _____

Affiliation _____

Address _____

City/State/Zip _____

Phone _____ E-mail _____

For a free demo, visit us on the web at: therascribe.wiley.com   ⊛ **WILEY**

Treatment Planners cover all the necessary elements for developing formal treatment plans, including detailed problem definitions, long-term goals, short-term objectives, therapeutic interventions, and DSM-IV™ diagnoses.

❑ **The Complete Adult Psychotherapy Treatment Planner,** Second Edition
0-471-31924-4 / $49.95

❑ **The Child Psychotherapy Treatment Planner,** Second Edition
0-471-34764-7 / $49.95

❑ **The Adolescent Psychotherapy Treatment Planner,** Second Edition
0-471-34766-3 / $49.95

❑ **The Addiction Treatment Planner,** Second Edition
0-471-41814-5 / $49.95

❑ **The Couples Psychotherapy Treatment Planner**
0-471-24711-1 / $49.95

❑ **The Group Therapy Treatment Planner**
0-471-37449-0 / $49.95

❑ **The Family Therapy Treatment Planner**
0-471-34768-X / $49.95

❑ **The Older Adult Psychotherapy Treatment Planner**
0-471-29574-4 / $49.95

❑ **The Employee Assistance (EAP) Treatment Planner**
0-471-24709-X / $49.95

❑ **The Gay and Lesbian Psychotherapy Treatment Planner**
0-471-35080-X / $49.95

❑ **The Crisis Counseling and Traumatic Events Treatment Planner**
0-471-39587-0 / $49.95

❑ **The Social Work and Human Services Treatment Planner**
0-471-37741-4 / $49.95

❑ **The Continuum of Care Treatment Planner**
0-471-19568-5 / $49.95

❑ **The Behavioral Medicine Treatment Planner**
0-471-31923-6 / $49.95

❑ **The Mental Retardation and Developmental Disability Treatment Planner**
0-471-38253-1 / $49.95

❑ **The Special Education Treatment Planner**
0-471-38872-6 / $49.95

❑ **The Severe and Persistent Mental Illness Treatment Planner**
0-471-35945-9 / $49.95

❑ **The Personality Disorders Treatment Planner**
0-471-39403-3 / $49.95

❑ **The Rehabilitation Psychology Treatment Planner**
0-471-35178-4 / $49.95

❑ **The Pastoral Counseling Treatment Planner**
0-471-25416-9 / $49.95

❑ **The Juvenile Justice and Residential Care Treatment Planner**
0-471-43320-9 / $49.95

❑ **The Psychiatric Evaluation & Psychopharmacology Treatment Planner**
0-471-43322-5 / $49.95 (available 2/02)

❑ **The Adult Corrections Treatment Planner**
0-471-20244-4 / $49.95 (available 6/02)

❑ **The School Counseling and School Social Work Treatment Planner**
0-471-08496-4 / $49.95 (available 8/02)

Progress Notes Planners contain complete prewritten progress notes for each presenting problem in the companion Treatment Planners.

❑ **The Adult Psychotherapy Progress Notes Planner**
0-471-34763-9 / $49.95

❑ **The Adolescent Psychotherapy Progress Notes Planner**
0-471-38104-7 / $49.95

❑ **The Child Psychotherapy Progress Notes Planner**
0-471-38102-0 / $49.95

❑ **The Addiction Progress Notes Planner**
0-471-10330-6 / $49.95

- -

Name_____

Affiliation_____

Address_____

City/State/Zip_____

Phone/Fax_____

E-mail_____

On the web: practiceplanners.wiley.com

To order, call 1-800-225-5945
(Please refer to promo #1-4019 when ordering.)
Or send this page with payment* to:
John Wiley & Sons, Inc., Attn: J. Knott
605 Third Avenue, New York, NY 10158-0012

❑ Check enclosed   ❑ Visa   ❑ MasterCard   ❑ American Express
Card #_____

Expiration Date_____

Signature_____

*Please add your local sales tax to all orders.

Practice Management Tools for Busy Mental Health Professionals

Homework Planners feature dozens of behaviorally based, ready-to-use assignments that are designed for use between sessions, as well as a disk (Microsoft Word) containing all of the assignments—allowing you to customize them to suit your unique client needs.

❑ **Brief Therapy Homework Planner**
0-471-24611-5 / $49.95

❑ **Brief Couples Therapy Homework Planner**
0-471-29511-6 / $49.95

❑ **Brief Child Therapy Homework Planner**
0-471-32366-7 / $49.95

❑ **Brief Adolescent Therapy Homework Planner**
0-471-34465-6 / $49.95

❑ **Chemical Dependence Treatment Homework Planner**
0-471-32452-3 / $49.95

❑ **Brief Employee Assistance Homework Planner**
0-471-38088-1 / $49.95

❑ **Brief Family Therapy Homework Planner**
0-471-385123-1 / $49.95

❑ **Grief Counseling Homework Planner**
0-471-43318-7 / $49.95

❑ **Divorce Counseling Homework Planner**
0-471-43319-5 / $49.95

❑ **Group Therapy Homework Planner**
0-471-41822-6 / $49.95

❑ **The School Counseling and School Social Work Homework Planner**
0-471-09114-6 / $49.95 (available 8/02)

Documentation Sourcebooks provide a comprehensive collection of ready-to-use blank forms, handouts, and questionnaires to help you manage your client reports and streamline the record keeping and treatment process. Features clear, concise explanations of the purpose of each form—including when it should be used and at what point. Includes customizable forms on disk.

❑ **The Clinical Documentation Sourcebook, Second Edition**
0-471-32692-5 / $49.95

❑ **The Psychotherapy Documentation Primer**
0-471-28990-6 / $45.00

❑ **The Couple and Family Clinical Documentation Sourcebook**
0-471-25234-4 / $49.95

❑ **The Clinical Child Documentation Sourcebook**
0-471-29111-0 / $49.95

❑ **The Chemical Dependence Treatment Documentation Sourcebook**
0-471-31285-1 / $49.95

❑ **The Forensic Documentation Sourcebook**
0-471-25459-2 / $95.00

❑ **The Continuum of Care Clinical Documentation Sourcebook**
0-471-34581-4 / $85.00

To order by phone, call TOLL FREE 1-800-225-5945

Or contact us at:
John Wiley & Sons, Inc., Attn: J. Knott
605 Third Avenue, New York, NY 10158-0012
Fax: 1-800-597-3299
Online: www.practiceplanners.wiley.com

WILEY

The
Family Therapy
Treatment Planner

PRACTICE *PLANNERS*™ SERIES

Treatment *Planners*

The Chemical Dependence Treatment Planner
The Continuum of Care Treatment Planner
The Couples Psychotherapy Treatment Planner
The Employee Assistance Treatment Planner
The Pastoral Counseling Treatment Planner
The Older Adult Psychotherapy Treatment Planner
The Complete Adult Psychotherapy Treatment Planner, Second Edition
The Behavioral Medicine Treatment Planner
The Group Therapy Treatment Planner
The Gay and Lesbian Psychotherapy Treatment Planner
The Child Psychotherapy Treatment Planner, Second Edition
The Adolescent Psychotherapy Treatment Planner, Second Edition
The Family Psychotherapy Treatment Planner
The Severe and Persistent Mental Illness Treatment Planner
The Mental Retardation and Developmental Disability Treatment Planner
The Neuropsychological Treatment Planner
The Social Work and Human Services Treatment Planner

Homework *Planners*

Brief Therapy Homework Planner
Brief Couples Therapy Homework Planner
Chemical Dependence Treatment Homework Planner
Brief Child Therapy Homework Planner
Brief Adolescent Therapy Homework Planner
Employee Assistance Homework Planner

Documentation *Sourcebooks*

The Clinical Documentation Sourcebook
The Forensic Documentation Sourcebook
The Psychotherapy Documentation Primer
The Chemical Dependence Treatment Documentation Sourcebook
The Clinical Child Documentation Sourcebook
The Couple and Family Clinical Documentation Sourcebook
The Clinical Documentation Sourcebook, Second Edition
The Continuum of Care Clinical Documentation Sourcebook

Presentation *Planners*

The Couples and Family Presentation Planner
The Life Skills Presentation Planner
The Work Skills Presentation Planner

Progress Notes *Planners*

The Adult Psychotherapy Progress Notes Planner
The Child Psychotherapy Progress Notes Planner
The Adolescent Psychotherapy Progress Notes Planner

The Family Therapy Treatment Planner

Frank M. Dattilio

Arthur E. Jongsma, Jr.

JOHN WILEY & SONS, INC.

New York • Chichester • Weinheim • Brisbane • Singapore • Toronto

This book is printed on acid-free paper.♾

Copyright © 2000 by John Wiley & Sons. All rights reserved.
Published simultaneously in Canada.

All references to diagnostic codes and the entire content of Appendix B are reprinted with permission from the *Diagnostic and Statistical Manual of Mental Disorders, Fourth Edition.* Copyright 1994, American Psychiatric Association.

No part of this publication may be reproduced, stored in a retrieval system or transmitted in any form or by any means, electronic, mechanical, photocopying, recording, scanning or otherwise, except as permitted under Sections 107 or 108 of the 1976 United States Copyright Act, without either the prior written permission of the Publisher, or authorization through payment of the appropriate per-copy fee to the Copyright Clearance Center, 222 Rosewood Drive, Danvers, MA 01923, (978) 750-8400, fax (978) 750-4744. Requests to the Publisher for permission should be addressed to the Permissions Department, John Wiley & Sons, Inc., 605 Third Avenue, New York, NY 10158-0012, (212) 850-6011, fax (212) 850-6008, E-Mail: PERMREQ@WILEY.COM.

This publication is designed to provide accurate and authoritative information in regard to the subject matter covered. It is sold with the understanding that the publisher is not engaged in rendering professional services. If legal, accounting, medical, psychological or any other expert assistance is required, the services of a competent professional person should be sought.

Designations used by companies to distinguish their products are often claimed as trademarks. In all instances where John Wiley & Sons, Inc. is aware of a claim, the product names appear in initial capital or all capital letters. Readers, however, should contact the appropriate companies for more complete information regarding trademarks and registration.

Note about Photocopy Rights

The publisher grants purchasers permission to reproduce handouts from this book for professional use with their clients.

ISBN 0-471-34768-X (book only)
ISBN 0-471-34769-8 (book with disk)

Printed in the United States of America.

10 9 8 7 6 5

To my wife Maryann and children Roseann, Tara, and Michael, who taught me most of what I need to know about families.

—Frank M. Dattilio

To Jennifer Byrne, who is my thoroughly organized, faithful assistant and a perseverant transcriptionist to whom I am sincerely grateful.

—Arthur E. Jongsma, Jr.

CONTENTS

PRACTICE *PLANNERS* SERIES PREFACE

The practice of psychotherapy has a dimension that did not exist 30, 20, or even 15 years ago—accountability. Treatment programs, public agencies, clinics, and even group and solo practitioners must now justify the treatment of patients to outside review entities that control the payment of fees. This development has resulted in an explosion of paperwork.

Clinicians must now document what has been done in treatment, what is planned for the future, and what the anticipated outcomes of the interventions are. The books and software in this Practice *Planners* series are designed to help practitioners fulfill these documentation requirements efficiently and professionally.

The Practice *Planners* series is growing rapidly. It now includes not only the second editions of the *Complete Adult Psychotherapy Treatment Planner,* the *Child Psychotherapy Treatment Planner,* and the *Adolescent Psychotherapy Treatment Planner,* but also treatment *Planners* targeted to specialty areas of practice, including chemical dependency, the continuum of care, couples therapy, employee assistance, behavioral medicine, therapy with older adults, pastoral counseling, family therapy, group therapy, neuropsychology, therapy with gays and lesbians, and more.

In addition to the treatment *Planners,* the series also includes *TheraScribe: The Computerized Assistant to Psychotherapy Treatment Planning*—as well as adjunctive books, such as the *Brief, Chemical Dependence, Couple, Child,* and *Adolescent Therapy Homework Planners;* the *Psychotherapy Documentation Primer;* and the *Clinical, Forensic, Child, Couple and Family, Continuum of Care,* and *Chemical Dependence Documentation Sourcebooks*—containing forms and resources to aid in mental health practice management. The most recent addition to this series is progress note *Planners* for adolescents, children, and adults, respectively. The goal of the series is to provide practitioners with the resources they need in order to provide high-quality care in the era of accountability—or, to put it simply, we seek to help you spend more time on patients, and less on paperwork.

—ARTHUR E. JONGSMA, JR.

PREFACE

The divorce rate has clearly had a major impact on the traditional family unit over the past several decades. The number of divorced persons in the United States alone has nearly quadrupled, from 4.3 million in 1970 to 16.7 million in 1993, representing 9 percent of all adults aged 18 and over in 1993 (Markman, Stanley, and Blumberg, 1996). Such statistics dramatically elevate the risk for family problems and future divorce for children, establishing the vital need for family intervention.

Consequently, the field of family therapy has grown exponentially since its introduction in the 1950s. Virtually all graduate programs in the field of mental health now offer some curriculum in family therapy (Piercy, Sprenkle, and Wetchler, 1996), and almost all 50 states maintain licensing laws for marital and family therapists. In addition, 40 percent of mental health referrals involve marital and family problems (Budman and Gurman, 1988).

With this explosive growth has come the increasing acceptance of family therapy interventions in the mental health service delivery system. In fact, a recent consumer report cited family therapy as one of the most effective forms of psychotherapeutic treatment in today's market (*Consumer Reports,* 1995). In addition, recent research has begun to demonstrate that marriage and family therapy treatments have a positive effect on physical health and health care usage (Crane, 1998). Hence, it is no surprise that insurance companies and managed care programs have increased their awareness and acceptance of family therapy as a mode of treatment for a number of mental health problems and have included it as a reimbursable intervention. Some 120 million patients receive their mental health care through a managed care arrangement (Shore, 1996), and the numbers are rising on a daily basis. It is therefore essential that clinicians have access to structured treatment plan materials that efficiently meet their needs.

This book also goes hand-in-hand with the *Couples Psychotherapy Treatment Planner* since very often family conflicts emanate from problems in the spouses' relationship. In such cases, the therapist should refer to the *Couples Psychotherapy Treatment Planner* (O'Leary, Heyman, and Jongsma) for more specific suggestions regarding the couples' relationship. With this concept in mind, the reader should also expect that there will at times be some overlap between the *Family Therapy* and *Couples Psychotherapy Treatment Planners.* We acknowledge our indebtedness to Dan O'Leary and Rick Heyman for their thorough work on the *Couples Planner.*

We wish to thank a number of people for their help and support in the preparation of this manuscript. These include Florence Kaslow, PhD, for her expertise in reviewing the drafts of each chapter, as well as the executive editor at Wiley, Kelly Franklin. Both of these individuals have provided us with the type of support that is vital during the assembly of this manuscript.

And how can a book reach publication without tedious attention to the details of the preparation of the many drafts of a manuscript? This book had that attention from Jennifer Byrne, Art Jongsma's extremely capable assistant. Thank you Jen, for your dedication and perseverance right to the day of sending the final master document off to Wiley. Many thanks also goes to Frank Dattilio's typist, Carol Jaskolka, whose expertise in the assembly of this book was crucial.

Finally, we thank our family members, who put up with our temporary "Family/Activity Imbalance" while we focused much of our energy and time on this project. We are back!

—FRANK M. DATTILIO
—ARTHUR E. JONGSMA, JR.

INTRODUCTION

Formalized treatment planning, which began in the medical sector in the 1960s, has become an integral component of mental health service delivery in the 1990s. To meet Joint Commission on Accreditation of Healthcare Organizations (JCAHO) standards, and help clients qualify for third-party reimbursement, treatment plans must be specific as to goal selection, problem definition, objective specification, and intervention implementation. The treatment plan must be individualized to meet the client's needs and goals and measurable in terms of setting milestones that can be used to chart the client's progress.

Although they are now a necessity, many clinicians lack formal training in the development of treatment plans. This is one area that most graduate school training programs fail to address, which often leaves the student at a disadvantage when embarking on clinical practice. The problems of quickly generating accurate, customized treatment plans are compounded by the need to acknowledge the family's treatment modality but enable the members to qualify for reimbursement under insurance plans more commonly geared to individual treatment. The purpose of this book is to clarify, simplify, improve, and accelerate the family therapy treatment planning process and to effectively deal with some of the hurdles that come with obtaining third-party authorization for family treatment. It is also designed to serve as a framework for clinicians to follow as they plot an effective course of treatment with challenging cases.

TREATMENT PLAN UTILITY

Detailed written treatment plans can be beneficial to clients, the therapist, the treatment team, the insurance community, treatment agencies, and the overall mental health profession. The clients are served by a written plan which clearly delineates the issues that are the focus of treatment. It is very easy for both the therapist and the clients to lose

1

sight of the issues that initially brought the clients into treatment. The treatment plan is a guide that structures the focus of the therapeutic contract and hopefully will help the therapist remain on track. Since issues can change as treatment progresses, the treatment plan must be viewed as a dynamic schematic or "road map" that can, and must, be updated to reflect any major change of problem, definition, goal, objective, or intervention. It also serves as a tracking system for therapists to use when attempting to explain periods of impasse during the process of treatment.

Recognizing that the plan will in most cases continue to evolve throughout the treatment process, it remains important to settle on initial treatment goals at the outset. Behaviorally based, measurable objectives clearly focus the treatment endeavor and provide a means of assessing treatment outcome. Clear objectives also allow the family members to channel their efforts into specific changes that will lead to the long-term goal of conflict resolution and healthy interaction.

Therapists are aided by treatment plans because they are forced to think analytically, and critically, about which interventions are best suited for objective attainment for each family member. In multi-provider settings, treatment plans are not only designed to help clarify objectives, but also serve the important function of delineating which clinician is responsible for what interventions. By providing a common language, the *Family Therapy Treatment Planner* can ensure consistent and clear communication among members of the treatment team.

Good communication improves quality of care and mitigates risk to the therapist. Malpractice suits are unfortunately increasing in frequency, and insurance premiums are consequently soaring. The first line of defense against allegations of malpractice is a complete clinical record detailing the treatment process. A written, customized, formal treatment plan that has been reviewed and signed by the clients, coupled with problem-oriented progress notes, is a powerful defense against false claims.

Every treatment agency or institution is constantly looking for ways to increase the quality and uniformity of the documentation in the clinical record. The demand for accountability from third-party payers and health maintenance organizations (HMOs) is only increasing and is partially satisfied by a written treatment plan and complete progress notes. A standardized, written treatment plan with problem definitions, goals, objectives, and interventions in every client's file enhances that uniformity of documentation and offers a means of improving care.

Finally, the psychotherapy profession stands to benefit from the use of more precise, measurable objectives to evaluate success in mental health treatment. With the advent of detailed treatment plans, outcome data can be more easily collected to document that interventions are effective in achieving specific goals.

HOW TO DEVELOP A FAMILY TREATMENT PLAN

The process of developing a treatment plan involves a logical series of steps that build on one another. The foundation of any effective treatment plan is the data gathered in a thorough biopsychosocial assessment. As family members present themselves for treatment, the therapist must sensitively listen in order to understand the issues the family is struggling with—in terms of family-of-origin issues, current stressors, emotional status, social network, physical health, coping skills, interpersonal conflicts, power control, and so on. Assessment data may be gathered from a social history, physical exam, clinical interview, psychological testing inventories, or through the use of genograms. The integration of the data by the therapist or the multidisciplinary treatment team members is critical in understanding the family members' individual issues and their family dynamics as a whole. Once the assessment is complete, following the six steps listed here will help to ensure the development of a sound treatment plan.

Step One: Problem Selection

This *Family Therapy Treatment Planner* offers 38 problems to select from. Although family members may discuss a variety of issues during the assessment phase, the clinician must ferret out the most significant problems on which to focus the treatment process. Usually a primary problem will surface; secondary problems are more covert and may become evident later. Some problem issues may have to be set aside as insufficiently urgent to warrant treatment at this time. These can be identified as tertiary issues and addressed later. An effective treatment plan can only deal with a few selected problems, or treatment will lose its direction. Thus, priority schedules can and should be used within the treatment planning process.

In choosing which problems to focus on, it is important to note which problems are most acute or disruptive to family members' functioning independently or as a family, and which concerns are most important to the individual members. The family's motivation to participate in and cooperate with the treatment process depends, to some extent, on the degree to which treatment addresses their greatest needs. Obviously, this step will vary depending on the specific family therapy treatment modality the clinician chooses to employ. While some therapeutic approaches lend themselves to outlining problems and issues more clearly than others, the clinician is advised to attempt to modify these steps to accommodate their respective approach.

Step Two: Problem Definition

Every family presents with a unique set of dynamics as to how a problem emotionally or behaviorally reveals itself in the course of their interaction together. Therefore, each problem that is selected for treatment focus requires a specific definition regarding how it is evidenced for that particular family. The symptom pattern should be associated with diagnostic criteria and codes such as those found in the *Diagnostic and Statistical Manual of Mental Disorders, Fourth Edition (DSM-IV)* or the *International Classification of Diseases*. The *Family Therapy Treatment Planner,* following the pattern established by *DSM-IV,* offers an array of behaviorally specific problem definition statements. Each of the presenting problems listed in the table of contents has several behavioral symptoms to choose from. These prewritten definitions may also be used as models in crafting additional definitions.

Step Three: Goal Development

The next step in the treatment planning stage is to set broad goals for the resolution of the target problem. These statements need not to be crafted in measurable terms but, instead, should focus on the global, long-term outcomes of treatment. Although the *Family Therapy Treatment Planner* suggests several possible goal statements for each problem, it is only necessary to select one goal for each treatment plan.

Step Four: Objective Construction

In contrast to long-term goals, objectives must be stated in behaviorally measurable language. It must be clear when the family has achieved the established objectives. Review agencies (e.g., JCAHO), HMOs, and managed care organizations insist that treatment results be measurable. As a result, the objectives presented in this *Family Therapy Treatment Planner* are designed to meet this demand for accountability. Numerous alternatives are presented to allow construction of a variety of treatment plan possibilities for the same presenting problem. The therapist must exercise professional judgment as to which objectives are most appropriate for a given family and how these objectives fit with their particular modality of therapy.

Each objective should be developed as a step toward attaining the broad treatment goal. In essence, objectives can be thought of as a series of steps that, when completed, will result in the achievement of the long-term goal. There should be at least two objectives for each problem, but the therapist may select as many as necessary for goal achievement. Target attainment dates should be listed for each objective. New objectives may be added to the plan as treatment progresses. When all of the necessary objectives have been achieved, the family should have resolved the target problem successfully, or at least be well en route to doing so.

Step Five: Intervention Creation

Interventions are the actions of the therapist designed to help the family complete the objectives. There should be at least one intervention for every objective. If the clients do not accomplish the objective after the initial intervention, new interventions should be added to the plan.

Interventions should be selected on the basis of the family members' needs and the therapist's full treatment repertoire. This *Family Therapy Treatment Planner* contains interventions from a broad range of therapeutic approaches, including cognitive, dynamic, behavioral, pharmacological, systems-oriented, experiential/expressive, and solution-focused brief therapy. It should be kept in mind, however, that not all modalities of treatment adhere to treatment planning in the same way. Depending on the specific modality of treatment, the mere concept of a treatment plan at all may be incongruous with the basic tenet of the approach. Consequently, it is left to the treating clinician to chose a treatment modality that will lend itself to effective treatment planning.

Step Six: Diagnosis Determination

The determination of an appropriate diagnosis is based on an evaluation of the family's complete clinical presentation. The therapist must compare the behavioral, cognitive, emotional, and interpersonal symptoms that the family members present to the criteria for diagnosis of a mental illness as described in *DSM-IV.* Careful assessment of behavioral indicators facilitate a more accurate diagnosis and more effective treatment planning.

One of the issues inherent with this step is indicating an *identified patient* to assign the diagnosis. With some therapeutic modalities, such as the structural or systems approach to family therapy, the notion of an identified patient (IP) is dispelled in an attempt to remove the IP from that role and focus more on the family as a whole. In cases such as this, viable alternatives are offered.

HOW TO USE THIS PLANNER

Acquiring skill in composing effective treatment plans can be a tedious and difficult process for many therapists. The *Family Therapy Treatment Planner* was developed as a tool to aid therapists in quickly writing treatment plans that are clear, specific, and customized to the particular needs of each family. Treatment plans should be developed by moving, in turn, through each of the following steps:

1. Choose one presenting problem with the family that you have identified in the assessment process. Locate the corresponding page number for that problem in the *Family Therapy Treatment Planner's* table of contents.
2. Select two or three of the listed behavioral definitions and record them in the appropriate section on the treatment plan form.
3. Select a single long-term goal, and record it in the Goals section of the treatment plan form.
4. Review the listed objectives for this problem and select the ones clinically indicated for the family. Remember, it is recommended that at least two objectives be selected for each problem. Add a target date or the number of sessions allocated for the attainment of each objective.
5. Choose relevant interventions. The numbers of the interventions most salient to each objective are listed in parentheses following the objective statement. Feel free to choose other interventions from the list, or to add new interventions as needed in the space provided.
6. *DSM-IV* diagnoses that are commonly associated with the problem are listed at the end of each chapter. These diagnoses are meant to be suggestions for clinical consideration. Select a diagnosis listed or assign a more appropriate choice from the *DSM-IV.*

    Note: To accommodate those practitioners who tend to plan treatment in terms of diagnostic labels rather than presenting problems, Appendix B lists all of the *DSM-IV* diagnoses that are included in the *Planner,* cross-referenced to the problems related to each diagnosis.

Following these steps will facilitate the development of complete, customized treatment plans ready for immediate implementation and presentation to the clients. The final plan should resemble the format of the sample plan presented at the end of this introduction.

ELECTRONIC TREATMENT PLANNING

As paperwork mounts, more and more therapists are turning to computerized record keeping. The presenting problems, goals, objectives, interventions, and diagnoses in the *Family Therapy Treatment Planner* are available in electronic form as an add-on upgrade module to the popular software *TheraScribe 3.0 and 3.5 for Windows: The Computerized Assistant to Treatment Planning*. For more information on TheraScribe or the family therapy add-on module, call John Wiley & Sons at 1-800-379-4539, or mail in the information request coupon at the back of this book.

A WORD OF CAUTION

Whether using the print *Planner* or the electronic version, it is critical to remember that effective treatment planning requires that each plan be tailored to the specific family's problems and needs. Treatment plans should not be mass-produced, even if families have similar problems. Each family member's strengths and weaknesses, unique stressors, social network, individual circumstances, and interactional patterns must be considered in developing a treatment strategy. The clinically derived statements in this *Planner* can be combined in thousands of permutations to develop detailed treatment plans. In addition, readers are encouraged to add their own definitions, goals, objectives, and interventions to the existing samples, particularly as they pertain to their respective mode of treatment. Clinicians are also urged to proceed with treatment planning in a manner that ensures the utmost confidentiality.

SAMPLE TREATMENT PLAN

PROBLEM: ANGER MANAGEMENT

Definitions: Expressions of anger that include threats, breaking objects, violating others' individual space, and refusal to speak to certain family members.

Expressions of anger that are perceived by others as demeaning, threatening, or disrespectful.

Disagreement among family members about the threat created by the angry member.

Goals: Terminate expressions of anger that are demeaning, threatening, disrespectful, or violent.

Get in touch with feelings of emotional pain and express them verbally in appropriate ways rather than through angry outbursts.

Objectives

1. Each family member identifies the destructive effects that his/her uncontrolled anger has had on all family members, including self.

2. Identify any secondary gain that has been derived through expressing anger in an intimidating style.

3. Implement assertiveness as a replacement for angry aggression to declare independence.

Interventions

1. Have each family member describe how his/her respective expression of anger is counterproductive to himself/herself and to other family members; assist them in identifying uncontrolled anger's negative effects (fear, withdrawal, guilt, revenge, etc.) on others.

1. Assist family members in identifying what secondary gain (acquiescence to demands, fear-based service, etc.) is derived from uncontrolled anger.

1. Clearly define examples of nonassertive, assertive, and aggressive expressions of anger and then have each family member give personal examples of each to demonstrate their understanding of the concept (see *Your Perfect Right* [Alberti and Emmons]).

(Continued)

4. Report on the use of the subjective units of discomfort (SUD) scale to measure anger escalation.

5. Identify the various cues for anger as it escalates.

6. Implement the use of the "turtle" technique of retreat to control anger escalation.

2. Use role-playing and modeling to teach assertiveness as an alternative to angry aggressiveness used to declare independence.

1. Instruct family members in the use of a subjective units of discomfort (SUD) scale from 0 to 100 as a barometer for measuring their anger.

1. Teach family members how to identify the cognitive, affective, behavioral, and physiological cues of anger and how to differentiate low, moderate, and high ranges. (Focus on verbal as well as nonverbal cues.)

1. Teach the use of the "turtle" technique, in which family members imagine themselves individually retreating into their shells until they cool down.

Diagnosis: 312.34   Intermittent Explosive Disorder

Note: The numbers in parentheses accompanying the short-term objectives in each chapter correspond to the list of suggested therapeutic interventions in that chapter. Each objective has specific interventions that have been designed to assist the client in attaining that objective. Clinical judgment should determine the exact intervention to be used, including any outside of those suggested.

ACTIVITY/FAMILY IMBALANCE

BEHAVIORAL DEFINITIONS

1. Tension develops in the family as a result of one of the family member's excessive time given to outside activities (parent's job or sport, a child's activity, etc.).
2. Family members question the issue of priorities because of the unusual amount of time that is dedicated to the outside activities.
3. Conflict and tension arise over the fact that certain duties and responsibilities are being shifted onto other family members unfairly due to the time absorbed by the external activity.
4. Jealousy and envy brew between family members, sparking arguments.
5. Family members compete over time with the often-absent family member, leading to disagreements (e.g., children arguing over time with parent).
6. A family member's excessive involvement with external activities is due to a mental illness (e.g., bipolar disorder).

__. _____
_____
__. _____
_____
__. _____
_____

LONG-TERM GOALS

1. Eliminate family tension as a result of admitting to the excessive outside activity and giving more time to family matters.

2. Find an acceptable balance between the competing demands of external activities and family responsibilities.
3. Implement a fair and equal system for assignment of chores and responsibilities among family members.
4. Family members strive to spend equal amount of time with each other.
5. Obtain treatment for mental illness in order to restore balance and proper priorities to allocation of time.

—. _____
   _____
   _____
—. _____
   _____
   _____
—. _____
   _____

SHORT-TERM OBJECTIVES

1. Define the external activity that is contributing to family disharmony. (1, 2, 3, 4)
2. Trace the history of the activity/family imbalance problem and what contributed to its origin. (5, 6, 7)
3. Each family member lists his/her time allocation priorities in a rank-ordered fashion. (8, 9)
4. Agree on a list of activity priorities that all members can endorse. (10, 11)
5. Each member identifies the expectations he/she believes the family holds for him/her. (12)
6. List the home-based duties, chores, and responsibilities that are assigned to each family member. (13, 14)

THERAPEUTIC INTERVENTIONS

1. Allow each family member to have their say about who is absent too often from the family and for what activity (e.g., dad and work; sibling and sports); discuss any differences in perception.
2. Facilitate the ventilation of feelings as experienced by each family member over the family member's absence.
3. Have each family member take ownership of their feelings and behaviors.
4. Help the family identify the problem and define the specifics (e.g., mom works too much and does not have time for us).
5. Trace how the activity/ family imbalance problem

7. Agree on an assignment of chores that all find equitable. (15)

8. Each family member acknowledges a responsibility to work on behalf of the family unit, not just self-interest. (16)

9. Agree to argue with each other over activity issue in a respectful, constructive manner. (17, 18, 19)

10. Verbalize feelings and beliefs over the lack of quality time family members spend together. (20, 21)

11. Each family member lists the pros and cons about being close with one another. (22, 23, 24)

12. Implement activities that build family unity and bonding. (24, 25)

13. Identify symptoms of a mental illness in the too-often-absent family member or in his/her family of origin. (26, 27, 28)

14. Accept referral for psychological treatment of the mentally ill family member. (29, 30, 31)

15. Verbalize acceptance of the presence of a mental illness and the need to obtain treatment for it. (32, 33)

evolved (e.g., due to financial need; learned behaviors from family of origin).

6. Utilize assessment techniques to help define the problem and its historical roots (e.g., genograms, Family-of-Origin Scale [Hovestadt, Anderson, Piercy, Cochran, and Fine], or Family of Origin Inventory [Stuart]).

7. Solicit each family member's opinion on why the excessive energy is directed outside of the family.

8. Have each family member express their priorities for how time is spent (family time, work, recreation, friends, Internet, etc.). Request that they rank order them according to what each perceives as being most important.

9. Have family members compare their lists of priorities and discuss how and why they are different; also explore how the priorities have come to be so different.

10. Develop a joint family list of priorities by attempting to facilitate agreement between members on what the ranking of priorities in the family should be.

11. Explore issues that may be interfering with the cohesive, rank-ordered list of priorities (e.g., need for attention or fear of not having enough income).

—· _____
    _____
—· _____
    _____
—· _____
    _____

12. Explore the perceived expectations the family members hold for one another (e.g., dad's belief of what his wife and children expect of him; an oldest child's perception of his family's expectation of him); compare these to actual expectations.

13. Open up a forum for the discussion of what home-based duties and responsibilities have been assigned to individual family members; poll each family member on what they believe would be a fair distribution of duties and responsibilities and why.

14. Bring to the surface any underlying beliefs about how the delegation of chores should be based on income earners versus nonincome earners, adults versus children, and so on.

15. Assist the family in developing a fair method for assigning chores to various family members (e.g., suggest using a lottery drawing to randomize assignment of chores).

16. Confront family members who appear to be attempting to shirk their responsibilities. Discuss the need to take responsibility for their own behavior and to work for the good of the family unit, not just themselves.

17. Explore the issue of jealousy and envy and how this

plays into the conflicts between family members over the activity/family imbalance issue.

18. Focus on specific arguments over time allocation within the family and how these have developed.

19. Suggest some appropriate, more constructive means of expressing disagreement over the activity issue (e.g., using "I" statements rather than "you" statements; staying calm and respectful in tone).

20. Facilitate family members in ventilating their feelings about the lack of time they have with each other or the unequally great amount of time spent with a specific family member.

21. Probe whether certain family members may be avoiding each other or avoiding intimacy by remaining overly involved in the external activities.

22. Ask each family member to list the pros and cons of being a part of a close family unit. Assess whether the family has a problem with being closely knit.

23. Use an assessment inventory to define the nature of relationships within the family (e.g., the Index of Family Relations [IFR] in the *Walmyr Assessment Scales Scoring Manual* [Hudson]).

24. Discuss the results of the assessment inventory and the implications for family relationships.

25. Suggest ways to build family intimacy, such as social or recreational activities or playing the UnGame (Zakich) together.

26. Investigate whether there is a history of mental health problems in the family of origin of the too-often-absent member.

27. Determine whether the family member who is spending excessive time outside the home may be struggling with a mental health issue (e.g., obsession, addiction, or a more serious psychiatric problem, such as bipolar disorder).

28. Suggest a more in-depth evaluation via referral of the too-often-absent member to another mental health professional (clinical psychologist, psychiatrist, etc.).

29. Discuss the various treatment options for the mentally ill family member (outpatient, inpatient, etc.).

30. Assist the family in identifying methods for supporting the mentally ill family member (intervention, support groups, etc.).

31. Discuss using a buddy system for family members both within and outside of the family (e.g., local chapter of Families of the Men-

tally Ill or the American Red Cross) to gain support in coping with mental illness in the family.

32. Confront the issue of denial of mental illness on the part of any family member, including the one with the diagnosed illness.

33. Attempt to uncover any enabling process within the family system that may be reinforcing the denial of mental illness.

—. _____
   _____

—. _____
   _____

—. _____
   _____

DIAGNOSTIC SUGGESTIONS

Axis I: 309.24   Adjustment Disorder With Anxiety
             309.0   Adjustment Disorder With Depressed Mood
             309.28   Adjustment Disorder With Mixed Anxiety and Depressed Mood
             309.3   Adjustment Disorder With Disturbance of Conduct
             300.4   Dysthymic Disorder
             300.02   Generalized Anxiety Disorder
             296.2x   Major Depressive Episode, Single Episode
             V61.20   Parent-Child Relational Problem
             296.5x   Bipolar I Disorder
             296.89   Bipolar II Disorder
             301.13   Cyclothymic Disorder

             _____   _____
             _____   _____

Axis II: 301.81   Narcissistic Personality Disorder
301.6   Dependent Personality Disorder
301.9   Personality Disorder NOS
301.5   Histrionic Personality Disorder

_____   _____

_____   _____

ADOLESCENT/PARENT CONFLICTS

BEHAVIORAL DEFINITIONS

1. Parents experience conflicts with adolescent child that begin to interfere with the family's overall functioning.
2. Parents argue with each other over how to respond to the adolescent's disruptive nonconforming behaviors.
3. Family members resent the adolescent-centered conflict, increasing tension in the home.
4. Parents feel a loss of control and the adolescent feels empowered by parent's dilemma, making his/her own rules and resisting parental intervention.
5. Adolescent acts out in areas of substance abuse, sexuality, school performance, and/or delinquency.

___. _____
_____

___. _____
_____

___. _____
_____

LONG-TERM GOALS

1. Parents arrive at some level of agreement regarding how to respond to the adolescent.
2. Parents reduce the effects of the adolescent's misbehavior on other family members.
3. Parents learn new methods for working together to achieve harmony and balance in the family.

4. Parents devise and enforce a set of rules and standards that promote peace and harmony in the family.
5. Parents feel empowered to take control of the family and react firmly to adolescent acting out.

—. _____
_____
_____

—. _____
_____
_____

—. _____
_____
_____

SHORT-TERM OBJECTIVES

1. Define the specifics about what needs to change in the adolescent's behavior. (1, 2)
2. Parents clarify philosophy on parenting expectations for the adolescent. (3)
3. Parents and adolescent cooperate with psychological testing to identify specific areas of parent/child conflict. (4, 5)
4. Identify family, school, or marital factors that may be contributing to the adolescent's undesirable behavior. (6, 7)
5. Parents identify their strengths and weaknesses in parenting style. (8, 9)
6. Parents read books and watch videotapes on parenting adolescents. (10)
7. Parents develop and implement a monitoring system for the adolescent's where-

THERAPEUTIC INTERVENTIONS

1. Open up the forum for family members to share their perception of the adolescent's behavior and discuss feelings about the adolescent's behavior.
2. Assess whether the adolescent's acting-out behavior is transient or is a more stable pattern.
3. Have parents share their philosophy on parenting and what expectations they have for their son or daughter.
4. Use specific questionnaires and inventories to assess specific areas of conflict and how the family may be contributing to the problems (e.g., Adolescent Coping Orientation for Problem Experiences [A-COPE] in *Family Assessment Inventories for Research and Practice* [McCubbin and Thompson]).

abouts, and indicate any deficiencies in the monitoring
system. (11, 12, 13)

8. Parents identify and record
the occurrence of a specific
desirable behavior of the
adolescent's that they would
like to see increase in frequency. (14)

9. Implement a behavioral
contract to increase the frequency of the adolescent's
target behavior. (15)

10. Increase the frequency of
positive social- or activity-
oriented interactions be-
tween parents and the
adolescent. (16)

11. Establish and implement
consequences for negative
adolescent behavior (e.g., the
use of response cost). (17)

12. Parents identify and make
an effort to terminate any
undesirable behaviors that
they may be modeling for
the adolescent. (18, 19)

13. Parents confer with each
other frequently to increase
mutual support in parent-
ing. (20, 21)

14. Parents use structured
dialogue techniques to
ensure good parental com-
munication for problem
solving. (22)

15. Parents minimize criticism
of the other's parenting efforts. (23)

16. Parents discuss disagreements only at times when
discussion is likely to be con-

5. Assess the family members'
belief system about appropriate versus inappropriate
behavior by utilization of
interviews and question-
naires (e.g., Family Beliefs
Inventory [Roehling and
Robin] or Parent-Adolescent
Relationship Questionnaire
[Robin, Koepke, and Moye]).

6. Explore familial interaction
patterns or dynamics that
may be exacerbating the
conflict between adolescent
and parents (underlying conflicts, family-of-origin issues,
unrealistic expectations,
marital problems, etc.).

7. Explore environmental
stressors that may be exacerbating the adolescent's
acting out (e.g., family transitions, inconsistent rules,
school or social difficulties,
peer relationships, or peer
pressure).

8. Role-play a parent/adoles-
cent conflict to assess how
parents solve the problem;
give parents feedback re-
garding the strengths and
weaknesses of their ap-
proach.

9. Teach how the adolescent's
strengths can be augmented
and his/her weaknesses di-
minished.

10. Recommend parents read
books on parenting tech-
niques (e.g., *Understanding
the Adolescent* [Orvin]; *Parents, Teens, and Boundaries:
How to Draw the Line*

structive, and not in the presence of the children. (24)

17. Parents identify and replace distorted cognitive beliefs that relate to parenting their teenager. (25, 26)

18. Family members hold family meetings regularly and conform to the rules of interaction. (27, 28)

19. Family members demonstrate empathy and respect for other individuals' points of view by paraphrasing or reflecting speaker's position before responding. (28, 29)

20. Parents list alternatives to their current parenting methods. (30)

21. Parents enact alternative parenting styles and evaluate their effectiveness. (31)

22. Identify and challenge unreasonable beliefs and expectations regarding adolescent behaviors. (32)

23. Parents establish consistent house rules and regulations. (33, 34)

24. Family establishes a regular dinner hour and sets rules regarding how often members will be present. (35, 36)

25. Parents go out alone at least one night per week for socialization and/or recreation. (37)

[Bluestein]; *Parents and Adolescents: Living Together,* vol. 1, *The Basics,* and vol. 2, *Family Problem Solving* [Patterson and Forgatch]; or *Living with a Work in Progress: A Parents Guide to Surviving Adolescence* [Goldberg-Freeman]).

11. Ask parents to develop monitoring for their adolescent, knowing *where* he/she is, *who* he/she is with, *what* he/she is doing, and *when* he/she will be home.

12. Assign parents to record their joint monitoring efforts with the adolescent as a homework assignment.

13. Ask parents to discuss their successes at monitoring and to identify events or situations in which monitoring requires improvement.

14. Ask parents to select a behavior of the adolescent's that they would like to see decrease or diminish. Ask them to record its occurrence every day for a week, and notice the behaviors or situations that precede it (antecedents) and follow it (consequences).

15. Have parents decide on an appropriate reward system (e.g., verbal praise, use of the car, allowance) to reinforce the positive target behavior of the adolescent; seek agreement between parents and adolescent for this behavioral contract.

—. _____

_____

—. _____

_____

—. _____

_____

16. Recommend that each parent increase the number of parent-initiated, casual, positive conversations with the adolescent.

17. Develop with parents a response cost/procedure to use in conjunction with the adolescent's targeted negative behavior; assign implementation and review success.

18. If parents are modeling for the adolescent the behavior they would like to extinguish (e.g., yelling or becoming sarcastic), have parents become aware and contract to change their own behavior before trying to change the same behavior in the adolescent.

19. Teach parents techniques of anger control to better mediate conflict.

20. Ask parents to role-play support for each other regarding their reaction to the adolescent's misbehavior; have the supportive parent ask (in a supportive, nonthreatening manner) how the other parent deals with the misbehavior and whether the supportive parent can do anything in the future to help.

21. Have parents contract to support the other's parenting by not interfering during the other's parent/adolescent interactions or with the other's decisions (i.e., avoid

splitting their parental unity).

22. Teach parents communication and problem-solving skills (see *Relationship Enhancement* [Guerney]) to use with the adolescent as well as each other (e.g., problem definition, brainstorming solutions, evaluation of alternatives, solution enactment, and enactment evaluation).

23. Help each parent identify when they are engaging in criticizing the other parent in a nonconstructive manner.

24. Help parents establish a practice of meeting in private so they can discuss parenting decisions and come to a mutual agreement before presenting it to the adolescent.

25. Ask parents to track their thoughts and emotional reactions during problematic situations with their adolescent.

26. Identify and challenge unreasonable beliefs by asking parents to provide evidence for the truth of their beliefs and persuasively illuminating the illogical premise involved (e.g., "If my daughter stays out late, she will become pregnant or a drug addict" can be replaced by "I can make my opinions and the house rules known, but ultimately her behavior is up to her").

27. Have parents initiate regular family meetings for constructive problem solving and evaluation of earlier contracts. Family meetings should be time-limited (starting with 15 minutes) and should observe set ground rules (see page 117 of *Parents and Adolescents: Living Together,* vol. 2: *Family Problem Solving* [Patterson and Forgatch]).

28. Family meetings should use respectful communication rules, such as taking turns talking, treating each other with respect, and no lecturing (see page 118 of *Parents and Adolescents: Living Together,* vol. 2: *Family Problem Solving* [Patterson and Forgatch]).

29. Reinforce family members' use of communication skills (see *Relationship Enhancement* [Guerney] and *Fighting for Your Marriage* [Markman, Stanley, and Blumberg]).

30. Have parents brainstorm alternative styles of parenting that they have learned as a result of their assigned readings, speaking with other parents (through parenting groups, etc.), or previous family therapy sessions. Recommend books such as *Tough Love* (York, York, and Wachtel).

31. Ask parents to try the alternative parenting style to

evaluate its effectiveness. Also, facilitate parents in providing each other with critical feedback afterward as to how well they perceived the alternative to work.

32. Have parents and adolescents list what they each believe is reasonable and unreasonable in adolescent behavior.

33. Have parents establish consistent house rules. Consequences for rule violation and compliance should be specified. Rules can be modified and negotiated in family meetings if necessary.

34. Reinforce the need for parents to follow through on praise for following rules as well as consequences for not following rules.

35. Discuss the feasibility of the family eating meals together; set rules about frequency and attendance.

36. Ask parents to meet with the adolescent (in session or as homework) to discuss and agree to eating dinner together as a family at least once or twice a week.

37. Encourage the parents to have one or two nights per week out alone together, or with adult friends, when children are not the focus of conversation or of the relationship.

__.   _____
      _____
__.   _____
      _____
__.   _____
      _____

DIAGNOSTIC SUGGESTIONS

Axis I:	309.3	Adjustment Disorder With Disturbance of Conduct
	309.4	Adjustment Disorder With Mixed Disturbance of Emotions and Conduct
	V61.21	Neglect of Child
	995.5	Neglect of Child (Victim)
	V61.20	Parent–Child Relational Problem
	V61.1	Partner Relational Problem
	995.5	Physical Abuse of Child (Victim)
	V61.21	Sexual Abuse of Child
	995.5	Sexual Abuse of Child (Victim)
	313.81	Oppositional Defiant Disorder
	312.9	Disruptive Behavior Disorder NOS
	312.8	Conduct Disorder, Adolescent Onset Type
	314.01	Attention-Deficit/Hyperactivity Disorder, Combined Type
	_____	_____
	_____	_____

ADOPTION ISSUES

BEHAVIORAL DEFINITIONS

1. Parents struggle with the issue of infertility and are considering contacting a child adoption agency or making a private adoption arrangement.
2. Parents struggle with a sense of failure and disconnectedness with the adopted child due to the lack of a biological link.
3. Parents struggle with when and if to inform the child that he/she is adopted, and become overprotective and overindulgent.
4. Adopted child feels different, isolated, and removed from the parents and siblings, and struggles with abandonment issues regarding his/her biological parents.
5. Parents feel a lack of connection with the adopted child as opposed to biological children.
6. Tension exists between biological and adopted children, with the adopted child sustaining badgering and ridicule from siblings, extended family-of-origin members, and so on.
7. Adopted child questions the whereabouts of their biological parents and make overtures to search for them.
8. Adopted child fantasizes and idealizes the biological parents.
9. Adoptive parents feel a sense of threat, rejection, abandonment, and even betrayal by adopted child's overtures to search for his/her biological parents and/or biological siblings.
10. Adopted child successfully locates biological parents and/or biological siblings and begins to form a bond, creating friction among the adoptive family members.
11. Adopted child encounters a cold and/or rejecting reception from biological parents and experiences negative emotions as a result.
12. Adoptive parents meet adopted child's biological parents, and tension results for all parties involved.

—. _____
    _____
    _____

—. _____
    _____
    _____

—. _____
    _____

LONG-TERM GOALS

1. Parents work through their struggles over their inability to conceive and accept this as a dysfunction of their genetic/biological disposition as opposed to a sense of failure.
2. Parents accept and bond with adopted and biological children equally.
3. Adopted child develops positive feelings regarding adoptive family.
4. Parents educate themselves on the issue of when and if they should inform a child that he/she is adopted.
5. Adopted and biological children resolve tension between themselves.
6. Parents decide when and if to provide the adopted child with information regarding biological parents, and deal appropriately with any threat that develops as a result of the child's inquiry.
7. Adopted child accepts the outcome of meeting his/her biological parents regardless of whether their reaction is positive or negative.

—. _____
    _____
    _____

—. _____
    _____
    _____

—. _____
    _____

SHORT-TERM OBJECTIVES

1. Identify the negative impact that infertility and its treatment have had on each

THERAPEUTIC INTERVENTIONS

1. Allow the couple to ventilate about the hardship of enduring the infertility process.

partner and on the relationship. (1, 2)

2. Parents verbalize an understanding that the inability to conceive is a matter of genetic/biological factors and not due to personal failure. (3, 4)

3. Parents identify the pros and cons of telling the child of his/her adoption. (5)

4. Parents agree as to when and what to tell the adopted child regarding his/her adoptive origins. (6)

5. Adopted child expresses feelings associated with being adopted. (7, 8, 13)

6. Parents accept the responsibility for the child learning of his/her adoption from a source outside of their immediate adoptive family. (9, 10)

7. Adopted child verbalizes positive feelings toward adoptive family. (11, 12, 13)

8. Parents identify the factors that cause them to experience a lack of connection with the adopted child, as opposed to their biological children. (14, 15, 16)

9. All family members identify the true source of tension between biological children and the adopted child. (17)

10. Parents verbalize acceptance of the child's need to search for his/her biological parents. (18, 19)

2. Explore the stress and strain that infertility has had on the couple's relationship and how it may be precluding their ability to conceive. Recommend *Infertility and Identity* (Deveraux and Hammerman).

3. Educate the couple on the biological factors of failure to conceive via referral to fertility experts and readings (e.g., *The Long-Awaited Stork* [Glazer]). Also, help the couple locate an infertility support group in their area, either through their obstetrician/gynecologist or the American Red Cross directory.

4. Discuss with the parents the notion that giving birth to a child is only a small part of the picture, that parenting is independent of birthing, and that a strong bond can form irrespective of the biological connection.

5. Review with the parents the pros (e.g., not having the child learn from someone else accidentally) and cons (e.g., risking the child's withdrawal from the adoptive family to search for his/her biological parents) and timing regarding telling the child of his/her adoption; refer them to readings (e.g., *The Adoption Resource Book* [Gilman]).

6. Help the parents make an initial decision regarding

11. Parents and the adopted child verbalize and resolve their fear of rejection and/or guilt about the adopted child investigating into his/her biological parents. (20)

12. Parents and the adopted child prepare for the possibility of the adopted child's biological parents having a negative reaction to an inquiry. (21, 22)

13. Parents accept the fact that an adopted child who is of age may choose to reside with or close to his/her biological parents or siblings after locating them. (23)

—. _____
   _____

—. _____
   _____

—. _____
   _____

what and when a child should be told about his/her adoption. Explain to them that this decision is not carved in stone and can be reevaluated and changed later.

7. Allow the adopted child to vent his/her feelings regarding adoption in family therapy. Focus on productively processing these feelings.

8. Teach the family members that the adoptive child's emotions (e.g., anger, isolation, acting-out behaviors, and depression) over being adopted are not uncommon.

9. Help the parents process their guilt over not having informed the child of his/her adoption, which has resulted in the child experiencing anger and rage.

10. Process how the parents arrived at the decision not to inform the child through family therapy sessions, so that the child can better understand their logic.

11. Encourage family activities that will promote the rebonding of the adopted child to parents and siblings (parental nurturing behaviors, games, family outings, one-to-one activities for the child and a parent, etc.).

12. Facilitate contact between the child and older adopted children outside of the immediate family who have accepted being adopted.

13. Recommend that child and parents read books on how it feels to be adopted (e.g., *How It Feels to Be Adopted* [Krementz]).

14. Assist the parents in identifying possible factors (lack of physical resemblance, absence of time in utero, etc.) that could contribute to differences in bonding with adopted versus biological children.

15. Help the parents to resolve any differences in their feelings for their adopted and biological children and to understand how this is likely to affect the entire family. (If it is identified as a more individual issue, consider referring for individual psychotherapy.)

16. Suggest to the parents that a separate couple's meeting take place between them and the therapist so that the issue of a lack of bonding with the adopted child may be addressed without any of the children present.

17. Address the entire family on the tension between the biological and adopted children. Search for any conflict between the parents to explain why this might exist. Also, help the children mediate their tensions or feuds regarding their differences.

18. Help the parents accept the fact that it is very natural

and common for adopted children to be curious about their biological parents.

19. Reinforce with the parents that the adopted child's inquiries are not an overture of rejection, but a quest for his/her existence and origin.

20. Reassure all family members that their feelings are not unusual and that fear of rejection and guilt are very common.

21. Discuss how the parents and children of the family can support one another in the event that the biological parents reject any inquiry by either the adoptive parents or the adopted child.

22. Use stress inoculation techniques and specific coping skills as advance preparation for any potential negative experiences (brainstorming with all family members their potential reactions to meeting the biological parents and how they feel about it, role-playing the initial meeting with biological parents, etc.).

23. Help the parents and family members to accept the adopted child's decision and his/her need to rebond with his/her biological family of origin.

—.   _____
     _____

—.   _____
     _____

—.   _____
     _____

DIAGNOSTIC SUGGESTIONS

Axis I: 309.0   Adjustment Disorder With Depressed Mood
             309.24   Adjustment Disorder With Anxiety
             309.28   Adjustment Disorder With Mixed Anxiety and
                       Depressed Mood
             309.4   Adjustment Disorder With Mixed Disturbance
                       of Emotions and Conduct
             309.3   Adjustment Disorder With Disturbance of
                       Conduct
             303.9   Alcohol Dependence
             305.00   Alcohol Abuse
             300.4   Dysthymic Disorder
             296.x   Major Depressive Disorder
             V61.1   Partner Relational Problem
             V61.1   Physical Abuse of Adult
             V61.20   Parent–Child Relational Problem
             995.81   Physical Abuse of Adult (Victim)
             309.81   Posttraumatic Stress Disorder

             _____   _____

             _____   _____

Axis II: 301.6   Dependent Personality Disorder
             301.83   Borderline Personality Disorder
             301.5   Histrionic Personality Disorder
             301.7   Antisocial Personality Disorder
             301.4   Obsessive-Compulsive Personality Disorder
             301.81   Narcissistic Personality Disorder

             _____   _____

             _____   _____

ALCOHOL ABUSE

BEHAVIORAL DEFINITIONS

1. The regular excessive use of alcohol by one or more members of a family unit leads to interference with functioning at work or school; to ignoring the dangers to health; to vocational, social, or legal problems; and to family and/or marital conflict.
2. Verbal or physical abuse associated with alcohol abuse leads to serious conflicts between family members.
3. Alcohol abusers make continued failed promises to discontinue use, despite family members' pleas.
4. Violence or threats of violence have occurred, during periods of intoxication as well as during sobriety, which has placed family members at risk.
5. Communication between family members has deteriorated to such a level that familial interaction is greatly reduced, and members simply coexist without any cohesiveness.
6. Non-substance-abusing family members function in a manner that serves to enable the abusers by generating excuses for their drinking.
7. All members engage in denial of the seriousness of the alcohol abuse and the effects that this has had on the family dynamics.
8. Serious financial problems have developed as a result of excessive or frivolous spending, frequent work absences, loss of employment, and so on.
9. Social alienation between family members develops as the substance abuser gravitates toward socializing with other abusers.
10. Children engage in acting-out behaviors as a result of the lack of structure and boundaries in the family.
11. Alcohol-abusing parents overlook children's alcohol use and inadvertently reinforce early substance-abusing patterns in children.
12. Isolation from extended family and friends as alcoholic member has become unavailable or unwelcome by others.

13. Bills are not paid, checks bounce, and there is no follow-through on daily responsibilities.
14. Family experiences shame and humiliation and makes excuses for the alcohol abuser's behavior to save face.

__. _____

_____

_____

__. _____

_____

_____

__. _____

_____

LONG-TERM GOALS

1. Alcohol-abusing family members accept the need for abstinence and become proactive in a recovery program.
2. Alcohol-abusing family members successfully achieve a sustained and consistent reduction in frequency and amount of alcohol consumption, avoiding further negative effects on the family as a whole.
3. Family achieves improved communication and problem solving, and positive family reactions.
4. The non-alcohol-abusing family members unite and become a strong entity to support the alcohol-abusing family members in recovery.
5. Family members engage in 12-step programs such as Alcoholics Anonymous (AA) and Al-Anon, or an alternative program, such as the Sobell method or Solutions-Focused Therapy for Alcoholics.
6. Alcohol abusers terminate any physical, sexual, or verbal abuse.
7. Alcohol abusers develop coping strategies for dealing with the issues related to establishing long-term sobriety (e.g., depression and anxiety, as well as physical problems such as nutritional deficiencies and high blood pressure).
8. Extended family member or some other responsible adult takes over the parental role with the children, preventing the parentizing of the children.

__. _____

_____

__. _____

_____

__. _____

_____

SHORT-TERM OBJECTIVES

1. Identify the untoward effects of the substance abuse on the self-esteem, family life, employment, health, social relations, and personal finances of all family members. (1, 2)

2. Alcohol abuser signs a contract with respect to the controlled and moderate use of all alcohol. (3)

3. Alcohol abuser proves his/her ability to control alcohol consumption at moderate levels by keeping a record of frequency and quantity of use. (4)

4. Read literature on controlled drinking, the effects of alcohol abuse, and family dynamics of alcohol abuse. (5, 6)

5. All family members sign a contract to be completely free of mood-altering substances during sessions. (7)

6. All family members agree to mandatory attendance at all treatment sessions except in the case of serious physical illness. (7)

7. Alcohol abuser signs a contract for complete abstinence at all times from mood-altering substances and for attendance at AA or group or individual alcohol treatment. (8, 9)

THERAPEUTIC INTERVENTIONS

1. Gather family members' perspectives on the negative effects that the alcohol abuse has had on family members and the general family dynamics; also focus on the destructive effects on the substance abuser and the impact that denial has played in this process.

2. Consider using such inventories or rating scales as the Alcohol Beliefs Scale (Connors and Maisto) to evaluate attitudes toward alcohol and the effects of alcohol abuse on quality of the alcohol abuser's and the family's life.

3. Ask the alcohol abuser to sign a contract stipulating the parameters for controlled or social drinking, such as the Sobell method (see *Behavioral Treatment of Alcohol Problems* [Sobell and Sobell]). Solicit an agreement that should the contract be broken after a designated number of times (e.g., 2), then a complete alcohol abstinence contract will be signed.

4. Develop a daily record form to track the frequency and quantity of alcohol use, using this record to determine the alcohol abuser's ability to consistently control his/her alcohol intake.

8. All family members sign a behavioral contract that stipulates that no violence or threats will be engaged in toward any other family member. (10, 11)

9. Family members implement cognitive/behavioral techniques to manage their angry feelings. (12, 13)

10. Violent family member accepts referral for specialized behavioral treatment of explosive disorder. (14)

11. Alcohol abuser identifies attractions to or perceived benefits of the excessive use of alcohol. (15, 16)

12. Alcohol abuser implements alternative stress management actions to achieve the same desirable effects that alcohol has produced in the past. (17, 18)

13. Alcohol abuser implements assertiveness and other social skills as a replacement for alcohol use to cope with social anxiety. (19, 20)

14. All family members agree to engage in several weeks of "caring days" during which each member does something pleasing for the other family members without prompting. (21)

15. Identify opportunities for social interaction with other families, and develop a plan together to initiate contact for activities that do not involve alcohol consumption. (22)

Recommend *How to Cut Down on Your Drinking* (National Institute on Alcohol Abuse and Alcoholism).

5. Research and assign to the alcohol abuser and to family members the most appropriate reading materials regarding alcohol addiction and its effects, controlled drinking, and the family dynamics of alcoholism (see *Behavioral Treatment of Alcohol Problems* [Sobell and Sobell], *How to Control Your Drinking* [Miller and Muñoz], and *Alcoholism: Getting the Facts* [National Institute on Alcohol Abuse and Alcoholism]).

6. Facilitate a discussion on the materials recommended and have family members compare their reactions to what they read. Highlight the differences in perceptions of family members and explore how they perceive this to contribute to the overall problem.

7. Develop a joint family contract that all members sign, an agreement to attend all sessions unless ill and to be completely free of mood-altering substances (not including legitimate prescription medication).

8. If the controlled-drinking contract is broken, ask the alcohol abuser to sign an agreement of abstinence from all alcohol use, accom-

16. Identify alternative social or recreational actions that all family members could engage in and that would be rewarding to all. (22, 23, 24)

17. All family members identify what specific characteristics derail or impede healthy communication between themselves, with an emphasis on the abusing family member's specific behaviors. (25, 26, 27, 28)

18. All family members discuss an incident or conflict using a new mode of communication that is free from any blaming or condescending language. (27, 28, 29)

19. Verbalize an understanding of and implement techniques for problem solving. (30, 31)

20. Family members report on their perception of how the family has implemented the use of a problem-solving strategy at home, sharing their individual feelings about it. (32, 33)

21. Alcohol abusers formally apologize to other family members for the pain and suffering they have caused due to their substance abuse. (34, 35)

22. Alcohol abusers identify triggers to episodes of drinking and agree to alternative, nondrinking responses to cope with trigger situations. (36, 37)

panied by an agreement to attend a support group (AA) or group psychotherapy for substance abusers.

9. Refer the alcohol abuser to a psychiatrist specializing in alcohol abuse for evaluation for pharmacotherapy (e.g., Antabuse).

10. Construct a written family contract specifying that no member of the family will engage in aggressive or assaultive threats on any other family member.

11. Develop a refuge plan for the safety of family members if violence does erupt.

12. Teach the use of cognitive behavioral strategies (deep breathing, cognitive restructuring, etc.) for anger control and the implementation of stress inoculation techniques (see *Cognitive Behavior Modification* [Meichenbaum]).

13. Teach assertiveness and assign family members to read the book *Your Perfect Right* (Alberti and Emmons).

14. Assess the case for the appropriateness of either individual, couple, or family therapy and for referring the acting-out family member to another provider for individual or group treatment of explosive disorder.

15. Explore those perceived benefits that the alcohol

23. Family members who are not alcohol abusers acknowledge how they have been primary and secondary enablers of the alcohol abusers. (38, 39)

24. Family members confront each other about behaviors that continue the enabling process. (38, 39, 40)

25. The non-alcohol-abusing family members discuss assertive incidents whereby they have avoided enabling or taking responsibility for the alcohol abusers. (39, 40, 41)

26. Family members identify stressors that are affecting them all, especially those that encourage the alcohol use, and formulate a plan of attack. (42, 43)

27. Identify the genetic, emotional, and environmental factors that have fostered a pattern of alcohol abuse. (44)

28. Children identify the unhealthy role each has assumed in the family due to the dysfunctioning that alcoholism has brought. (45, 46, 47)

—. _____
_____

—. _____
_____

—. _____
_____

abusers are obtaining by engaging in alcohol use (acceptance by friends and peers; reduction of anxiety, social or otherwise; sleep induction; escape from family tensions; etc.).

16. Trace the alcohol abuser's history and help identify how this behavior has been reinforced at home and in the community.

17. Strategize with the alcohol abuser as to what specific behavioral exercises (meditation, relaxation, social skill or assertiveness training, etc.) can be used to replace alcohol use and/or intoxication but obtain the benefits sought.

18. Instruct the alcohol abuser on the use and implementation of stress management (deep breathing, progressive muscle relaxation, guided imagery, meditation, etc.).

19. Use modeling and role-playing to teach assertiveness and social skill techniques, helping the alcohol abuser to weigh the pros and cons of using such techniques.

20. Administer measurement scales to assess any progress made as a result of the assertiveness and social skills training (e.g., Assertiveness Self-Report Inventory [Herzberger, Chan, and Katz] and the Social

Solving Inventory [D'Zurilla and Nezu]).

21. Instruct family members on the technique of "caring days" (see *Helping Couples Change: A Social Learning Approach to Marital Therapy* [Stuart]) in which each member does something pleasant for other members (e.g., do a special chore without being asked; pay a nice compliment).

22. Encourage and assist the family in formulating a plan for social activities with other couples or families that do not include alcohol consumption. Suggest church, hobby, and recreational groups or work associates as possible social network opportunities for outreach.

23. Schedule a specific family recreational activity in which each family member is assigned a specific role in making the activity happen, using the Inventory of Rewarding Activities (Birchler) to brainstorm and develop a list of recreational or educational activities that might be enjoyed by the family.

24. Assign the family to choose one social or recreational activity and assess how they fare on the outcome. Have them keep notes on what they enjoy about the activity and what they do not.

25. Have each family member reflect on the manner in which they obstruct the smooth, productive course of communication (cut the others off during conversation, refuse to respond, etc.).

26. Attempt to track and resolve the origins of any miscommunication patterns that have developed (family-of-origin patterns of dysfunctional communicating, foreign language, etc.).

27. While discussing communication skills, review rules for the speaker and for the listener (see *Fighting for Your Marriage* [Markham, Stanley, and Blumberg]).

28. Use role-playing, empty chair, or psychodrama techniques to have family members work out a conflict, with the emphasis on using nondegrading, assertive methods of communication.

29. Reinforce positive changes toward well-mannered, respectful, empathetic communication between family members.

30. Teach the following five steps of conflict resolution: (1) define the problem (with the help of the therapist, if necessary); (2) generate many solutions, even if some are not practical, allowing for creativity; (3) evaluate the pros and cons of the proposed solutions; (4) obtain agreement on the

proposed solution; and (5) implement the solutions (see family applications of problem-solving methods in "Language System and Therapy: An Evolving Idea" [Goolishian and Anderson] or the *Family Therapy Sourcebook* [Piercy, Sprinkle, and Wetchler]).

31. Promote family discussion of a conflictual issue in the session to view how members deal with an area of conflict, and then model implementation of problem-solving steps.

32. Assign homework regarding the use of problem-solving techniques, using specific problems that are germane to what is currently happening in the family.

33. Review family members' experience with problem solving at home, reinforcing success and redirecting for failures.

34. Recommend that the alcohol abuser formally apologizes for the pain caused to other family members due to his/her substance abuse.

35. Help family members obtain closure on the ritual of apology so that it minimizes any barriers to the alcohol abuser's future progress.

36. Help the family identify triggers of relapse of alcohol use and instruct them on what can be done to help avoid future relapses.

37. Suggest to the family members that they develop index cards with alternative strategies for coping with alcohol abuse in the face of stimuli that trigger relapse (connecting with sponsors at AA or support groups, using stress inoculation techniques, etc.).

38. Help the non-alcohol-abusing family members identify the behaviors that they engage in (e.g., lying to cover up for the alcohol abuser's irresponsibility, minimizing the seriousness of the alcohol abuser's drinking problem, taking on most of the family responsibilities, tolerating the verbal, emotional, and/or physical abuse) that support the continuation of the alcohol abuser's abusive drinking.

39. Use role-playing of family scenarios to guide the non-alcohol-abusing family members in not accepting responsibility for the alcohol abuser.

40. Review instances of family interaction at home in which family members have avoided enabling behaviors.

41. Brainstorm ideas among the family members as to how to more constructively respond to situations that previously precipitated enabling behaviors (not making excuses for broken

promises or unfulfilled responsibilities, telling the truth regarding intoxication even if it brings painful consequences, reporting physical abuse to police, etc.).

42. Explore and identify stressors facing each member of the family.

43. Assist the family members in devising a strategy for dealing with each of the identified stressors (financial restructuring; job search; apologies to friends, neighbors, or extended family members; tutoring assistance, etc.).

44. Investigate the emotional, social, and genetic factors that facilitate the alcohol abuse and that reinforce the need for abstinence.

45. Teach family members the roles usually adopted by children of alcoholic parents (e.g., the family hero, the scapegoat, the lost child, and the mascot; see *Another Chance* [Wegscheider-Cruse] and *Bradshaw on the Family* [Bradshaw]). Help the children identify the role (or roles) each has adopted.

46. Encourage the children to give up their unhealthy role assumptions and express their needs, feelings, and desires directly and assertively.

47. Help the children brainstorm how they can develop

alternative behaviors to the
healthy ones.

—. _____
    _____

—. _____
    _____

—. _____
    _____

DIAGNOSTIC SUGGESTIONS

Axis I: 303.9   Alcohol Dependence
         305.00   Alcohol Abuse
         300.4   Dysthymic Disorder
         V61.1   Partner Relational Problem
         V61.20   Parent–Child Relational Problem

         _____   _____

         _____   _____

Axis II: 301.6   Dependent Personality Disorder
         301.82   Avoidant Personality Disorder

         _____   _____

         _____   _____

ANGER MANAGEMENT

BEHAVIORAL DEFINITIONS

1. Expressions of anger that include threats, breaking objects, violating others' individual space, and refusal to speak to certain family members.
2. Intimidation and coercion of some family members into relinquishing their rights in response to another member's expression of anger.
3. Hostile, aggressive behavior that alienates neighbors, extended family members, and school personnel, as well as nuclear family members.
4. Expressions of anger that are perceived by others as demeaning, threatening, or disrespectful.
5. Disagreement among family members about the threat created by the angry member.

Anger can be a volatile subject, particularly when it is expressed in violent, destructive ways. This can impede the progress of the therapeutic process if not directed appropriately. Therapists should ensure against potentially violent outbursts among family members by using anger assessment inventories such as the Novaco scales (Novaco, 1975) or other anger and temperament measures. In the event that a family member's anger becomes disruptive during a family session, individual sessions should be utilized to deescalate the anger in a nonpunitive fashion. If anger outbursts are chronic and accompanied by explosive rage, then a referral to a psychiatrist or neurologist should be made, especially if the individual experiences sleepiness or drowsiness after each and every anger outburst. This may be suggestive of a neurological problem.

—. _____
  _____
  _____
—. _____
  _____
  _____
—. _____
  _____

LONG-TERM GOALS

1. Terminate expressions of anger that are demeaning, threatening, disrespectful, or violent.
2. Learn the precursors of inappropriate anger escalation as a step in temper control.
3. Get in touch with feelings of emotional pain and express them verbally in appropriate ways rather than through angry outbursts.
4. Family members support each other during periods when one or more of them is expressing hurt or vulnerability.
5. Recognize the various levels of anger expression and identify when and how to intervene to avoid explosive tirades and destructive outbursts.
6. Understand the impetus for the anger and how certain needs get set aside when acquiescing to threats of violation of the rights of others.

—. _____
  _____
  _____
—. _____
  _____
  _____
—. _____
  _____

SHORT TERM OBJECTIVES

THERAPEUTIC INTERVENTIONS

1. Verbalize an understanding of anger as an emotion necessary to the human survival mechanism but must be controlled. (1, 2, 3)

1. Verify the notion that anger is a necessary and useful emotion that needs to be harnessed and recognized

2. Each family member identifies the destructive effects that his/her uncontrolled anger has had on all family members, including self. (4)

3. Recall an incident in which one family member's strategy for managing anger may have been misinterpreted by the others. (5)

4. Identify any secondary gain that has been derived through expressing anger in an intimidating style. (6)

5. Each family member cites at least one example each of incidents in which his/her anger was expressed constructively and destructively. (6, 7)

6. Family members sign a contract stipulating that they will attempt to manage their anger with the support and guidance of family therapy. (8, 9, 10)

7. Each family member identifies an anger control technique that seems to work for him/her. (11, 12)

8. Each family member identifies his/her three main reasons for becoming angry. (13)

9. Each family member identifies an example from his/her own behavior of anger that was used to manipulate. (14)

10. Demonstrate the use of healthy, direct, respectful communication of a desire

as a sign that something is amiss or troubling.

2. Review some of the positive uses of anger—namely, as a reaction to a perceived threat and a means of communicating that some personal violation has occurred.

3. Educate family on the need for anger management and control as a method of better expressing one's feelings in order to obtain a positive outcome (see *Anger Workout Book* [Weisenberger] and *The Anger Workbook* [Carter, and Minirth]).

4. Have each family member describe how his/her respective expression of anger is counterproductive to himself/herself and to other family members; assist them in identifying uncontrolled anger's negative effects (fear, withdrawal, guilt, revenge, etc.) on others.

5. Ask family members to take turns volunteering and explaining examples of how their anger has been misinterpreted.

6. Assist family members in identifying what secondary gain (acquiescence to demands, fear-based service, etc.) is derived from uncontrolled anger.

7. Review various means of anger expression that have worked well in the past, as

for change in the behavior of another family member. (15)

11. Each family member identifies an example from his/her own behavior of anger that was used to assert independence. (16)

12. Implement assertiveness as a replacement for angry aggression to declare independence. (17, 18)

13. Identify expressions of anger that are in reaction to a perceived threat or means of defense against fear. (19)

14. Acknowledge the difference between uncontrolled anger outbursts while at home as opposed to controlled expression while in public. (20)

15. Each family member gives examples of his/her own use of passive-aggressive behavior and states how assertiveness could have been used instead. (21)

16. Report on the use of the subjective units of discomfort (SUD) scale to measure anger escalation. (22)

17. Identify the various cues for anger as it escalates. (23)

18. Verbalize an understanding of the steps in using time-out as an anger control technique. (24)

19. Report on the use of time-out at home to control anger. (25)

20. State a verbal agreement to not manipulate or intimidate using anger. (26)

contrasted with ways in which anger has been expressed destructively.

8. Urge family members to sign a contract agreeing to accept responsibility for containing their own anger and managing it effectively.

9. Discuss methods for instituting family support systems in helping each other control their anger levels (signaling time-out, breathing cues, etc.). Also recommend reading *Don't Sweat the Small Stuff with Your Family* (Carlson).

10. Discuss the dilemma of how each family member needs to express anger, while finding the difficult balance of doing it appropriately.

11. Evaluate specific techniques for anger control (thought stopping, controlled breathing, counting to 10, self-talk, etc.) and determine which one suits each family member.

12. Use paradoxical intention techniques by instructing family members to try cues that cause them to become angry one at a time. Highlight how difficult it is to become angry when we deliberately attempt to provoke it in ourselves.

13. Explore with each family member his/her three primary reasons for becoming angry.

21. Implement the use of the "turtle" technique of retreat to control anger escalation. (27)

22. Report on the successful development of sensitivity to the feelings of anger developing within and to the precursors of anger. (28, 29)

—. _____
   _____

—. _____
   _____

—. _____
   _____

14. Assist family members in identifying instances when their expression of anger was used as a means of manipulation.

15. Use modeling and role-playing to teach alternative methods (using "I" messages, making calm, respectful requests for change, etc.) to achieve goals without manipulating one another with anger.

16. Assist family members in identifying instances when their expression of anger was an attempt at asserting independence.

17. Clearly define examples of nonassertive, assertive, and aggressive expressions of anger and then have each family member give personal examples of each to demonstrate their understanding of the concept (see *Your Perfect Right* [Alberti and Emmons]).

18. Use role-playing and modeling to teach assertiveness as an alternative to angry aggressiveness used to declare independence.

19. Help family members identify internal and external cues for anger both at home as well as in public.

20. Point out how anger is often controlled while in public but uncontrolled at home, indicating that the ability to control is present.

21. After clearly defining for family members the definition of passive-aggressive behavior, have each of them recall specific examples in which their past behaviors have fit into this category; redirect this behavior into appropriate assertiveness.

22. Instruct family members in the use of a subjective units of discomfort (SUD) scale from 0 to 100 as a barometer for measuring their anger.

23. Teach family members how to identify the cognitive, affective, behavioral, and physiological cues of anger and how to differentiate low, moderate, and high ranges. (Focus on verbal as well as nonverbal cues.)

24. Teach family members the five steps in using time-out to control anger: (1) *self-monitoring* for escalating feelings of anger and hurt, (2) *signaling* to another family member that verbal exchange is not a good idea, (3) *acknowledgment* of the need for the other family members to back off, (4) *separation* to cool down and use cognitive self-talk to regain composure, and (5) *returning* to calm verbal exchange.

25. Assign family members to implement the time-out technique at home; review results, reinforcing success and redirecting for failures.

26. Develop family agreement to begin talking about angry feelings and thoughts earlier as opposed to allowing them to reach the level of intense behavioral expression, passive-aggressive maneuvers, or manipulative behaviors.

27. Teach the use of the "turtle" technique, in which family members imagine themselves individually retreating into their shells until they cool down.

28. Utilize the exercise of a pillow fight or a fight using batacas (foam-covered bats) between family members in order for them to get in touch with their individual anger levels.

29. Assign homework to each family member that utilizes anger-tracking exercises, identifying the precursors to anger along with the accompanying emotions and behaviors that fuel it.

—. _____
   _____

—. _____
   _____

—. _____
   _____

DIAGNOSTIC SUGGESTIONS

Axis I:	309.0	Adjustment Disorder With Depressed Mood
	309.3	Adjustment Disorders With Disturbance of Conduct
	312.34	Intermittent Explosive Disorder
	296.5x	Bipolar I Disorder
	296.x	Major Depressive Disorder
	V61.1	Partner Relational Problem
	V61.1	Physical Abuse of Adult
	995.81	Physical Abuse of Adult (Victim)
	V61.21	Physical Abuse of Child
	995.5	Physical Abuse of Child (Victim)
	V61.20	Parent–Child Relational Problem
	_____	_____
	_____	_____
Axis II:	301.7	Antisocial Personality Disorder
	301.83	Borderline Personality Disorder
	301.81	Narcissistic Personality Disorder
	301.0	Paranoid Personality Disorder
	_____	_____
	_____	_____

ANXIETY

BEHAVIORAL DEFINITIONS

1. One or more family members experience excessive worry or a sense of impending doom that precludes their daily normal functioning in their individual roles in the family.
2. One or more family members experience jitteriness, restlessness, insomnia, high-level autonomic activity, palpitations, sweaty palms, and so on.
3. One family member's symptoms of anxiety have caused undue distress within the family to the point that concessions are made to him/her.
4. Ruminations or controlling behaviors by the anxiety-ridden family member agitate other family members and alienate him/her from the others.
5. Anxiety symptoms in a parent or older family member lead to a child's dysfunctional behavior.
6. One or more family members experience the inability to fly, travel by boat, or drive on the superhighway due to irrational phobic fears.

—. _____
   _____
—. _____
   _____
—. _____
   _____

LONG-TERM GOALS

1. Utilize cognitive and behavioral techniques to reduce anxiety.
2. Confront anxiety-producing stimuli gradually to overcome debilitating fears.
3. Resolve the underlying biochemical, interpersonal, or emotional issues that result in symptoms of anxiety.
4. Family members learn about the symptoms, origins, and treatment of anxiety.
5. Family members provide support to one another in learning to reduce anxiety.
6. Family members learn their appropriate role in supporting the anxious family member in employing specific techniques for reducing anxiety levels and avoidance behaviors.

—. _____

_____

—. _____

_____

—. _____

_____

SHORT-TERM OBJECTIVES

1. Identify the nature and precipitators of anxiety symptoms. (1, 2, 3)
2. Each family member lists the specific impact that the anxiety symptoms or disorders have had on him/her. (3, 4, 9)
3. Each family member assesses how he/she has dealt with the anxiety, as well as how the family as a whole has coped with the anxiety to this point. (4, 5)
4. Nonanxious family members identify how they try

THERAPEUTIC INTERVENTIONS

1. Have the anxious family member list the specific symptoms and avoidance behaviors by utilizing one of the many anxiety inventories (Beck Anxiety Inventory [Beck and Steer], Body Sensations Questionnaire [Chambless, Caputo, and Bright], State-Trait Anxiety Inventory [Spielberger], etc.).
2. Gather reports from extended family members and the anxious family member's imagery or recollec-

to be supportive of the anxious family member. (6)

5. Nonanxious family members identify any resentments they may have for the anxious family member. (7, 8)

6. Family members discuss how the anxiety problems have changed family roles, if applicable. (8, 9)

7. Family members verbalize an understanding that anxiety is a survival mechanism and its maladaptive patterns can be corrected with specific therapeutic interventions. (10, 11, 12)

8. Nonanxious family members verbalize a constructive role for themselves in support of the anxious family member without becoming enmeshed in an unhealthy way. (13, 14, 15)

9. Family members verbalize an understanding of the interplay between physiology, cognitions, emotions, and behaviors affecting the anxious family member. (16, 17)

10. Anxious family member identifies automatic thoughts that produce anxious feelings. (18, 19)

11. All family members verbalize an understanding of cognitive restructuring concepts and techniques. (20, 21, 22)

12. Nonanxious family members coach the anxious family member in the use of cognitive restructuring. (23)

tions of how anxiety developed, to assist all family members in understanding the symptomatic effects of anxiety.

3. Gather the nonanxious family members' perspectives on the anxiety and avoidance patterns and attempt to uncover information not mentioned by the anxious family member.

4. Ask each family member to select a mode of expression that best characterizes the impact that the anxiety disorder has had on him/her. This may be through dramatization or written or artistic expression.

5. Ascertain the current coping skills of each family member regarding the anxiety problem within the family, and attempt to determine which coping mechanisms have been effective.

6. Have the nonanxious family members describe how they have each tried to be supportive of the anxious family member.

7. Ask each nonanxious family member to identify specific incidents in which he/she has felt resentment as a result of the side effects of another family member's anxiety (e.g., family members having to forfeit activities due to the anxiety), and strategize ways in which to reduce this conflict.

13. Develop a common language for family members to discuss varying levels of anxiety discomfort among the anxious family members. (24, 25)

14. Practice the use of deep breathing and relaxation skills to reduce anxiety. (26, 27)

15. Anxious family member records daily anxiety symptoms, Subjective Units of Distress Scale (SUDS) rating, and anxiety triggers. (28)

16. Anxious member creates a hierarchy of external stimulus events that produce increasing levels of anxiety. (29)

17. Anxious family members expose themselves to gradually increasing levels of anxiety-producing situations. (30, 31, 32)

18. Anxious family member implements thought-stopping techniques to reduce anxiety-producing cognitions. (33)

19. Anxious family member takes antianxiety medication as prescribed. (34, 35)

—. _____
  _____

—. _____
  _____

—. _____
  _____

8. Discuss with each family member how the specific anxiety disorder has affected them and what role they have adopted in the situation (supporter, antagonist, etc.).

9. Explore how each family member came to assume their role in the family (supporter, comforter, etc.)—by choice or via assignment by another family member.

10. Focus on the psychoeducational aspect of treatment by informing family members of the specific role that anxiety plays in every human being's system—that it is a survival mechanism that can, at times, be misinterpreted to the point of causing distress and debilitating symptoms. (Attempt to simplify this information for young children).

11. Teach family members that anxiety is a survival mechanism to be managed and that it is not a dichotomous entity, but one that fluctuates in intensity.

12. Reinforce the notion that the anxious family member must constantly confront his/her anxiety or fear in order to reduce it to a manageable level.

13. Discuss particular methods of how family members can encourage the anxious family member to follow his/her

treatment plan (words of affection, encouragement, nonenabling behaviors, etc.).

14. Encourage the nonanxious family members to serve as a coach to the anxious family member. If more than one family member is anxious, employ "buddy systems," and so on.

15. Brainstorm potential problems or pitfalls (parentification of the child, secondary gain, etc.) of the use of other family members as coaches and supporting agents. Identify ways to circumvent these problems.

16. Educate the family members on the interaction between physiology, cognition, affect, and behavior and how this affects the anxiety condition. (Recommend *Anxiety and Its Treatment: Help Is Available* [Greist, Jefferson, and Marks] or *Don't Panic: Taking Control of Anxiety Attacks* [Wilson]).

17. Encourage the use of various educational materials on anxiety (e.g., *The Anxiety and Phobia Workbook* [Bourne]; or *Mastery of Your Anxiety and Worry* [Craske, Barlow, and O'Leary]).

18. Assist the anxious family member in identifying internal anxiety-producing stimuli (e.g., catastrophic thoughts).

19. Diplomatically point out the anxious family member's propensity to overestimate anxious situations and to catastrophize anticipated situations or events.

20. Teach the anxious family member to replace distorted, negative thoughts with positive, realistic thoughts that counteract anxiety. Recommend using *Mastering Your Anxiety and Panic—Patient's Workbook* (Barlow and Craske).

21. Operationally define certain terms for all family members (e.g., *catastrophizing* and *reframing*).

22. Use role-modeling techniques with the anxious family member to teach cognitive restructuring of catastrophic thoughts and distortions and how to restructure and reframe events.

23. Transfer the role-modeling over to the other family members so that they can aid in coaching the situation with the anxious family member.

24. Teach family members about the barometer used by the anxious family member to assess his/her level of anxiety, the Subjective Units of Distress Scale (SUDS).

25. Encourage a line of open communication between family members regarding

the SUDS anxiety level in order to increase their awareness of when the anxious family member is experiencing difficulty.

26. Teach all family members various methods of physio-behavioral techniques for reducing anxiety (e.g., deep breathing and progressive relaxation). Have them read *The Relaxation Response* (Benson). Teach these techniques to nonanxious family members to aid them in better understanding the techniques and helping the anxious family member not to feel like the identified patient.

27. Provide family members access to audio- or videotapes to assist them in practicing breathing retraining and relaxation methods. Have them practice several times per day for at least 10 to 15 minutes to support them in coaching the anxious family member, but also for their own personal health and stress reduction.

28. Assign the anxious family member to keep an anxiety diary on a daily basis, recording his/her anxiety symptoms and SUDS rating, tracking cues that trigger his/her anxiety symptoms, and noting how his/her symptoms diminish over time.

29. Assist the anxious family member in identifying anxiety-producing external situations or events and organizing them in a hierarchy with accompanying SUDS ratings.

30. Initiate imagery exposure to a stimulus situation associated with a low-anxiety situation or event while the anxious family member utilizes relaxation techniques.

31. Assign graduated *in vivo* exposure at home to the stimulus situations in the hierarchy, and ask the anxious family member to practice relaxation and record the results in his/her daily anxiety log.

32. Continue to reinforce anxiety inoculation techniques, and use reverse role-playing and role-modeling in the therapy sessions to teach how potential anxiety situations may be addressed.

33. Teach the use of thought-stopping techniques (e.g., shouting "Stop!" in your mind while imagining a stop sign; snapping a rubber band on the wrist to interrupt negative thoughts and control anxiety symptoms).

34. Assess the need for antianxiety medication and refer the anxious family member to a physician for evaluation and psychotropic treatment, if indicated.

35. Monitor the anxious family member's medication use as to compliance, effectiveness, and side effects.

—. _____

  _____

—. _____

  _____

—. _____

  _____

DIAGNOSTIC SUGGESTIONS

Axis I: 293.89   Anxiety Disorder Due to General Medical Condition
  300.00   Anxiety Disorder NOS
  300.02   Generalized Anxiety Disorder
  300.21   Panic Disorder With Agoraphobia
  300.01   Panic Disorder Without Agoraphobia
  300.29   Specific Phobia
  300.23   Social Phobia
  309.24   Adjustment Disorder With Anxiety
  309.28   Adjustment Disorder With Mixed Anxiety and Depressed Mood

  _____   _____

  _____   _____

Axis II: 301.6   Dependent Personality Disorder
  301.82   Avoidant Personality Disorder

  _____   _____

  _____   _____

BLAME

BEHAVIORAL DEFINITIONS

1. Family members incessantly blame one another for conflicts in the family relationships or for things not operating to their respective expectations.
2. One or more family members overtly express their disenchantment with relationships within the family system as a whole.
3. Those family members most vociferous in their discontent and blame are resistant to accepting responsibility for their own contribution to family conflict or disenchantment.
4. Blaming family members externalize the responsibility for their own behavior and emotions.
5. The majority of interactions between family members lean toward the shifting of blame as opposed to responsible and honest self-admission of fault.
6. The chronic blaming behaviors have significantly affected communication and cohesiveness within the family.
7. Family members who engage in the greatest degree of externalization of blame verbalize low self-esteem and demonstrate poor interpersonal skills.

__. _____
   _____
__. _____
   _____
__. _____
   _____

LONG-TERM GOALS

1. Minimize blame patterns among family members, replacing them with more effective methods of problem solving.
2. Reduce the anger and agitation that accompanies blaming behavior.
3. Reduce the frequency and intensity of derogatory comments that are associated with blaming behaviors.
4. Restructure the view of the causes of family conflicts so as to seek solutions rather than placing blame.
5. Family members agree on replacement behaviors for those that attribute blame in family conflicts.

—. _____

_____

—. _____

_____

—. _____

_____

SHORT-TERM OBJECTIVES

1. Identify and isolate conflicts in the family in a civil and productive fashion. (1, 2, 3)
2. Each family member accepts responsibility for his/her own contribution to the conflicts and to the pattern of blaming. (4, 5, 6)
3. Reduce the frequency of disrespectful blaming exchanges in communication among family members. (7, 8)
4. Increase the frequency of the use of "I" statements to communicate feelings. (7, 8)

THERAPEUTIC INTERVENTIONS

1. Take turns asking each family member to define the problems in their own words and to discuss the blaming habits of one another in an appropriate and respectful manner.
2. Explore what factors may be underlying the actions of blame with each family member (old injustices, physical abuse, alcohol abuse, etc.).
3. Use modeling, role-playing, and guidance in helping family members to achieve and improve mutual respect when interacting.

5. Family members engage in *quid pro quo* behaviors in attempts to be more pleasing to the others. (9)

6. Reduce the frequency and intensity of expressions of anger within the family. (10)

7. Express forgiveness to other family members for past hurts. (11)

8. Family members express ownership and responsibility for their respective thoughts, feelings, and behaviors. (7, 8, 12)

9. Family members identify pleasurable behaviors desired from others, as opposed to maintaining the same pattern of blame. (13)

10. Implement pleasing behaviors on a *quid pro quo* basis. (14, 15)

11. Compliment, praise, and express appreciation for other family members' engaging in behaviors that are pleasing. (14, 15, 16)

12. Increase the use of assertiveness to express needs or desires rather than using blame. (17)

13. Identify words or behaviors that tend to trigger anger blaming. (18)

14. Implement constructive alternatives to blaming when trigger behaviors occur. (19)

15. Verbalize an understanding that a means of meeting one's own needs is through

4. Encourage the family members to take responsibility for their respective contributions to the conflict in the family as opposed to the projection of all blame onto others. Recommend reading *Beyond Blame* (Lukeman and Lukeman) and *The Language of Letting Go* (Beattie).

5. Seek to help the family members equally divide the responsibility for satisfaction as well as for dissatisfaction in the family.

6. Using a typical example of a conflict in the family, have family members divide their responsibilities for contribution to the conflict.

7. Use role-playing, positive reinforcement, and modeling to shape constructive behaviors to facilitate members in adopting new noninflammatory communication.

8. Encourage the use of "I" statements for all family members, with the majority of the focus on the present tense.

9. Encourage family members to formally agree to *quid pro quo* contracts to promote cooperation.

10. If anger or resentment is interfering with a blaming family member's ability to change, then shift the focus to anger reduction (anger management techniques,

performing pleasing actions for others. (20)

16. Agree on the tasks (chores) each member will undertake to promote the smooth, efficient functioning of the household. (21, 22, 23)

17. Agree to remain flexible in renegotiating behaviors that will continue to increase satisfaction in the family. (23)

18. Identify the pain that blaming has brought and how to better express disappointment. (24)

19. Each family member lists specific external pressures that may contribute to blaming behaviors. (25)

20. Family members engage in problem-solving skills individually as well as as a unit in order to cope with the external stressors that arise in their lives and reduce their propensity to blame others. (26, 27)

—. _____
    _____

—. _____
    _____

—. _____
    _____

working through causes for anger, letter writing to explain hurt, cognitive restructuring to reduce distorted thinking, etc.).

11. Encourage the use of rituals (physical embrace, written letter of forgiveness, etc.) during the process of forgiveness, after anger issues are worked through. Also recommend the book *Forgiveness: The Healing Gift We Give Ourselves* (Carson).

12. Use modeling and positive reinforcement to teach members to accept responsibility for their own thoughts, feelings, and behaviors.

13. Assist the family members in each identifying two or more pleasing behaviors that each of the other members could engage in.

14. Assign specific homework exercises that will regularly allow family members to benefit from the pleasing behaviors *quid pro quo* (e.g., adapt Stuart's "caring days" exercise from *Helping Couples Change* to the family unit).

15. Assign family members the task of reinforcing other members for pleasing behaviors in order to encourage their recurrence so that a fluid pattern of a more satisfying interchange can emerge.

16. Ask the blaming family member to review occasions when he/she has complimented the behavior of another family member. Encourage and reinforce the blaming family member's behavior in shifting to a position of praise rather than criticism.

17. Reemphasize the use of assertiveness in order to circumvent aggressive or passive-aggressive behaviors.

18. Assist the family members in identifying the specific words or behaviors that trigger blaming.

19. Develop constructive alternatives to blaming ("I" messages, assertiveness, reinforcement of incompatible behavior, etc.) as a response to common triggers to blaming.

20. Teach the family members that they have specific choices as to the quality of their family life and the comfort of their own lives, underscoring the choice of performing pleasing actions for each other as a means of fulfilling their own needs.

21. Assist the family members in accepting "rules of the family"—that is, taking responsibility for basic chores or tasks for the sake of family functioning (e.g., the father should help put the children to bed; the mother

should assist in the yard work; the children will make their beds or pick up their toys).

22. Clarify how the "rules of the family" are being broken and how those rule violations evoke negative feelings.

23. Assist the family members in renegotiating rules and roles that are agreeable to each, as a means of reducing blaming behavior. Each member will have input into the rule making and a vote on how they should be reinforced.

24. Have each family member list how they have specifically been hurt by another family member's blaming and what future mode of expression (e.g., "I" message) should be followed to avoid blaming.

25. Assign each family member to list the external stressors that are placing pressure on him/her and that lead to irritability toward others.

26. Teach the family the five steps to problem solving: (1) define the problem in specific terms, (2) brainstorm alternatives, (3) choose a mutually acceptable alternative, (4) develop a plan to put the chosen alternative into practice, including a fall-back plan, and (5) evaluate the success of the chosen alternative.

27. Encourage family members
to help each other with
problem solving.

___. _____

_____

___. _____

_____

___. _____

_____

DIAGNOSTIC SUGGESTIONS

Axis I:	309.24	Adjustment Disorder With Anxiety
	309.0	Adjustment Disorder With Depressed Mood
	309.3	Adjustment Disorder With Disturbance of Conduct
	309.28	Adjustment Disorder With Mixed Anxiety and Depressed Mood
	309.4	Adjustment Disorder With Mixed Disturbance of Emotions and Conduct
	305.00	Alcohol Abuse
	303.9	Alcohol Dependence
	296.x	Major Depressive Disorder
	312.34	Intermittent Explosive Disorder
	V61.1	Partner Relational Problem
	V61.20	Parent–Child Relational Problem
	_____	_____
	_____	_____
Axis II:	301.0	Paranoid Personality Disorder
	301.7	Antisocial Personality Disorder
	301.83	Borderline Personality Disorder
	301.81	Narcissistic Personality Disorder
	_____	_____
	_____	_____

BLENDED FAMILY PROBLEMS

BEHAVIORAL DEFINITIONS

1. Biological parent's and stepparent's parenting practices conflict.
2. Child's loyalty is to the absent biological parent.
3. Child's behavioral and/or emotional problems arise due to the adjustment to a new third parent (e.g., child rejects the stepparent's enforcement of rules and regulations).
4. Biological parent who lives outside of the home encourages child to protest against the stepparent.
5. Biological parent and stepparent conflict over issues of power, control, and favoritism.
6. Family experiences monetary pressures arising from a reduction in or loss of child support.
7. Rivalry develops between children of the blended family due to differences in parenting style and resentment of attention to others.
8. Jealousy and/or insecurity arise as a result of a parent displaying affection for the stepchild, causing tension in the marriage and guilt in the child.
9. Conflict arises between the noncustodial parent and the custodial parent over the visitation schedule (spending more visitation time

---

The term *blended family* includes two or more families living together as a result of a divorce, a foster family situation and/or an adoptive situation. Blended family problems are probably among the most frequent and challenging problems that family therapists will face. Due to the high divorce rate, the likelihood that marriages will include children from previous marriages is escalating. In fact, it has been estimated that by the beginning of the new millennium, as many as 50 percent of children and adults will belong to a blended family (Kaufman and Coale, 1993). This problem only intensifies when the blended family consists of adolescents or children with emotional or behavioral problems. Most parents struggle with their biological adolescent offspring, let alone having to interact with their spouse's adolescents.

than agreed upon, ex-spouse deliberately undermining wishes of the child's custodial parent, etc.).

10. An ex-spouse interferes with family issues that pertain to the blended family's lifestyle (e.g., curfew, rules, and regulations).

11. Parent and/or stepparent personalizes the child's behavioral problems, causing fragmentation within the family.

12. Children of the blended family feel they are treated unfairly or ignored by the stepparent.

13. Grown children living outside of the family of origin ask for financial support, causing conflict within the blended family.

—. _____

_____

_____

—. _____

_____

_____

—. _____

_____

LONG-TERM GOALS

1. Family members accept the responsibility of the adjustment that comes with joining a new family and agree to make exceptions in order to live together more harmoniously.

2. Children of the blended family accept the new spouse as a coparent and display respect to him/her as an adult and an equal caretaker.

3. Parents learn to be flexible in parenting their spouse's children in order to develop a positive relationship.

4. Stepparent interacts civilly and productively with the spouse's ex-partner.

5. Parents of the blended family achieve agreement over issues of power and control.

6. Parents terminate displaying favoritism so as to create harmony in the family.

7. Family members accept difficulties caused by a lack of child support.

8. Parents avoid criticizing the ex-spouse in front of the children.

9. Stepparent sensitively and respectfully displays affection for the spouse's children.

10. Parents reduce or eliminate the ex-spouse's interference in the blended family's issues.

11. Stepparent remains conscientious about not ignoring or treating the spouse's children unfairly.

12. Parents establish family rules about adult offsprings requesting financial support.

—. _____

_____

—. _____

_____

—. _____

_____

SHORT-TERM OBJECTIVES

1. Each family member defines, from his/her own perspective, the specific conflicts and issues between family members. (1, 2)

2. Identify issues of the stepparent's rule enforcement or discipline. (3, 4, 5)

3. Spouses terminate blaming an ex-spouse for the conflicts within the current marriage and blended family. (6)

4. Spouses implement communication skills to strengthen the bond between them. (7)

5. Biological parent living outside of the home attends a session with parents and stepparent to discuss parenting. (8)

6. Parents and ex-spouse agree to set aside their differences and cooperate in the parenting task. (9)

7. Parents identify and resolve conflicts between them-

THERAPEUTIC INTERVENTIONS

1. Establish a neutral zone for family members to express themselves without fear of retaliation by other family members.

2. Utilize such techniques as metaphors (see *Problem-Solving Therapy* [Haley]) or family sculpting (see *The New People Making* [Satir]) to facilitate family members in talking openly about their feelings and emotions over present conflicts with one another.

3. Facilitate open dialogue between the disgruntled children and the stepparent or adoptive parent. Explore the child's feelings of disloyalty to his/her biological parents.

4. Facilitate release of the child's feelings (fear of control, fear of abandonment, displaced anger toward absent parent, etc.) that may

selves as to parenting patterns. (10, 11)

8. Parents agree to cooperate and communicate so as to eliminate their being manipulated by the children. (12)

9. Identify the effect that the loss or decrease of child support has had on the family. (13, 14, 15)

10. List actions that can reduce the tension over reduced child support. (15)

11. Parents identify any insecurity or jealousy regarding affection displayed between a parent and a stepchild. (16, 17)

12. Biological parents reach agreement on a visitation schedule with the children. (18, 19)

13. Children express and identify the basis for their feelings that they are treated unfairly by the stepparent. (20, 21)

14. All family members agree on changes necessary to facilitate a feeling of equality in treatment of the children by both parents. (22, 23)

15. Verbalize agreement about if and when any financial assistance will be given to adult children of either spouse who reside outside of the home. (24, 25, 26)

be inhibiting acceptance of the stepparent's directives.

5. Assess the strictness or rigidity of the stepparent's style and whether it may be interfering with acceptance by the children. Use role-playing and modeling to help the parent consider more flexible alternative methods.

6. Assess the parent and stepparent's potential for unfairly and too easily blaming an ex-spouse for internal conflicts within their marriage and blended family.

7. Teach assertiveness and communication skills (use of "I" messages, empathetic listening and reflective responding, undivided attention and good eye contact, respectful and controlled expression of emotions, etc.) to the parents to strengthen their relationship and reduce the impact of an ex-spouse. Recommend reading *Core Communications, Skills and Processes* (Miller and Miller).

8. Invite the biological parent or ex-spouse into a conjoint session with the other biological parent and/or the stepparent in order to discuss differences in parenting philosophies, strategies, and misperceptions. Suggest the use of a unified parenting program such as STEP or PET (see *Parents*

__.__ _____

_____

__.__ _____

_____

__.__ _____

_____

and Adolescents, vol. 2, *Family Problem Solving* [Forgatch and Patterson]).

9. Meet with the biological parents alone to resolve any residual feelings about their prior union.

10. Conduct a conjoint meeting with parents of the blended family and address personal insecurities, feelings of loss of power, and needs to demonstrate favoritism. Suggest alternative methods for dealing with these issues and how spouses can be supportive of each other. (See *The Couples Psychotherapy Treatment Planner* [O'Leary, Heyman, and Jongsma]). Also recommend reading *Step-Families* (Bray and Kelly).

11. Use role exchange and role alternatives to reduce parental conflicts. Have them consider the advantages and disadvantages of behavioral change and deal with the emotional fear that accompanies this change.

12. Address the potential manipulation of the child in playing one parent against the other for power and territorial advantages.

13. Discuss the anger and resentment that has risen between family members regarding the financial effect of a reduction in child support.

14. Encourage the children to express their feelings regarding finances to both biological parents.

15. Brainstorm financial (e.g., adding part-time jobs for family members) or emotional (e.g., more time spent in family activities that are free or low cost) solutions to the cut in income due to the reduction in child support.

16. Assess whether a display of affection by a parent to a stepchild may arouse anxiety, anger, suspicion, or jealousy in the biological parent. Explore how this may relate to the biological parent's own neglect or abuse in his/her family of origin.

17. Suggest ways in which the biological parent can deal with his/her insecurities and reframe their expression in the family system. Teach alternative ways of viewing the situation (e.g., "It's an honor to have my spouse show such fondness toward my son or daughter").

18. Reassure the children that they are not responsible for their parents' disagreements regarding visitation scheduling and that these conflicts do not reflect their parents' love for them.

19. Suggest a meeting between the custodial and the non-custodial parent in order to

address the issue of visitation. If this proves fruitless, then suggest professional mediation.

20. Facilitate the children in expressing directly or through a letter the basis for their feelings of being treated unfairly by a stepparent.

21. Explore whether the parent is consciously or unconsciously ignoring the stepchildren. Review methods for increasing their awareness of this (e.g., have parents listen to the children's feedback and evaluate whether they are listening to them; suggest the use of reflective listening, in which parent and child give each other feedback on what is being said) and obtain a commitment from them toward involvement.

22. Negotiate between the children and the stepparent as to actions that would be perceived as more fair by the children.

23. Suggest a list of special activities that the parent and the stepchildren can do to reduce their feelings of alienation from each other.

24. Review the pros and cons of lending money or giving gifts to adult offspring. Brainstorm the potential resentments that may occur on the part of either the

spouse or other family members.

25. Take a family vote on whether and how adult members will be assisted. Address how to deal with the tension that arises from feelings of guilt and anger.

26. Encourage assertiveness for parents who are afraid of negative responses from children to whom they refuse financial assistance.

___. _____

_____

___. _____

_____

___. _____

_____

DIAGNOSTIC SUGGESTIONS

Axis I:	V61.20	Parent–Child Relational Problem
	V61.1	Partner Relational Problem
	V61.8	Sibling Relational Problem
	_____	_____
	_____	
Axis II:	301.9	Personality Disorder NOS
	_____	_____
	_____	_____

CHILD/PARENT CONFLICTS

BEHAVIORAL DEFINITIONS

1. Children under the age of 13 have behavioral problems that cause conflict for the parents and the rest of the family members (e.g., acting out, destructive behaviors, or refusal to go to school).
2. The children's behavior sparks ongoing arguments and dissension between the parents, weakening their effectiveness with the children.
3. Boundaries weaken and issues of power and control surface, contributing to the decreasing effectiveness of the parents.
4. The children's behavioral problems spread to the community (neighborhood or school), causing added stress to the family.
5. All family members experience tension and conflict due to the dysfunction in the home.
6. The children pick up on the parents' schism and play one against the other.
7. The parents become angry with each other and engage in undercutting behavior that escalates the children's misbehavior to more serious levels.

—. _____
   _____
—. _____
   _____
—. _____
   _____

LONG-TERM GOALS

1. Reduce or eliminate the children's behavioral problems that cause conflict for the parents and other family members.
2. Parents work together as a team in making clear and firm decisions regarding discipline.
3. Reduce or eliminate tension and conflict in the family by improvement of coping skills and communication.
4. Reduce the children's manipulative behavior and increase the parent's alignment and control.

__. _____
 _____
__. _____
 _____
__. _____
 _____

SHORT-TERM OBJECTIVES

1. Operationally define the behavioral problems that are occurring with the children and how they impact the family. (1, 2, 3)
2. Identify the family interactional patterns that are contributing to the problematic behavior. (4, 5)
3. Identify external factors that may be contributing to the behavioral problems. (6, 7)
4. Parents list their strengths and weaknesses as caretakers and disciplinarians. (8, 9)
5. Parents identify ways to support each other in disciplining the children. (10, 11)

THERAPEUTIC INTERVENTIONS

1. Help the family specifically outline the problematic behavior and conceptualize the problem.
2. Have each family member express how he/she is being affected by the children's misbehaviors.
3. Utilize some specific inventories that will define the behavioral problem and help determine whether they are individual or part of the system or both (e.g., Child Behavior Checklist—Ages 4–18 [Achenbach]).
4. Search for specific familial interaction patterns that may be subtly or overtly supporting problematic be-

6. Parents verbalize an understanding of the principles of effective parenting and behavior modification. (12, 13)

7. Parents confront and resolve disagreements between themselves discreetly and not in the presence of the children. (14, 15)

8. All family members list specific behaviors that they may be engaging in that are negative modeling for the child. (16)

9. Implement healthy alternative behaviors and agree to attempt to serve as a positive role model for younger children. (17, 18, 19)

10. Family members identify and challenge their own unreasonable or unrealistic expectations of the children. (20, 21)

11. Implement new methods of effective communication and problem solving between family members. (22, 23, 24)

12. Implement family meetings to increase mutual understanding and improve overall family communication. (25, 26)

13. Child reduces the frequency of manipulating behaviors and increase the frequency of the acceptance of limits by the parents. (10, 14, 15, 27, 28, 29)

14. Parents express their own emotions and frustrations

haviors (dissension between parents, favoritism, etc.).

5. Assess the specific characteristics the children may have that contribute to their behavior problems (hyperactivity, temperament, etc.).

6. Explore for any emotional and/or environmental stressors that may be precipitating the problem (e.g., family transitions, inconsistent rules, school or social difficulties).

7. Develop a plan for how to reduce the amount of stress from external factors. Refer to books such as *Coping Cat Workbook* (Kendall).

8. Have each parent list his/her own strengths and weaknesses as a parent and the strengths and weaknesses of the partner as a parent.

9. Brainstorm how each parent can capitalize on his/her strengths and reduce the impact of his/her weaknesses.

10. Assist parents in identifying methods for supporting each other and not undercutting each other's attempts at setting limits on the children.

11. Role-play scenarios with parents and children in which discipline is required, and model appropriate support for the parent who

in a controlled, respectful manner. (30, 31)

—. _____

   _____

—. _____

   _____

—. _____

   _____

takes the lead in setting limits.

12. Assign the use of readings and videotapes that may increase parenting skills (e.g., the STEP Program [Dinkmeyer, McKay, and Dinkmeyer], *Positive Parenting from A to Z* [Joslin], or *S.O.S. Help for Parents* [Clark]).

13. Teach the principles of behavioral reinforcement, response cost, and rewards for positive behavioral change.

14. Discuss the necessity for parents not to allow the children too much information about their disagreements in order to strengthen their unity.

15. Recommend to parents strategies for controlling their urges to bicker in the presence of the children (e.g., utilize self-talk or nonverbal signals to each other as a cue for curtailing their statements).

16. Solicit examples from family members of behaviors that are negative models for younger children (e.g., temper tantrums, aggressive verbalizations, disrespectful name-calling, or ignoring another family member).

17. Brainstorm healthy alternatives to the negative behavior models.

18. Role-play the implementation of healthy alterna-

tives to negative behavior models.

19. Contract with all family members to seek to implement positive alternative behavior and to be positive role models for younger family members.

20. Have family members track their thoughts and emotional reactions during problematic behaviors with their children, identifying distorted cognitions.

21. Help family members to challenge unreasonable expectations by persuasively illuminating the illogical premise involved (e.g., "This behavior will never change and therefore my child is doomed to be a social misfit").

22. Provide the family members with some basic communication training (e.g., see *Relationship Enhancement* [Guerney]) and problem-solving skills training (e.g., see *The Parents Handbook: STEP* [Dinkmeyer, McKay, and Dinkmeyer]).

23. Encourage a trial of *in vivo* use of newly learned communication and problem-solving skills.

24. Have parents rate the effectiveness of the newly learned skills and discuss their positive and negative experiences with them.

25. Discuss the concept of family meetings held at home on a regular basis in which all members express their thoughts and feelings; establish a set of basic rules to follow at meetings (length, frequency, attendance requirements, leadership, participation, etc.).

26. Assign family meetings on a regular basis that include all family members. Have family members vote on days and times for family meetings.

27. Help parents to recognize when there is inconsistency in their parenting and encourage them to communicate with each other so that the children do not successfully manipulate them.

28. Ask parents to schedule parenting meetings with each other in order to review the children's behavior of past weeks and confront the children about their manipulations.

29. Help parents become aware of how they are undercutting each other due to frustration and how this may be inadvertently facilitating the children's manipulations.

30. Help parents to get in touch with their own emotions and frustrations associated with the trials of parenting.

31. Devise strategies for increasing anger control and

frustration tolerance (deep
breathing, cognitive self-
talk, diversion techniques,
etc.).

—. _____
   _____
   _____
—. _____
   _____
—. _____
   _____

DIAGNOSTIC SUGGESTIONS

Axis I: 309.3   Adjustment Disorder With Disturbance of
                    Conduct
            309.4   Adjustment Disorder With Mixed Disturbance
                    of Emotions and Conduct
            V61.21 Neglect of Child
            995.5   Neglect of Child (Victim)
            V61.2   Parent–Child Relational Problem
            V61.1   Partner Relational Problem
            V61.21 Physical Abuse of Child
            995.5   Physical Abuse of Child (Victim)
            V61.21 Sexual Abuse of Child
            995.5   Sexual Abuse of Child (Victim)
            313.81 Oppositional Defiant Disorder
            312.9   Disruptive Behavior Disorder NOS
            312.8   Conduct Disorder, Adolescent Onset Type
            314.01 Attention-Deficit/Hyperactivity Disorder,
                    Combined Type

            _____ _____
            _____ _____

COMMUNICATION

BEHAVIORAL DEFINITIONS

1. Family members are experiencing frequent arguments and misinterpretations with one another.
2. Certain family members elect not to verbally express themselves much at all, due to either their inhibitions or passive-aggressive behaviors, causing a breakdown in communication.
3. Basic as well as complex verbal exchanges in the family are fraught with misconstrued information and miscommunication.
4. Positive affirmations and compliments are rarely or never expressed, contributing to alienation between family members.
5. In order to reach conclusions, family members rely on "mind reading" or "assumptions" based on observing nonverbal behaviors of other family members.
6. Little attentive listening and thoughtful responding are practiced by family members.
7. Family members often interrupt or talk over each other.

__. _____
   _____
   _____
__. _____
   _____
   _____
__. _____
   _____

LONG-TERM GOALS

1. Communication improves to the point that intrafamilial conflict and dysfunction are significantly reduced.

2. Gradually discuss particularly volatile topics with reduced tension and conflict.
3. Address the issues that underlie nonverbal expressions with one another (anger, need for control, resentment, etc.).
4. Improved speaker/listener techniques allow for reduced misconstrual of verbal miscommunications.
5. Improve and increase the rate of positive verbal comments and pleasurable exchanges between family members.
6. Learn to avoid relying on assumptions and inferences (mind reading) through the improved use of communication skills and assertive behaviors.
7. Individuals stop interrupting one another and cease other rude behavior.
8. Work toward more family cohesiveness, more of a sense of engagement, and less isolation.

—. _____
   _____
—. _____
   _____
—. _____
   _____

SHORT-TERM OBJECTIVES

1. All family members admit to and assume responsibility for poor communication and related tensions. (1, 2, 3)
2. Identify problem areas of communication. (4)
3. All family members cease and desist blaming each other for poor communication and take personal responsibility for their own faults. (5, 6)
4. Terminate relying on nonverbal communication or

THERAPEUTIC INTERVENTIONS

1. Use defining and identifying techniques to clarify the communication problems.
2. Develop a genogram or use another family-of-origin exploration technique to determine communication problems that have trickled down from the parents' families of origin (see *Family of Origin Inventory* [Stuart]).
3. Reinforce family members who readily admit to communication problems and

speaking through other family members. (7, 8)

5. Identify any underlying dynamics that may be hindering or confounding communication. (9)

6. Reduce expressions of anger that are triggered by poor communication in the family. (10, 11)

7. Increase the frequency of assertive communication as a replacement for passive withdrawal or aggressive attacking. (12)

8. Implement constructive problem-solving techniques to resolve differences. (13, 14)

9. Share feelings that underlie the isolation behavior. (15, 16)

10. List the benefits and risks of becoming a more cohesive, open, close family. (17, 18)

11. Identify potential pitfalls that may contribute to any backsliding into poor communication and disengagement/alienation. (19, 20)

12. Eliminate or reduce the frequency and duration of isolation that occurs among family members. (21, 22, 23)

13. Agree to use family meetings for communication and problem solving in the future. (21, 22, 24, 25)

14. Provide positive feedback to other family members as communication progress is observed. (26, 27)

confront those who deny them.

4. Have the family select a topical issue to discuss and observe or videotape the discussion and identify times when they each engage in faulty communication.

5. Contract with the family members to shift away from blaming each other and practice using "I" statements; role-play members taking responsibility for their own faulty communication skills. Start with the parents first, particularly if the children are resistant or oppositional.

6. Discuss a family record system for when family members are successful in not blaming each other and in taking personal responsibility.

7. Introduce the use of the speaker-listener technique (see *Fighting for Your Marriage* [Markman, Stanley, and Blumberg] or *Core Communications, Skills and Processes* [Miller and Miller]) to structure family conversations. Model reflective listening and teach rephrasing of confusing statements and requesting clarification when something is not understood.

8. Confront patterns of speaking through other family

15. Implement actions that are designed to please the other family members as a means of serving each other. (27)

16. Parents monitor the family progress and keep everyone motivated. (28, 29, 30)

—. _____
   _____

—. _____
   _____

—. _____
   _____

members or using only non-verbal communication; instruct members to speak directly, clearly, and for themselves.

9. Explore for any underlying dynamic that may be affecting the communication process (e.g., hidden resentment, avoidant behavior).

10. Teach cognitive-behavioral techniques (e.g., deep breathing, cognitive restructuring) to help family members mediate anger or frustration that results from problems in communication. Recommend the *Anger Workout Book* (Weisenberger) and *The Anger Workbook* (Carter and Minirth).

11. Have family members practice alternative behaviors for venting their frustration (e.g., journaling, sports activities) and report on their experiences. Recommend books such as *Journaling for Joy* (Chapman).

12. Use assertiveness training techniques to counter passivity or aggression in family members (recommend *Your Perfect Right* [Alberti and Emmons]).

13. Teach problem-solving techniques as outlined in *Fighting for Your Marriage* [Markman, Stanley, and Blumberg].

14. Have family members attempt to reverse roles and

review a problem from the other family member's perspective; process the experience.

15. Discuss with family members how they have gravitated away from each other and probe for a desire to become closer together.

16. Explore the feelings of fear, anger, hurt, or depression that may contribute to isolation between family members.

17. Empathize with the family about how becoming more cohesive may take time and feel different or unusual.

18. Facilitate the process of family members sharing their feelings about getting closer. Discuss the pros and cons of a more cohesive family from each member's perspective.

19. Brainstorm about what may cause the family member to slide back into old habits of isolation (laziness, strength of old patterns, crisis, etc.).

20. Review techniques for how to avoid any backslides into old habits (monitoring, family meetings, etc.).

21. Help the family members to set up a structure for regular family meetings held once per week or once per month as needed.

22. Discuss in detail how the family meetings should be conducted and how commu-

nication techniques/skills should be practiced.

23. Reinforce all family members when they contribute to open, respectful communication and reduce the isolation between family members.

24. Develop an agreement about the way failing communication should be addressed and establish the fact that any family member has a right to call a family meeting at any time he/she feels it is necessary.

25. Utilize role-play and modeling techniques to teach how to implement the family meeting to deal with failed communication.

26. Use modeling or role-playing techniques to teach and practice the process of family members giving positive feedback to one another.

27. Discuss and assign the implementation of "pleasing behaviors" (doing chores for one another, etc.) in order to support and promote positive/productive family interaction.

28. Suggest the planning of some family outings or activities in order to strengthen family interaction and then have the family discuss their reactions to the exercise.

29. Suggest that the parents consider reading certain materials (e.g., *Changing*

Families [Fassler, Lash, and Ivers]).

30. Consider follow-up visits with the parents to reinforce their role in supporting the family change.

—. _____
    _____
—. _____
    _____
—. _____
    _____

DIAGNOSTIC SUGGESTIONS

Axis I:

309.24	Adjustment Disorder With Anxiety
309.0	Adjustment Disorder With Depressed Mood
309.3	Adjustment Disorder With Disturbance of Conduct
309.28	Adjustment Disorder With Mixed Anxiety and Depressed Mood
309.4	Adjustment Disorder With Mixed Disturbance of Emotions and Conduct
305.00	Alcohol Abuse
303.9	Alcohol Dependence
296.x	Bipolar I Disorder
300.4	Dysthymic Disorder
296.x	Major Depressive Disorder
V61.21	Physical Abuse of Child
995.5	Physical Abuse of Child (Victim)
V61.2	Parent–Child Relational Problem
_____	_____
_____	_____

Axis II:

301.7	Antisocial Personality Disorder
301.83	Borderline Personality Disorder
301.5	Histrionic Personality Disorder
301.81	Narcissistic Personality Disorder
_____	_____
_____	_____

COMPULSIVE BEHAVIORS

BEHAVIORAL DEFINITIONS

1. A family member engages excessively in an activity to the point where it interferes with daily functioning (e.g., gambling, shopping, Internet use, or health/exercise).
2. Family members' response to the individual's excessive behavior leads to a change in the pattern of relationships and contributes to tension and conflict within the family.
3. Verbal and/or physical abuse occurs when the family member is confronted about the excessive behavior.
4. Enabling by family members contributes to the ongoing pattern of addictive behavior.
5. Dysfunctional communication, loss of work and/or financial support, or medication problems result from the excessive behavior pattern.
6. Children act out as a result of the long-term effects of a lack of structure or boundaries in the environment that are a consequence of the excessive behavior.
7. The family member becomes isolated from extended family and friends due to the preoccupation with the excessive activity.
8. Bills are not paid, checks bounce, and there is no follow-through on daily responsibilities because of the time spent on the excessive activity.
9. The family experiences shame and humiliation and makes excuses for the family member's excessive behavior in order to save face.

—. _____

_____

—. _____

_____

—. _____

_____

LONG-TERM GOALS

1. Achieve a significant reduction or elimination of the compulsive behavior.
2. Eliminate the verbal, physical, and/or psychological abuse in the home.
3. Redirect enabling behaviors and develop new, healthier patterns of familial interaction.
4. An extended family member or some other responsible adult takes over the parental role with the children, preventing the parentizing of the children.

—. _____

_____

—. _____

_____

—. _____

_____

SHORT-TERM OBJECTIVES

1. Identify the excessive behavior and give evidence that it is engaged in compulsively. (1, 2)

2. Identify the untoward effects of the excessive behavior on the self-esteem, family life, employment, health, social relations, and

THERAPEUTIC INTERVENTIONS

1. Use interviewing and/or inventories to determine the degree of compulsivity or excessive engagement in activities (e.g., the Daily Activity chart in *Cognitive Therapy: Basics and Beyond* [Beck] or "Measuring Non-Pathological and Compul-

personal finances of all family members. (3)

3. Sign a contract with respect to controlled and moderate involvement in the excessive activity/behavior. (4, 5)

4. Prove the ability to control the excessive behavior to moderate levels by keeping a record of the frequency of the activity/behavior. (6)

5. Read literature on controlling compulsive behaviors and on the effects of excessive behavior on family dynamics. (7, 8)

6. Sign a contract agreeing to attend meetings with openness and honesty. (9, 10)

7. Compulsive family member cooperates with referral to a physician for a medication evaluation. (11)

8. Compulsive family member signs a behavioral contract that stipulates that no violence or threats will be engaged in toward any other family member. (12, 13)

9. Implement the use of cognitive/behavioral techniques to manage angry feelings. (14)

10. Violent family member accepts referral for specialized behavioral treatment of explosive disorder. (15)

11. Compulsive family member identifies attractions to or perceived benefits of the excessive behavior. (16)

siveness" [Kagan and Squires]).

2. Poll all family members about why they believe the activity is excessive or compulsive.

3. Gather family members' perspectives on the negative effects that the compulsive behavior has had on all family members and the family dynamics; focus on the impact that denial has played in this process.

4. Assign the compulsive family member to follow a structured format for controlling the excessive behavior (e.g., use of a stipulated, written activity schedule and/or attendance at a 12-step program). Solicit an agreement that, should the contract be broken a designated number of times (e.g., twice), a complete abstinence contract will be instituted.

5. Ask the compulsive family member to sign a written contract that stipulates the moderate frequency of behavior to be engaged in on a daily and weekly basis.

6. Develop a daily record form to track the frequency and intensity of compulsive behaviors, using this record to determine the family member's ability to consistently control the behaviors.

12. List and implement alternative behaviors that can replace the compulsive behavior and still produce the benefits sought. (17, 18, 19)

13. Compulsive family member implements assertiveness and other social skills as replacements for the excessive behavior. (19)

14. Engage in "caring days," when each member does something pleasing for the other family members without prompting. (20)

15. Identify opportunities that exist for social interaction with other families and together develop a plan for initiating contact for activities that do not involve compulsive behavior. (21, 22)

16. Identify alternative social/recreational activities that all family members could engage in that would be rewarding to all. (22)

17. Compulsive family member apologizes to other family members for the pain and suffering he/she has caused by his/her excessive behaviors. (23)

18. Identify triggers to episodes of compulsive behavior and agree to alternative responses to cope with situations. (24, 25)

19. Acknowledge how primary and secondary enabling has occurred. (26, 27)

7. Research and assign reading materials regarding the compulsive behavior and its effects, controlled behavior, and the family dynamics of addiction (e.g., *Sex, Drugs, Gambling, and Chocolate: A Workbook for Overcoming Addictions* [Horvath and Hester]; *Compulsive Gamblers and Their Families* [McEnvoy]; *Caught in the Net* [Young]; and *Consuming Passions: Help for Compulsive Shoppers* [Catalano and Sonenberg]).

8. Hold a discussion session with family members to process the material that they have read and focus on new insights.

9. Develop a joint family contract that all members sign, agreeing to attend all sessions and to be completely open about any compulsive behaviors that they may engage in themselves.

10. If the session attendance contract is broken, ask the compulsive family member to sign an agreement of abstinence from all excessive behaviors accompanied by an agreement to attend a support group (e.g., Gambler's Anonymous [GA] or group psychotherapy).

11. Refer the compulsive family member to a psychiatrist specializing in obsessive-compulsive behavior to evaluate for the use of phar-

20. Cite assertive incidences whereby enabling or taking responsibility for the compulsive family member has been avoided. (28)

21. Confront each other's behaviors that continue the enabling process. (29)

22. Children identify the unhealthy role in the family that each has assumed as a result of the dysfunction the compulsive behaviors have brought. (30, 31)

___. _____

_____

___. _____

_____

___. _____

_____

macotherapy (e.g., SRI antidepressants).

12. Develop a written contract stipulating that no member of the family will engage in aggressive or assaultive threats on any other family member.

13. Develop a refuge plan for the safety of family members if violence does erupt when compulsive behavior is challenged.

14. Teach the use of cognitive-behavioral strategies, such as controlled breathing, thought stopping, and Meichenbaum's stress inoculation techniques (*Cognitive Behavior Modification* [Meichenbaum], for anger and stress control.

15. Refer the acting-out family member to another provider for individual or group treatment of the explosive disorder.

16. Explore those perceived benefits that the compulsive family member is obtaining by engaging in the excessive behaviors (acceptance by friends/peers, reduction of social or other anxiety, escape from family tensions, etc.).

17. Strategize about the specific behavioral exercises (e.g., meditation, relaxation, social skill or assertiveness training) that can be used to replace compulsive be-

haviors, while still obtaining the benefits sought.

18. Teach stress management techniques (deep breathing, progressive muscle relaxation, guided imagery, meditation, etc.) as replacements for compulsive behaviors.

19. Use modeling and role-playing to teach assertiveness and social skill techniques, helping the compulsive family member to weigh the pros and cons of using such techniques.

20. Instruct family members in the technique of "caring days" (see *Helping Couples Change: A Social Learning Approach to Marital Therapy* [Stuart]), in which each family member does something pleasant for other members (e.g., performing a special chore without being asked; paying a nice compliment).

21. Encourage and assist in formulating a plan for social activities with other couples or families that does not include the compulsive activity. Suggest church, hobby, work associates, and recreational groups as possible social network opportunities for outreach.

22. Schedule a specific family recreational activity in which each family member is assigned a specific role in making the activity happen (consider using the Inven-

tory of Rewarding Activities [Birchler] to brainstorm and develop a list of recreational/educational activities that might be enjoyed by the family).

23. Recommend that the compulsive family member formally apologize for the pain caused to other family members as a result of the excessive behavior and time taken away from the family.

24. Help the family identify triggers of relapse for the compulsive behavior and what may help to avoid future relapse.

25. Suggest to the family that they develop index cards listing alternative coping strategies for compulsive behaviors in the face of stimuli that trigger relapse (e.g., connecting with sponsors at the support groups; using stress inoculation techniques).

26. Address the issue of subtle enabling or cover-up behaviors by family members. Use educative techniques to make the nonconscious more aware and use more direct confrontation when necessary.

27. Using role-play techniques of family scenarios, guide the noncompulsive family members in not accepting responsibility for the compulsive member's choices.

28. Review instances of family interaction at home in which family members have avoided enabling behaviors.

29. Brainstorm ideas among family members about how to more constructively respond to situations that previously precipitated enabling behaviors.

30. Teach family members the roles (see *Another Chance* [Wegscheider-Cruse]) usually adopted by children of addictive parents (e.g., the family hero, the scapegoat, the lost child, and the mascot). Help children identify the role (or roles) each has adopted.

31. Encourage children to give up their unhealthy role assumptions and express their needs, feelings, and desires directly and assertively.

___. _____
     _____

___. _____
     _____

___. _____
     _____

DIAGNOSTIC SUGGESTIONS

Axis I: 300.3   Obsessive-Compulsive Disorder
               296.40   Bipolar I Disorder
               300.4   Dysthymic Disorder
               296.2x   Major Depressive Disorder, Single Episode

	V61.1	Partner Relational Problem
	V61.2	Parent–Child Relational Problem
	_____	_____
	_____	_____

Axis II:	301.83	Borderline Personality Disorder
	301.4	Obsessive-Compulsive Personality Disorder
	301.5	Histrionic Personality Disorder
	_____	_____
	_____	_____

DEATH OF A CHILD

BEHAVIORAL DEFINITIONS

1. The accidental, sudden death of a child occurs, causing grief to the surviving family members.
2. The death of a child occurs in utero (stillborn) or at birth, causing expecting parents and family members to grieve over the loss.
3. The death of a child occurs following a long terminal illness (e.g., congenital heart disease, cystic fibrosis, or muscular dystrophy).
4. The death of a child occurs due to an acute illness (e.g., brain tumor or cancer).
5. The parents and/or family members witness and/or participate in the accidental death of a child (e.g., auto accident), causing extreme guilt and trauma.
6. The child's death has an impact on the family dynamics and the way siblings reorder their lives with one another in order to cope with the loss.
7. The parents have a fear of future loss and display overprotectiveness of the surviving children.

—. _____
   _____
—. _____
   _____
—. _____
   _____

LONG-TERM GOALS

1. Adjust to the shock and trauma of the death/loss and learn to cope effectively with the grief and the absence of the deceased family member.
2. Come to grips with the notion that death is part of life and can occur at any time, whether it be in utero or during the developmental life span.
3. Become aware of the various stages of grief and prepare for dealing with the emotions that accompany those stages.
4. Learn to mediate guilt, whether it be a result of being a survivor or due to some peripheral or direct involvement in the child's accidental death.
5. Parents and family members resolve the need to overprotect the surviving children.

—. _____
   _____

—. _____
   _____

—. _____
   _____

SHORT-TERM OBJECTIVES

1. Each family member expresses his/her grief associated with the shocking death of the child. (1, 2, 3)
2. Family members verbalize an understanding of the various stages of grief associated with the loss of a loved one. (4)
3. Implement cognitive and behavioral techniques for coping with the loss of a loved one. (5, 6)

THERAPEUTIC INTERVENTIONS

1. Allow the family to vent their grief as a family and express the loss as a whole.
2. Promote a sense of unity and facilitate cohesiveness among the surviving family members.
3. Facilitate each family member expressing how the grief has affected him/her on an individual basis and define how the experience differs from those of other family members.

4. Family members reaffirm their faith-based beliefs regarding death. (7, 8)

5. Family members identify those aspects within themselves that were touched by the deceased while he/she was alive. (9, 10, 11)

6. Verbalize the resolution of guilt surrounding the death of the family member. (12, 13)

7. Parents acknowledge their propensity to be overprotective of the surviving children, both as a natural reaction and as a means of assuaging guilt. (14)

8. Parents identify the negative impact of being overprotective of surviving children. (15)

9. Parents and/or family members cooperate with the assessment and treatment of preexisting anxiety or depression that has been exacerbated by the death. (16, 17)

10. Siblings express any irrational feelings of responsibility for the death of the child. (18, 19)

11. Family members terminate blaming of themselves or each other for the child's death. (19)

4. Educate the family about the stages of grief for survivors; recommend that adults read *How to Survive the Loss of a Child* (Sanders) and that children read *The Fall of Freddie the Leaf* (Buscaglia).

5. Discuss with the family methods for coping with the loss of a child and sibling. Explore the use of various rituals (e.g., wearing certain clothing that belonged to the deceased or constructing a shrine).

6. Teach cognitive behavioral coping strategies for grief (e.g., imagery that suggests how the deceased would want the survivors to go on, how the deceased would be dealing with the reverse situation if the circumstances had been different).

7. Explore with family members their religious beliefs about life after death. Reinforce the notion that the deceased is safe and free from pain. Recommend the book *After the Death of a Child* (Finkbeiner).

8. Explore with the family the possibility of making arrangements for a memorial service to honor the deceased and reaffirm their faith.

9. Consider holding a family session at the graveside of the deceased child to allow family members to express

__. _____

_____

__. _____

_____

__. _____

_____

thoughts and feelings to each other and the deceased.

10. Have each family member share his/her favorite image or photo of the deceased child with the other family members in order to keep the deceased alive in spirit.

11. Speak about how the deceased lives within each family member spiritually and recognize the characteristics of the deceased when they appear.

12. Discuss in detail the actual circumstances of the child's death; differentiate between survivor guilt and guilt for not being able to do more to save the child from death or ease pain and suffering.

13. Educate the family members about survivor guilt and how this is a natural stage of grief and loss; suggest that adults read *When the Worst That Could Happen Already Has* (Wholey).

14. Help family members to recognize their excessive overprotective behaviors and to look at alternative ways of self-reassurance and letting go of the deceased.

15. Review with family members potential negative side effects of being overprotective of the surviving children.

16. Conduct an assessment of any preexisting psychopathology that may have been brought to a head by the death of the child.

17. Refer individual family members to a therapist or psychiatrist for treatment of any determined preexisting emotional disorder.

18. Explore for the presence of irrational guilt in siblings (especially young siblings) for the death of the child.

19. In a family session, expose any hidden blame for the child's death that may exist.

__. _____
    _____

__. _____
    _____

__. _____
    _____

DIAGNOSTIC SUGGESTIONS

Axis I:	296.2x	Major Depressive Disorder, Single Episode
	296.3x	Major Depressive Disorder, Recurrent
	300.4	Dysthymic Disorder
	311	Depressive Disorder NOS
	309.81	Posttraumatic Stress Disorder
	309.0	Adjustment Disorder With Depressed Mood
	309.24	Adjustment Disorder With Anxiety
	309.28	Adjustment Disorder With Mixed Anxiety and Depressed Mood
	308.3	Acute Stress Disorder
	V61.2	Parent–Child Relational Problem
	V61.1	Partner Relational Problem
	V62.82	Bereavement
	V62.89	Religious/Spiritual Problem

———   ————————————

———   ————————————

Axis II: 301.6   Dependent Personality Disorder
301.83   Borderline Personality Disorder
301.5   Histrionic Personality Disorder

———   ————————————

———   ————————————

DEATH OF A PARENT

BEHAVIORAL DEFINITIONS

1. The accidental, sudden death of a parent leaves a single-parent or parentless home, causing grief to the survivors.
2. The death of a parent occurs following a long terminal illness (heart disease, cancer, leukemia, etc.).
3. The death of a parent occurs due to an acute illness (heart attack, auto accident, etc.).
4. The spouse and/or family members of the deceased witness and/or participate in the accidental death of a parent (e.g., auto accident, drowning), causing extreme guilt and trauma.
5. The parent's death has an impact on the family dynamics and the way surviving family members reorder their lives with one another in order to cope with the loss.
6. Survivors have a fear of future loss of other family members and display overprotectiveness of one another.
7. Financial hardships fall on the surviving family, which causes undue stress in addition to the stress of losing the parent.

__. _____
   _____
__. _____
   _____
__. _____
   _____

LONG-TERM GOALS

1. Adjust to the shock and trauma of the death/loss and learn to cope effectively with the grief and the absence of the deceased parent.

2. Come to grips with the notion that death is an unavoidable part of life and can occur at any time during the developmental life span.

3. Become aware of the various stages of grief and prepare for dealing with the emotions that accompany those stages.

4. Learn to mediate guilt, whether it be a result of being a survivor or due to some peripheral or direct involvement in the parent's accidental death.

5. Surviving parent and family members work through their resistance to and rejection of parental replacements (relatives, foster parents, etc.).

—. _____

_____

—. _____

_____

—. _____

_____

SHORT-TERM OBJECTIVES

1. Each family member expresses his/her grief associated with the shocking death of the parent. (1, 2, 3)

2. Family members verbalize an understanding of the various stages of grief associated with the loss of a loved one. (4)

3. Implement cognitive and behavioral techniques for coping with the loss of a loved one. (5, 6)

4. Family members reaffirm their faith-based beliefs regarding death. (7, 8)

5. Family members identify those aspects within themselves that were touched by

THERAPEUTIC INTERVENTIONS

1. Allow the family to vent their grief as a family and express the loss as a whole.

2. Promote a sense of unity and facilitate cohesiveness among the surviving family members. Also, focus on how the caretaking role will be fulfilled in the family.

3. Each family member will express how the grief has affected him/her on an individual basis and define how the experience differs from those of the others. (For adults, use journaling, poetry, etc. For children under the age of 12, utilize picture drawings, music, etc.).

the deceased while he/she was alive. (9, 10, 11)

6. Verbalize the resolution of guilt surrounding the death of the parent. (12, 13)

7. Acknowledge the propensity to be overprotective with the surviving family members, both as a natural reaction and as a means of assuaging guilt. (14)

8. Identify the negative impact of being overprotective of surviving family members. (15)

9. Parents and/or family members cooperate with the assessment and treatment of preexisting anxiety or depression that has been exacerbated by the death. (16, 17)

10. Children express any irrational feelings of responsibility for the death of the parent. (18, 19)

11. Family members terminate blaming of themselves or each other for the parent's death. (19)

12. Children express resistance to bonding with a parental substitute or replacement. (20, 21)

13. Family members express frustration with financial hardships that result from the death of the parent. (22)

4. Educate the family regarding the stages of grief for survivors; recommend that adults read *How to Survive the Loss of a Child* (Sanders) and that children read *The Fall of Freddie the Leaf* (Buscaglia).

5. Discuss with the family methods for coping with the loss of a spouse/parent. Explore the use of various rituals (e.g., wearing certain clothing that belonged to the deceased, constructing a shrine). If meeting with the family prior to the viewing or burial service, consider having family members place certain symbolic items in the deceased's coffin, provided that it is not contrary to the survivors' religious beliefs.

6. Teach cognitive behavioral coping strategies for grief (e.g., imagery that suggests how the deceased would want the survivors to go on, how the deceased would be dealing with the reverse situation if the circumstances had been different). Recommend reading *Grief: Climb Toward Understanding* (Davies).

7. Explore with family members their religious/spiritual beliefs about life after death. Reinforce the notion that the deceased is safe and free from pain. Recom-

—. _____
_____
—. _____
_____
—. _____
_____

mend reading *How We Die* (Nuland).

8. Explore with the family the possibility of making arrangements for a memorial service to honor the deceased and reaffirm their faith.

9. Consider holding a family session at the graveside of the deceased parent to allow family members to express thoughts and feelings to each other and to the deceased.

10. Have each family member share his/her favorite image or photo of the deceased parent with the other family members in order to keep the deceased alive in spirit (e.g., children or adults could wear a picture in a locket).

11. Speak about how the deceased lives within each family member spiritually and recognize the deceased's characteristics when they appear.

12. Discuss in detail the actual circumstances of the parent's death; differentiate between survivor guilt and guilt for not being able to do more to save the parent from death or ease pain and suffering.

13. Educate the family member about survivor guilt and how this is a natural stage of grief and loss; suggest that adults read *When the*

Worst That Could Happen Already Has (Wholey), and that children read *How to Survive the Loss of a Parent* (Akner).

14. Help family members to recognize their excessive overprotective behaviors and to look at alternative ways of self-reassurance and letting go of the deceased. For children, begin to identify other potential role models (older siblings, aunt/uncle, etc.).

15. Review with family members potential negative side effects of being overprotective of each other and assess whether or not this is a healthy aspect of survival.

16. Conduct an assessment (use psychological testing, inventories, history taking, etc.) of any preexisting psychopathology that may have been brought to a head by the parent's death.

17. Refer individual family members to a therapist or psychiatrist for treatment of any determined preexisting emotional disorder.

18. Explore for the presence of irrational guilt in children (especially young children) for the death of the parent.

19. In a family session, expose any hidden blame that may exist for the parent's death.

20. Facilitate the process of extended family members

bonding with the children as a replacement for the deceased parent (relative, stepparent, etc.). Also, focus on how this individual can never replace the deceased, but can only follow in his/her footsteps; allow for the children's expressions of resistance and fear of bonding.

21. Recommend that the children talk about the missing parent as much as possible and be allowed to keep a log or diary to write to them on a regular basis.

22. Search for alternative means of financial support and begin to face the need to do with less. Process the anger and resentment among family members over having to do with less.

__. _____
   _____
   _____

__. _____
   _____

__. _____
   _____
   _____

DIAGNOSTIC SUGGESTIONS

Axis I:	296.2x	Major Depressive Disorder, Single Episode
	296.3x	Major Depressive Disorder, Recurrent
	300.4	Dysthymic Disorder
	311	Depressive Disorder NOS
	309.0	Adjustment Disorder With Depressed Mood
	309.24	Adjustment Disorder With Anxiety

	309.28	Adjustment Disorder With Mixed Anxiety and Depressed Mood
	308.3	Acute Stress Disorder
	309.21	Separation Anxiety Disorder
	300.02	Generalized Anxiety Disorder
	313.89	Reactive Attachment Disorder of Early Childhood
	V62.89	Religious/Spiritual Problem
	V62.82	Bereavement
	_____	_____
	_____	_____
Axis II:	301.6	Dependent Personality Disorder
	301.83	Borderline Personality Disorder
	301.5	Histrionic Personality Disorder
	_____	_____
	_____	_____

DEPENDENCY ISSUES

BEHAVIORAL DEFINITIONS

1. One family member has an extreme need to be taken care of by other family members, which leads to clinging and submissive behaviors.
2. The family member displays overt expression of a fear of abandonment.
3. Dependency issues place tension and a burden of responsibility onto others, causing friction in the home.
4. The family member seeks reassurance from others and does everything possible to avoid disagreement and conflict.
5. The family member experiences guilt readily, leading to low self-esteem.
6. The family member is unable to render independent decisions without confirmation and support from other family members.
7. Nondependent family members enable the dependent family member by giving in to frequent demands for contact and reassurance, and to manipulative behaviors.
8. The dependent family member experiences anxiety and depression during periods of absence from other family members.
9. The dependent family member experiences loss of purpose and meaning in life when he/she perceives insufficient support from other family members.

__. _____

_____

__. _____

_____

__. _____

_____

LONG-TERM GOALS

1. Eliminate the pressure for caretaking by others and display less clingy and submissive behaviors.
2. Increase assertiveness and demonstrate self-reliance.
3. Eliminate feelings of guilt and increase self-esteem.
4. Eliminate unrealistic fear of abandonment.
5. Nondependent family members recognize their enabling behavior and give in less frequently to the dependent family member's demands and manipulations.
6. Increase tolerance for separation from family members.
7. Dependent family member makes decisions without reassurance from others.

—. _____

_____

—. _____

_____

—. _____

_____

SHORT-TERM OBJECTIVES

1. Identify those specific behaviors that constitute the dependency. (1, 2)
2. Describe the impact the dependency has had on family members. (3)
3. Identify the history of the development of dependency. (4, 5)
4. Verbalize an increased awareness of the nature and dynamics of dependency. (4, 5, 6, 7)
5. Dependent family member identifies the unrealistic fear of abandonment. (8, 9)

THERAPEUTIC INTERVENTIONS

1. Ask each family member to describe the evidence for excessive dependency in one family member.
2. Assist the family in developing operational definitions or, possibly, metaphors to identify specific dependent behaviors and dynamics that need to change.
3. Have each family member express how the dependency issues have affected him/her personally and the behaviors it has changed.
4. Promote acceptance by everyone in the family that

6. List constructive behavioral and cognitive coping activities to overcome the fear of abandonment. (10)

7. Describe the tension that the dependency places on the entire family. (3, 11, 12)

8. Identify how conflicts are avoided due to the irrational fear of rejection. (13, 14, 15)

9. Dependent family member acknowledges irrational guilt and implement cognitive restructuring to overcome it. (16, 17, 18, 19)

10. Identify fears associated with making independent decisions. (20, 21)

11. Increase the frequency of independent decision making and report a reduction in the fear associated with it. (22, 23, 24)

12. Acknowledge enabling behaviors on the part of the nondependent family members. (25, 26, 27)

13. List behaviors of the family that will encourage independence in the dependent member. (28)

14. All family members increase the frequency of the assertive expression of beliefs and emotions. (29, 30)

15. Implement changes in roles within the family unit that foster growth in independence. (31, 32)

this problem truly exists and explore the dynamics of how it may have developed.

5. Explore the parents' families of origin and/or use genograms to make connections with other possible dependent people in the family.

6. Educate the family as a whole about the dynamics of unhealthy dependency.

7. Suggest specific readings such as the codependency series by Beattie (e.g., *Codependent No More* and *Beyond Codependency*) and discuss with the family members the concepts involved.

8. Explore the dependent family member's fears of abandonment and what it means to him/her to be alone. Utilize techniques for helping reframe his/her fear (e.g., see *Cognitive Therapy of Personality Disorders* [Beck, Freeman, and associates]).

9. Ask other family members to share their beliefs about being alone and contrast these with those of the dependent member.

10. Encourage brainstorming on how family members can overcome irrational thoughts regarding abandonment (e.g., utilize rational self-talk; fill free time with constructive activity).

—. _____
_____
—. _____
_____
—. _____
_____

11. If family members have difficulty expressing themselves, utilize such techniques as family sculpting (see "Family Sculpture and Relationship Wrapping Techniques" [Constantine]; *Satir Step-by-Step* [Satir and Baldwin]) or reverse role-playing.

12. Have individual family members take responsibility for their contributions to the overall tension in the family.

13. Discuss the issue of avoidance of conflict and how each family member feels about dealing with this issue.

14. Identify irrational thoughts about conflict such as that one will be totally rejected by other family members if disagreement arises.

15. Review methods of conflict resolution and styles of disagreement; reinforce the notion that all families experience conflict and that it is necessary for family growth and development.

16. Have family members engage in role-playing to demonstrate the thoughts they have in response to guilt.

17. Compare family members' thoughts associated with guilt to those of the dependent family member and help him/her revise or re-

structure the way of dealing with guilt.

18. Educate the family about the dynamics of guilt and how most guilt is self-inflicted.

19. Recommend homework from *Ten Days to Self-Esteem* (Burns) to teach cognitive restructuring techniques that will reduce guilt and build self-esteem.

20. Facilitate family discussion about decision making and fears of making bad decisions or failing.

21. Help the family adopt a less perfectionistic style and a more accepting attitude about making bad decisions or failing.

22. Teach structured techniques to assist in decision making (e.g., using a decision tree, listing the pros and cons of choices). Attempt to address this as a family behavior with less emphasis on the dependent family member.

23. Encourage family members to use positive reinforcement when the dependent family member makes independent decisions and displays less of a need to rely on other family members.

24. Discuss incidents when the dependent family member has successfully made decisions, and use rituals to reinforce.

25. Encourage family members to admit that they have enabled the dependent member and discuss how that enabling may have developed.

26. Explore for the origins of guilt in other family members that may be underlying their enabling behaviors.

27. Assess the need of family members to keep the dependent family member dependent (for their own self-esteem; because of power issues, fears, etc.).

28. Assist the family in identifying alternative behaviors on the part of the nondependent family members that will contribute to the support of overall family change (refusal to respond to the dependent member's calls for reassurance of being loved or being capable, reinforcing independent behaviors, etc.).

29. Define the differences between assertive and aggressive expressions of emotions; use role-playing and modeling to teach assertive expressions of thoughts and feelings.

30. Refer the dependent family member to specific assertiveness training classes.

31. Utilize role reversal exercises to foster support for role changes among family

members (the dominant decision maker becoming more passive, the quiet member becoming more expressive, the passive member becoming more assertive, etc.).

32. Have family members discuss how they feel when reversing roles or trying out new roles in the family.

___. _____

_____

___. _____

_____

___. _____

_____

DIAGNOSTIC SUGGESTIONS

Axis I:	311	Depressive Disorder NOS
	300.4	Dysthymic Disorder
	296.x	Major Depressive Disorder
	313.89	Reactive Attachment Disorder of Early Childhood
	_____	_____
	_____	_____
Axis II:	301.6	Dependent Personality Disorder
	301.82	Avoidant Personality Disorder
	_____	_____
	_____	_____

DEPRESSION IN FAMILY MEMBERS

BEHAVIORAL DEFINITIONS

1. Ongoing sadness, hopelessness, or pessimism.
2. Disengagement with or disinterest in normally enjoyable activities in life (e.g., visiting relatives or dining out).
3. A decrease in the ability to remain focused or to concentrate, (frequent daydreaming, losing place while reading or doing schoolwork, etc.).
4. Insomnia (onset or interrupted sleep) with excessive fatigue or a general malaise.
5. Decreased sense of self-worth.
6. Social withdrawal.
7. Psychomotor agitation or retardation (slowed movement, low motivation, etc.).
8. Feelings of guilt and lack of desire to live.
9. Suicidal ideation and/or gestures to incur harm to oneself.
10. Outright rejection of antidepressant medication or poor response to any type of therapeutic intervention.
11. A decrease in energy level and appetite, and/or a chronic anhedonia.
12. Increased irritability and low frustration tolerance.

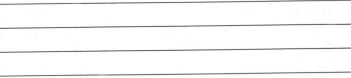

LONG-TERM GOALS

1. Resolve the depression and return to a normal level of participation in and contribution to family activities.
2. Resolve the grief and improve the overall coping skills.
3. Reduce feelings of helplessness and lack of control over one's life.
4. Eliminate suicidal beliefs and/or gestures with an increased desire to live and a lessened sense of general hopelessness.
5. Improve feelings of self-esteem.
6. Increase involvement with and enjoyment of normal social activities.
7. Reduce feelings of hopelessness and dissatisfaction with life.

—. _____
   _____
   _____
—. _____
   _____
   _____
—. _____
   _____

SHORT-TERM OBJECTIVES

1. Identify the signs of depression and the factors that may have triggered the depression. (1, 2)

2. Depressed family member cooperates with psychological testing to assess the depth of the depression. (3, 4, 5)

3. Family members identify how they have been affected by the symptoms of the depressed family member. (6, 7)

4. Agree that the depression clearly exists and is affecting the entire family. (1, 6, 8)

THERAPEUTIC INTERVENTIONS

1. Have each family member give his/her perception of the evidence for depression in one family member.

2. Assist family members in identifying any specific event that may have triggered the depressive symptomatology.

3. Administer diagnostic inventories of depression to the depressed family member (e.g., the Beck Hopelessness Scale [Beck] or the Children's Depression Inventory [Kovacs]).

4. Review the results of the assessment measures for

5. Agree to utilize an observational measure to monitor the depressed family member's symptoms and progress. (9, 10)

6. Depressed family member increases social engagement with other family members and friends. (11, 12, 13)

7. Depressed family member identifies negative, distorted cognitive messages and replace with positive, realistic self-talk that reduces depression and builds self-esteem. (14, 15, 16)

8. Depressed family member reports increased concentration and reduced brooding. (17)

9. Family encourages less daytime sleeping by depressed family member and an overall increase in activity. (12, 17, 18)

10. Depressed family member evidences improved self-esteem through his/her verbal expressions as well as the ability to take on more risk. (19)

11. Depressed family member decreases the frequency of avoidant behaviors. (20, 21)

12. Depressed family member expresses anger directly, respectfully, and under control. (21, 22, 23)

13. Depressed family member completes standardized assessment measures on a regular basis to evaluate

depression, hopelessness, and suicidality with the family and explain what they mean.

5. Use a chart or graph to measure depression recovery progress or regression on assessment measures administered.

6. Ask family members to share their perceptions of how the depression of the other member affects them individually.

7. Allow for the expression of negative emotions such as resentment from the nondepressed family members in reaction to the pall that is cast over the family by the depressed family member.

8. Inquire about any family member who might believe that the depression is not real or may be a means of manipulation.

9. Brainstorm about methods for monitoring or measuring the depressed family member's levels of depression and agitation other than inventories (e.g., observation of agitation, withdrawal).

10. Help family members monitor their propensity to project their own emotional issues when attempting to assess the depressed family member's level of depression.

11. Assess how the depression has contributed to the fam-

the level of depression and the risk of suicide. (24)

14. Family reviews and confronts the results of the assessment, sharing feedback regarding the results. (25, 26)

15. Agree to the implementation of a solid prevention plan to reduce the risk of suicide. (27, 28, 29, 30)

16. Nondepressed family members agree on criteria for sincere suicide risk versus a manipulation attempt. (31, 32)

17. Disclose any childhood history of abuse. (33)

18. All family members terminate attempts to inflict guilt subtly or directly. (34, 35)

19. Nondepressed family members terminate enabling behavior directed at maintaining depression. (36)

20. Obtain an assessment of the role of chemical imbalance, genetic predisposition, or other medical factors in the depression. (37, 38)

21. Depressed family member agrees to take antidepressant medication if necessary and/or accept more intensive treatment (e.g., individual psychotherapy, partial hospitalization, occupational therapy). (37, 38, 39, 40)

22. Depressed family member displays improved energy level and appetite and more

ily member's social disengagement or disinterest in regular activities.

12. Develop a behavioral contract and/or a weekly schedule of a specified number of social activities for the depressed family member with friends and family (see *Feeling Good: The New Mood Therapy* [Burns]).

13. Teach techniques to reduce behavioral deficits that contribute to the depression (e.g., teach assertiveness or social skills).

14. Assist the depressed member and other family members to recognize and identify distorted, negative cognitive messages that support depressed feelings and low self-esteem (recommend *The Feeling Good Handbook* [Burns] or *Mind over Mood* [Greenberger and Padesky]).

15. Teach positive, reality-based self-talk that can replaced distorted cognitive messages; encourage nondepressed family members to remind the depressed member to think positively and realistically.

16. Use genogram or family-of-origin techniques for discussing the history of self-perception and the overall level of mental health in the family.

17. Suggest techniques for maintaining the level of

zest for life, and other family members reinforce the improvement. (41, 42)

23. Nondepressed family members make unsolicited contact with the depressed member throughout the day. (43)

24. Increase the frequency and intensity of physical exercise. (44)

25. Identify markers for potential relapse into depression. (45)

___. _____
     _____

___. _____
     _____

___. _____
     _____

concentration and avoidance of daydreaming (e.g., staying active, engaging in brief reading activities, and practicing recall exercises).

18. Support nondepressed family members in encouraging the depressed member to sleep less and involve himself/herself in family activities.

19. Recommend that the family implement self-esteem-building exercises (see *Self-Esteem* [McKay and Fanning]).

20. Explore for a pattern of avoidant behaviors in the depressed family member; use techniques such as graded exposure and coping skills training to reduce avoidant behavior.

21. Explore how family members deal with anger issues; teach how suppressed anger can lead to avoidance behavior and depression.

22. Teach the use of assertiveness versus passivity, passive-aggressiveness, and aggressiveness as related to anger expression.

23. Incorporate techniques (e.g., journaling and artwork) as alternative forms of expression of anger and depression; facilitate positive processing and avoid any unnecessary attacking between family members.

24. Use standardized measures to assess the depression and level of change (e.g., the Beck Depression Inventory [Beck and Steer], the Beck Helplessness Scale [Beck]).

25. Assess the depressed family member's frustration if his/her mood does not seem to be improving.

26. Use brainstorming techniques to determine possible reasons to explain why the depression resolution is stalled.

27. Carefully assess the level of risk for suicide; implement a plan for the support and safety of the depressed family member.

28. List methods for family members to stay in contact with each other or to use a crisis hotline during periods of high suicide risk.

29. Develop a no-self-harm contract that is signed by all members of the family.

30. Obtain an agreement that immediate hospitalization will be used if any hopelessness symptoms are exacerbated into gestures of or attempts at suicide.

31. Discuss methods for determining when the suicide crisis is real and when it might be a means of manipulation on the depressed family member's part. Use specific criteria of risk (e.g., time, place, and method)

and scores on assessment inventories as collaborating evidence of depression. Also recommend readings such as *No One Saw My Pain* (Slaby and Garfinkel).

32. Review reasons that the depressed family member might attempt to manipulate the family with false gestures of suicide (e.g., a need for attention or to act out anger) and how these reasons can be eliminated.

33. Explore the possibility of early trauma (e.g., sexual, physical, or psychological abuse) and how this might be contributing to the depression.

34. Look for indications in the family dynamics that guilt may be subtly induced by other family members.

35. Discuss and consider alternatives to guilt-inflicting behaviors (other means of communication, etc.).

36. Address the issue of potential enabling behaviors on the part of other family members. Discuss matters such as the need for others to overpower or enhance control.

37. Assess for an extended family history of depression and make a referral to a psychiatrist or family physician to evaluate the need for psychotropic medication.

38. Educate family members about the time period needed for medication to become effective, the need to take it regularly, any potential side effects, and what to do if side effects are recognized. Underscore the need to work closely with the prescribing physician.

39. Brainstorm and develop a list of alternative treatments (hospitalization, day treatment programs, intensive individual and/or group psychotherapy, etc.).

40. Help the family develop a plan to enact alternate, more intensive treatments for depression.

41. Teach family members how to reinforce any improvement in the depressed family member's social involvement, energy level, or mood.

42. Assist family members in identifying the specific reinforcers that are effective for the depressed family member (e.g., verbal praise) and their implementation.

43. Facilitate an agreement from other family members to make unsolicited contact with the depressed family member throughout the day (e-mail, phone calls, etc.).

44. Devise a plan that involves all family members interacting in physical activities (e.g., swimming, going to the fitness center, playing

badminton or winter sports, ice skating).

45. Teach the family how to monitor progress after the symptoms have subsided and determine the markers (an increase in the level of depression, engaging in denial, etc.) for potential relapse in the future.

—. _____
_____

—. _____
_____

—. _____
_____

DIAGNOSTIC SUGGESTIONS

Axis I:	309.0	Adjustment Disorder With Depressed Mood
	296.xx	Bipolar I Disorder
	296.89	Bipolar II Disorder
	300.4	Dysthymic Disorder
	301.13	Cyclothymic Disorder
	296.2x	Major Depressive Disorder, Single Episode
	296.3x	Major Depressive Disorder, Recurrent
	295.70	Schizoaffective Disorder
	310.1	Personality Change Due to General Medical Condition
	V62.82	Bereavement
	_____	_____
	_____	_____
Axis II:	301.83	Borderline Personality Disorder
	301.82	Avoidant Personality Disorder
	301.6	Dependent Personality Disorder
	_____	_____
	_____	_____

DISENGAGEMENT/LOSS
OF FAMILY COHESION

BEHAVIORAL DEFINITIONS

1. Disengagement from one another and disillusionment with the state of the family's development.
2. No laughing or having fun together.
3. Feelings of alienation and estrangement from the family unit.
4. Entrenchment with individual activities and other relationships outside of the family unit.
5. Quick escalation of tension and conflict, especially when situations force family members to interact (e.g., crisis, death).
6. Negative reaction of external parties to family members because of the lack of communication, cohesion, and disharmony in the family (e.g., children, paramour begin to notice coldness in the family).
7. Appearance of negative psychological or behavioral side effects of the family's disengagement (e.g., mental or physical illness, substance abuse, criminal activity).
8. Lack of shared activities and joint celebrations.
9. Lost sense of self due to the effects of the family disengagement.

__. _____

_____

__. _____

_____

__. _____

_____

LONG-TERM GOALS

1. Family members admit to having a problem with intimacy and cohesiveness with each other.
2. Eliminate feelings of alienation through engagement in behaviors that facilitate cohesiveness and intimacy.
3. Achieve the ability to laugh and have fun together.
4. Redirect the focus of the family to devoting more time to immediate family members than to external relationships.
5. Devise methods for coping with tension and crisis situations in the family.

__. _____

_____

__. _____

_____

__. _____

_____

SHORT-TERM OBJECTIVES

1. Identify the evidence for and history of family disengagement. (1, 2, 3, 4)
2. Cooperate with psychological testing to assess family disengagement. (5)
3. Each family member expresses how he/she experiences a sense of alienation and estrangement from the others. (6, 7)
4. Accept individual responsibility for the contribution to the disengagement. (8, 9)
5. Articulate the external relationships and activities that have been replacements for the lack of family closeness. (10, 11)

THERAPEUTIC INTERVENTIONS

1. Facilitate a discussion about each family member's perception of the family and how it functions.
2. Explore the emotional responses and the behavioral displays that have been generated as a result of the family's disengagement.
3. Assist family members in defining in behavioral terms what is contributing to the disengagement. Consider using the Family of Origin Inventory (Stuart) to aid in determining how this may have been learned in childhood experiences.

6. Agree to make an effort to overcome resistance and rebuild family cohesion and communication through emotional investment. (12, 13, 14)

7. Describe the conflicts that develop as a result of reengaging with one another. (15, 16)

8. Implement conflict resolution techniques rather than withdrawal to cope with friction due to reengagement. (17, 18)

9. Implement healthy communication and problem-solving skills to overcome conflict. (19, 20)

10. Acknowledge and address any negative behavioral or psychological side effects that the disengagement has had. (21, 22, 23)

11. Troubled family member accepts referral for more individualized treatment. (24)

12. Troubled family member terminates blaming or projecting responsibility for his/her own behavior. (25)

13. Family members commit to rebuilding an active social life together and to engaging in more family celebrations. (26, 27, 28)

14. Report a reinforced sense of personal identity and identify how the family can fortify this in the future. (29, 30, 31)

4. Have each family member list what he/she feels is desirable but missing within the family, and discuss each family member's list in the session. Recommend the book *The Seven Habits of Highly Effective Families* (Covey).

5. Use test instruments to assess the family's cohesion (e.g., the Family Adaptability and Cohesion Scales [Olson] or the Family Sense of Coherence and Family Adaptation Scales [Antonovsky and Sourani]).

6. Consider having family members select a video that best exemplifies their sense of disengagement (e.g., a film such as *Ordinary People*).

7. Open a forum for each family member to express how he/she individually experiences the alienation and loss of closeness in the family. Use creative techniques (songs, poems, artwork, etc.) to achieve this.

8. Have each family member take responsibility for his/her own contribution to the family's gravitating toward disengagement.

9. Aim toward the reduction of blaming behaviors by having family members use "I" messages instead of "you" messages.

10. Discuss with family members their gravitation to out-

side activities and relationships and how this is a natural reaction to the situation.

11. Have each family member
acknowledge how he/she
has personally sought out
relationships with others
outside of the family and
how this has helped to fill
the void in their own family.

12. Discuss the fear of and difficulties inherent in gravitating back to the family unit
and how this will be an adjustment for everyone. Have
each family member de-
scribe how it will affect
him/her personally.

13. Brainstorm methods for
coping with the reinvest-
ment in the family and how
to respond to fears and resistance (e.g., taking one
step at a time, discussing
the risk involved with trust-
ing each other, considering
how to start spending time
with each other and what to
expect).

14. Encourage family members'
faith and trust in taking a
risk by reinvesting in their
own family.

15. Have each family member
describe the conflicts that
arise when they must interact with one another in a
crisis (see the Conflict Tactics Scale in *Physical Violence in American Families*
[Straus and Gelles]).

16. Prepare the family for tension and conflict to be a natural part of the rehabilitation process and discuss ways to inoculate against this (e.g., using progressive muscle relaxation, identifying likely areas of conflict and how to anticipate and resolve them, weighing alternative responses).

17. Teach conflict resolution strategies or tension-reducing techniques (e.g., time-out procedures, ventilation sessions, third-party mediators) to deal with tension and conflict.

18. Brainstorm ways to better prepare for interaction during family crises (e.g., a death in the family); use role-playing to practice these new ways to interact.

19. Teach the family principles of healthy communication and problem solving; utilize techniques such as the speaker/listener technique or pro-versus-con problem-solving strategies (see *Fighting for Your Marriage* [Markman, Stanley, and Blumberg]).

20. Use role-playing techniques to enact an actual situation of conflictual communication and coach the family through the process of using communication and problem-solving skills.

21. Assess for signs of physical or mental illness, substance

abuse problems, or criminal behavior in any of the family members.

22. Discuss whether the psychological or behavioral problems are directly or indirectly related to the disengagement within the family.

23. Facilitate the expression of feelings related to the psychological or behavioral problem of a family member.

24. Assess for the need for any adjunct therapeutic intervention and, if so, refer to the appropriate source (family physician, psychiatrist, etc.).

25. Confront the troubled family member for unnecessarily blaming or manipulating through his/her acting out.

26. Have family members generate a list of different family activities that they would like to see occur.

27. Ask each family member to fantasize about how the proposed family activities would unfold; discuss fear of failure and disappointment that may be present.

28. Brainstorm with family members on ways to avoid failures and to facilitate more successful and enjoyable family activities.

29. Have each family member list how he/she has experienced a weakened or lost part of himself/herself and compare this with the expe-

riences of other family
members.

30. Generate a list of family activities that may help to restore a sense of self and
connection between family
members (e.g., volunteering
time together to aid the less
fortunate; other activities
that involve survival and
working together, such as a
rafting trip).

31. Suggest including family-of-
origin members in a session
to address the lack of personal identity and allow for
a process of ventilation of
the emotion attached to it;
(see *Family-of-Origin Therapy: An Intergenerational
Approach* [Framo]).

__. _____
     _____
__. _____
     _____
__. _____
     _____

DIAGNOSTIC SUGGESTIONS

Axis I: 309.0   Adjustment Disorder With Depressed Mood
              305.00   Alcohol Abuse
              303.9   Alcohol Dependence
              300.4   Dysthymic Disorder
              296.x   Major Depressive Disorder
              V61.1   Partner Relational Problem
              V61.2   Parent–Child Relational Problem
              _____   _____
              _____   _____

Axis II: 301.20   Schizoid Personality Disorder
              301.82   Avoidant Personality Disorder
              V71.09   No Diagnosis
              799.9   Diagnosis Deferred

_____   _____

_____   _____

EATING DISORDER

BEHAVIORAL DEFINITIONS

1. Preoccupation with body weight and size related to a grossly unrealistic perception of oneself as being fat or heavy.
2. Denial of the effect that the weight loss has had on the body.
3. Severe weight loss with the deliberate refusal to maintain a minimal healthy weight.
4. Self-limiting intake of food and a high frequency of self-induced vomiting, excessive use of laxatives, and/or excessive strenuous exercise.
5. Females experience amenorrhea.
6. Periodic consumption of high-calorie foods and then the use of self-induced vomiting and/or an inappropriate use of laxatives to avoid gaining weight.
7. Desperate fear of losing control over weight gain and/or appearing fat or heavy.
8. Reduction in potassium and chloride levels in the body due to excessive vomiting and/or elimination.
9. Electrolyte and fluid imbalance due to the restriction of food intake and vomiting.
10. Reduced interest in sexual activities.
11. A change in the level of intimacy with others or a flattening of mood and affect.
12. Extreme defensiveness about eating patterns, particularly aspects of food selection and dieting.
13. Family tension surrounding eating habits.
14. Excessive exercise.

—. _____

—. _____

—. _____

LONG-TERM GOALS

1. Restore normal eating patterns, body weight, balanced fluid and electrolytes, and a realistic perception of body size.
2. Terminate the pattern of binge eating and purging behavior with a return to normal eating of enough nutritious foods to maintain a healthy weight.
3. Stabilize medical condition, resume patterns of food intake that will sustain life, and gain weight to a normal level.
4. Identify family patterns that are contributing to the cause or exacerbation of the eating disorder.
5. Eliminate conflict and dysfunctional family patterns involving control and the intake of food.
6. Facilitate an open environment for displaying emotions in the family.
7. Improve methods and strategies for conflict resolution and increased communication.
8. Stabilize physical and psychological condition.

—. _____

—. _____

—. _____

SHORT-TERM OBJECTIVES	THERAPEUTIC INTERVENTIONS
1. Identify the evidence for an eating disorder in a family member. (1, 2, 3)	1. Review the *DSM-IV* criteria for an eating disorder with all family members and

2. Identify conflicts within the family that might contribute to an eating disorder. (4, 5, 6)

3. Identify the history of and possible contributing factors to the eating disorder. (7)

4. Family members verbalize an increased understanding of the eating disorder's symptoms, causes, and treatments. (8, 9)

5. Family member with the diagnosed eating disorder obtains the level of care recommended by a team of professionals. (10, 11)

6. Family members support the use of hospitalization and/or medication for the member with the eating disorder. (11, 12)

7. Highlight positive attributes of the family member with the eating disorder and express his/her worth as a valued member of the family. (13)

8. Express anger and frustration over the effect that the eating disorder has had on the family dynamics. (14, 15, 16)

9. Each family member, including the family member with the eating disorder, acknowledges his/her role with respect to the eating disorder. (17)

10. Individual with the eating disorder agrees to comply with the dietary recommen-

highlight areas that are relevant.

2. Discuss the eating patterns among all family members and assess what is healthy behavior and what is not. Also urge family members to educate themselves through literature such as *Eating Disorders* (National Institute of Mental Health).

3. Use assessment instruments to further refine a diagnosis (e.g., Eating Disorders Inventory-2 [Garner] and the Family-of-Origin Scale [Hovestadt, Anderson, Piercy, Cochran, and Fine]).

4. Explore for patterns that may contribute to the eating disturbance in the family (e.g., criticism during mealtime).

5. Have the family member with the eating disorder share with the family details about his/her bingeing and purging and the specific cues that set them off (anger, etc.).

6. Once the cues that contribute to bingeing and purging are established, discuss with family members their role in the specific interaction with the family member suffering from the eating disorder.

7. Family members express their beliefs about how the eating patterns developed.

dations outlined by the treatment team. (18, 19)

11. Identify the role that obsessiveness and perfectionism play in maintaining the eating disorder. (20, 21, 22)

12. Agree to practice new communication skills and conflict resolution techniques. (23, 24)

13. Identify the role of a desire for control as the basis for the eating disorder. (25, 26)

14. Identify the role of perfectionism in relationship to the need for control and low self-esteem. (27, 28)

15. Report less fear of failure, reduced need for perfectionism, and increased feelings of self-esteem. (29, 30)

__. _____
   _____
__. _____
   _____
__. _____
   _____

Focus on specific dynamics of family members.

8. Family members discuss the knowledge they have acquired about eating disorders through the media, from reading, or from other people. Highlight accurate aspects of what they learned and how it applies to their family; correct misconceptions.

9. Have family members read materials on eating disorders to broaden their knowledge base (e.g., *Reviving Ophelia* [Pipher] and *The Secret Language of Eating Disorders* [Claude-Pierre]).

10. Assess the need for a referral of the family member with the eating disorder to a treatment team of professionals aside from the family therapist (e.g., a clinical psychologist/psychiatrist).

11. Solicit support from family members for the treatment team's decision to hospitalize the family member with an eating disorder if the condition becomes severe enough. (This may involve an involuntary commitment if the family member with the eating disorder refuses inpatient care.)

12. Ask all family members to talk openly about the necessity for medical treatment (e.g., hospitalization or psy-

chotropic medication) and
to give support to the family
member with the eating disorder.

13. Ask each family member to
list the positive traits and
talents as well as the value
of the member with the eating disorder.

14. Facilitate an expression of
family members' anger and
resentment and review constructive ways to appropriately express these feelings.

15. Assist family members in
identifying the behavioral,
cognitive, and affective cues
that their anger is escalating to a level of unhealthi-
ness (e.g., use scale from
0–10).

16. Teach family members
time-out procedures. Re-
view the components of
anger control (e.g., *self-
monitoring* for escalating
feelings of anger and hurt,
signaling to the family
member that verbal engagement should end, *acknowl-
edging* the need to
disengage, *separating, cool-
ing down,* and regaining
control and composure,
eventually returning to controlled verbal engagement).

17. Discuss with each family
member the need to take
ownership for specific behaviors that contribute to
the family dynamics. Use "I"
statements instead of "you"
statements. Also educate

family members about the tendency to externalize blame as a means of defense and denial over the eating disorder.

18. Refer the family to meet with a dietitian to review meal planning.

19. Encourage and reinforce the family support of a gradual movement toward a balanced diet and increased food intake by the family member with the eating disorder.

20. Educate the family about how compulsivity may be a means of expressing anger or compensating for feelings of low self-esteem or poor self-worth.

21. Suggest methods for dealing with perfectionism and control in one's life (e.g., deliberate exposure to situations in which the person experiences failure and has to live with it or being in situations where he/she is out of control).

22. Focus on the way criticism is expressed in the family and the impact this has had on the need to be compulsive and perfect.

23. Discuss how change in the family will affect the dynamics of the family interaction; highlight the need for improved communication and problem-solving skills.

24. Teach the family the use of communication skills as well as techniques for conflict resolution (see *From Conflict to Resolution: Skills and Strategies for Individual, Couple and Family Therapy* [Heitler] and *Relationship Enhancement* [Guerny]).

25. Address boundary issues with family members and encourage the use of enactments and imbalancing techniques for purposes of restructuring. Discuss alternatives for dealing with feelings of loss of control and redirection of power.

26. Explore with family members whether control has been an issue in the family in the past and the role this may have played in the development of the eating disorder.

27. Discuss how perfectionism may interfere with various aspects of the development of self-concept, control, relationships, communication, sexual functioning/acting out, and so on.

28. Educate the family about the link between perfectionism and eating disorders and how the disorder functions as a means of overcompensating for perceived inadequacy and unacceptability.

29. Brainstorm methods for replacing perfectionistic

schemas and behaviors with more healthy behaviors (e.g., accentuating positive qualities, providing each other with room for failure, and changing family schemas about making mistakes).

30. Ask the family member with the eating disorder to describe in some detail the specific positive feedback that is most desired and that will build self-esteem while he/she attempts to overcome the eating disorder. Also, consider the use of strategies (e.g., focus on other activities that involve skills that do not rely on body image such as crafts, etc.) for improving self-esteem and body image affected by perfectionism.

__. _____
     _____
__. _____
     _____
__. _____
     _____

DIAGNOSTIC SUGGESTIONS

Axis I: 307.1   Anorexia Nervosa
              307.51   Bulimia Nervosa
              307.50   Eating Disorder NOS
              296.x   Major Depressive Disorder
              V61.1   Partner Relational Problem
              300.3   Obsessive-Compulsive Disorder

_____		_____
_____		_____

Axis II: 301.83   Borderline Personality Disorder
301.6   Dependent Personality Disorder
301.4   Obsessive-Compulsive Personality Disorder
301.5   Histrionic Personality Disorder

_____		_____
_____		_____

EXTRAFAMILIAL SEXUAL ABUSE

BEHAVIORAL DEFINITIONS

1. A verbal demand to accede to sexual interaction is made to a family member by someone outside of the immediate and extended family (neighbor, coworker, stranger).
2. A physical threat or psychological coercion to fulfill sexual demands causes the victim to submit to ongoing abuse.
3. The abused family member is reluctant to share the trauma of the abuse with anyone, including other family members, for fear of rejection, retaliation, and so on.
4. The abused family member struggles with issues of guilt, shame, anger, resentment, and/or depression as a result of the abuse.
5. Family members are confused by the change in emotions and behaviors (agitation, avoidance, depression, withdrawal, etc.) of the abused family member and suspect that abuse may have occurred.
6. Family members experience a range of emotions, including rage, guilt, depression, and sorrow, in reaction to learning of the abuse.
7. The abused family member begins to act out sexually.
8. Family members pressure the victim of abuse to report the abuse to the authorities, causing the victim to press charges and enter the due process of the court system and adding additional stress to the situation.
9. The abuse victim is pregnant as a result of the rape.

Sexual abuse often occurs in combination with psychological abuse and can be accompanied by physical abuse as well. Psychological abuse and physical abuse are more common when the sexual abuse is extrafamilial (neighbor, stranger in community, etc.). Sexual interaction or demands may be defined by any type of intimate touch, including petting, frotteurism (rubbing against), or other forms of manual or oral contact. This definition can also include, but does not limit itself to, the perpetrator masturbating, exposing the victim to pornography, or performing other explicit sexual acts in the presence of the victim.

—. _____
   _____
   _____

—. _____
   _____
   _____

—. _____
   _____

LONG-TERM GOALS

1. Family members become educated about the trauma of sexual abuse and learn the effects of various types of sexual abuse (forcible rape, being exposed to pornography, etc.).
2. Family members learn how to comfort the victim and be supportive in helping the victim express feelings and slowly deal with the effects of the abuse.
3. Family members resolve their own reactions to the victim's abuse.
4. Family members help the victim with the decision of whether to report the abuse to the authorities.*
5. Family members cope with the victim's acting-out behaviors that result from the abuse.
6. Family members develop improved ways to protect each other from future abuse.
7. Family members aid the abuse victim in making the best decision regarding whether to abort the pregnancy.

—. _____
   _____
   _____

—. _____
   _____
   _____

—. _____
   _____

---

*We are not suggesting that any therapist should engage in supporting the failure to report any sexual violation, but that the therapist should be sensitive to helping the family come to the best decision, especially in those situations that may be borderline violations (e.g., exposing an 18-year-old family member to pornography).

SHORT-TERM OBJECTIVES

1. Victim talks openly about the sustained abuse. (1, 2, 3, 4)

2. List the common psychological effects of a sexual trauma. (5)

3. Victim identifies a mode of expression of feelings that promotes relief. (6)

4. List ways to support the victim's feelings regarding the perpetrator. (7)

5. Victim reports a reduction in fear of the perpetrator. (8, 9)

6. Verbalize an understanding of the effects of the abuse, both on the victim as well as on the family. (10)

7. List supportive techniques for helping the victim overcome trauma symptoms. (11, 12)

8. Family members learn how to share their own emotional and behavioral reactions to the abuse. (13, 14, 15)

9. Identify conflicts between family members that have developed since discovery of the abuse. (16)

10. Report a reduction in family conflict. (17)

11. Victim of abuse reports a reduction in feelings of vulnerability, guilt, and shame with the support of family members. (18)

THERAPEUTIC INTERVENTIONS

1. Facilitate being nonjudgmental, warm, accepting, and in good eye contact when the victim expresses feelings associated with the abuse.

2. Use indirect methods to facilitate expression of the effects of the abuse (i.e., play therapy, artwork, psychodrama, questionnaires/inventories such as the Modified Posttraumatic Symptom Scale [Resick, Falsetti, Resnick, and Kilpatrick] or the Sexual Assault Symptom Scale [Ruch, Gartell, Amedeo, and Coyne]).

3. Refer the abused family member to a victim's abuse group.

4. Introduce the family to some readings on sexual abuse and how it affects the victim (e.g., *Betrayal of Innocence* [Forward and Buck]).

5. Educate the family and the victim about the posttraumatic effects of sexual abuse (withdrawal, acting-out behaviors, etc.) and how the effects may vary from subtle to blatant.

6. Facilitate different modes of emotional expression for the victim (e.g., journaling or artwork) and assess what

12. Family and victim verbalize acceptance of periods of anxiety, depression, despair, and anger that result from the abuse. (19)

13. Family members refrain from informally confronting the perpetrator of the abuse, if they knew the perpetrator before the abuse occurred. (20)

14. Family members discuss and agree to the best way to proceed regarding reporting the perpetrator to legal authorities. (21, 22)

15. Make contact with the legal authorities to report the perpetrator. (23)

16. Family members agree to proceed in a manner that is sensitive to the feelings of the victim regarding the legal reporting of the abuse. (24, 25)

17. Each family member describes a specific role for himself/herself in dealing with the emotions and behaviors of the victim. (26)

18. Family members verbalize adherence to a goal of healing from the pain of the abuse and describe how to move on in light of what has occurred. (27, 28)

19. Identify family conflict or individual victim's factors that may be contributing to the victim's sexual acting out. (29, 30)

comforts him/her and what promotes anxiety.

7. Discuss/brainstorm ways in which the family can support the victim's feelings regarding the perpetrator (e.g., avoiding anything to do with the perpetrator or his/her family).

8. Address the issue of distortions that often occur on the part of the victim that lead to a fear of submitting the perpetrator to the authorities because it may hurt him/her.

9. Help the family to deal with the victim's fear of retaliation by the perpetrator by reassuring the victim of safety and support.

10. Educate the family members about both victims and perpetrators of sexual abuse: why it happens, how it starts, and so on. Specifically focus on the effects on the victim (refer to *Psychotherapy of Sexually Abused Children and Their Families* [Friedrich] or *A Sourcebook of Child Sexual Abuse* [Finkelhor, et al.].)

11. Brainstorm about both individual (e.g., rewriting a new rendition of the abusive event) and family group techniques (e.g., providing physical comfort such as hugs) for dealing with symptoms in the victim as they appear.

20. Family makes a decision about the option of relocation. (31)

—. _____
  _____

—. _____
  _____

—. _____
  _____

12. Caution the nonabused family members not to over-anticipate symptoms in the victim to the point of seeing what is not there and/or inducing it.

13. Redirect the focus onto the behaviors and emotions of other family members that have developed in reaction to the abuse experience.

14. Brainstorm and suggest various coping skills (e.g., cognitive restructuring of negative self-talk) for family members to deal with emotions such as anger, guilt, and despair.

15. Encourage the victim to become part of the healing process for the other family members as well (e.g., by expressing anger over his/her vulnerability).

16. Explore conflict that emerges among family members over the abuse (e.g., blaming of one another for not protecting the victim better; resentment by siblings that the victim is getting too much attention).

17. Use strategies (e.g., conflict resolution, behavioral contracts, or cognitive restructuring) to assist the family in reducing conflict among themselves. (See "Families in Crisis" [Dattilio].)

18. Help family members develop the best method of supporting the victim in dealing with his/her vulner-

ability (supportive listening, empathetic understanding, determination of comfort zones, etc.).

19. Help the family to develop strategies for dealing with the victim's anxiety and depression, using relaxation methods and other cognitive-behavioral techniques.

20. Help the family to understand how dealing with the perpetrator in an appropriate, legal manner may be the best course of action.

21. Process with the family their thoughts and feelings about reporting the perpetrator to legal authorities; arrive at a consensus decision about how to proceed, with the victim's feelings and comfort level being of paramount importance.

22. Refer the family to the victim's rights advocate and a support group that is usually associated with the local district attorney's office or police station.

23. Refer the family to the local authorities (police abuse unit, district attorney's office, etc.) to report the sexual abuse perpetrator.

24. Help nonabused family members see their own emotions as secondary and become sensitive to the pace of the victim (doing too much too quickly can have a negative effect on the vic-

tim, testifying can be intimidating, etc.).

25. Allow for the ventilation of the nonabused family members' emotions and frustrations, particularly over not having the prosecution move faster.

26. Discuss how each of the nonabused family members can best aid the victim in dealing with the victim's behavioral and emotional outbursts from the abuse (e.g., the differences between a parent comforting the victim and a sibling comforting the victim; using humor as opposed to physical embracing).

27. Brainstorm methods for going forward and healing from the effects of the abuse. Utilize such techniques as rituals and taking advantage of various community support programs.

28. Reinforce the agreement between family members not to revisit the trauma too often once healing has occurred and also not to use the event to blame or as an excuse for other, nonrelated, behaviors in the future.

29. Attempt to help family members sift through the aspects of the victim's sexual acting out that may be due to preexisting individual or family issues (i.e., lack of attention, low self-

esteem, need for additional comfort, anger toward men/women).

30. Assess the specific aspects of the victim's sexual acting out that can be dealt with familially, as well as what needs to be addressed in individual or group therapy.

31. If the situation is too intimidating to the victim, explore with the family the final option of relocating geographically. Weigh the pros and cons of this option.

—. _____
   _____

—. _____
   _____

—. _____
   _____

DIAGNOSTIC SUGGESTIONS

Axis I:	309.81	Posttraumatic Stress Disorder
	309.0	Adjustment Disorder With Depressed Mood
	309.24	Adjustment Disorder With Anxiety
	309.28	Adjustment Disorder With Mixed Anxiety and Depressed Mood
	309.3	Adjustment Disorder With Disturbance of Conduct
	309.4	Adjustment Disorder With Mixed Disturbance of Emotions and Conduct
	300.4	Dysthymic Disorder
	312.9	Disruptive Behavior Disorder NOS
	313.81	Oppositional Defiant Disorder
	V61.21	Sexual Abuse of Child
	995.53	Sexual Abuse of Child (Victim)
	V61.2	Parent–Child Relational Problem
	307.42	Primary Insomnia

	307.44	Primary Hypersomnia
	300.6	Depersonalization Disorder
	300.15	Dissociative Disorder NOS
	296.2x	Major Depressive Disorder, Single Episode
	296.3x	Major Depressive Disorder, Recurrent
	_____	_____
	_____	_____
Axis II:	301.20	Schizoid Personality Disorder
	301.83	Borderline Personality Disorder
	301.9	Personality Disorder NOS
	_____	_____
	_____	_____

FAMILY ACTIVITY DISPUTES

BEHAVIORAL DEFINITIONS

1. Strong disagreements arise over family activities, causing a sense of disengagement between family members.
2. Younger children complain about not being permitted to do the same activities as their older siblings.
3. The family splinters into doing separate activities, causing feelings of disengagement and loss of cohesion among family members.
4. Family members become more invested in other families' activities in order to compensate for what is missing from their own family.
5. Disagreements occur over how money should be spent for family needs, wants, and pleasurable pursuits.

—. _____
   _____
   _____
—. _____
   _____
   _____
—. _____
   _____

LONG-TERM GOALS

1. Reduce conflict over leisure-time family activities.
2. Younger members of the family learn to accept their need to wait until a more appropriate age in order to enjoy certain activities.
3. Accept the need for sharing and patience in planning and implementing family activities.
4. Reduce family members' involvement in activities that are meant to compensate for what is missing within their own family.

5. Eliminate tension and conflict between family members over the perceived violation of their own needs for recreation, stimulation, or learning.

—. _____

_____

—. _____

_____

—. _____

_____

SHORT-TERM OBJECTIVES

1. Define disagreement with each other over family activities by using specific operational terms. (1, 2)

2. Demonstrate tolerance for listening to the likes and dislikes of other family members for various activities in a civil and respectful manner. (3, 4)

3. Engage in several activities of differing lengths as an experiment to see what members like and dislike. (5, 6)

4. List the pros and cons as well as the impact of the activity. (6, 7)

5. Engage in activities that are enjoyable to some individual family members but not to all. (8, 9, 10)

6. Rate the degree of enjoyment for family social/recreational activities. (11)

THERAPEUTIC INTERVENTIONS

1. Facilitate a session in which members describe their discontent about family activity.

2. Encourage family members to use certain adjectives that help to define how they feel (selfish, cheated, left out, lonely, resentful, etc.).

3. Ascertain through interview and/or inventory what activities are pleasing and satisfying to each family member and identify where any overlap exists. Utilize such inventories as the Inventory of Rewarding Activities (Birchler) or the Family Inventory of Life Events and Changes in *Family Assessment Inventories for Research and Practice* (McCubbin and Thompson).

4. Assess whether certain family members lack toler-

7. List activities that are enjoyed by all family mem-
bers. (12)

8. Agree to participate in
other family members' en-
joyed activities because it is
a means of sacrificing self-
interest for the good of another. (13, 14, 15)

9. Schedule activities in combi-
nations such that various
things will appeal to different family members. (16, 17)

10. Identify any underlying
negative feelings or personality traits that may be contributing to the lack of
cooperation with each
other's activities.
(18, 19, 20, 21)

11. Agree to seek fairness and
balance in scheduling activities that are more enjoyable to some members than
to others. (22, 23, 24)

__. _____
   _____

__. _____
   _____

__. _____
   _____

ance and where this stems
from. Suggest certain exercises that would help to
build better tolerance (e.g.,
the use of positive talk and
weighing the shortcomings
of having to put their own
needs on hold).

5. Try to determine whether
the discontent with family
activities is an all-or-
nothing matter or there are
only aspects of the activities
that family members do not
care for. Have them con-
struct a list of specific objec-
tions and then review the
particulars.

6. Have family members share
their opinions on the pros
and cons of other family
members' activities.

7. Allow family members to
talk personally about the effect a particular activity
had on them. Help them to
evaluate whether this effect
is due to their own personality traits or to the dynamics of the activity or to both.

8. Facilitate a discussion
about maintaining an open
mind and remaining flexi-
ble about activities sug-
gested by other family
members.

9. Ask family members to
agree to try one of the other
member's activity sugges-
tions one time and evaluate
the outcome in the subse-
quent family visit.

10. Schedule an activity for all family members to attempt; using a list of each member's favorite activities. Start with activities that involve a minimal amount of time.

11. Have each family member rate the degree of enjoyment of an activity on a scale from 0 to 10 (or use the Family Time and Routines Index [McCubbin and Thompson]). Also allow for the expression of discontent with certain activities, but stipulate that family members must list positives along with negatives.

12. Use brainstorming and consult assessment results to develop a list of mutually enjoyable activities.

13. Encourage all family members to invest effort and cooperation into an activity that may not appeal to them initially.

14. Teach the concept of family members' sacrificing personal interest for the pleasure of another family member; this is a means of showing love, respect, and unity.

15. Ask family members to consider committing to sacrificing by displaying interest in an activity that they might not be pleased with and then weigh some of the potential rewards of such a

sacrifice (giving a gift of self, making other family members happy, learning a new activity, etc.).

16. Solicit agreement that after engaging in one family member's enjoyable activity, the family will eat at another family member's favorite restaurant in order to balance the scales.

17. Discuss additional ways to increase the attractiveness of certain activities that family members may not care for (e.g., pair together two activities that are enjoyed by different members).

18. Brainstorm with family members about what factors might be underlying disputes about family activities (jealousy, insecurity, favoritism, etc.).

19. Determine whether there are other issues that are influencing the conflict over family activities (e.g., the need to avoid social contact or the need for power and control).

20. Develop ways in which to address underlying conflicts or to compensate for personality traits in alternative ways other than by disagreeing over activities.

21. Assess the need to refer family members for individual counseling due to more ingrained issues (self-

centeredness, depression, narcissism, etc.).

22. Propose the idea of using a lottery or some type of random drawing to rotate activities.

23. Discuss the need for mutual courtesy and that activities should involve some tolerance for give-and-take.

24. Prepare the family for the idea that not everyone will always be pleased, that they need to inoculate themselves against disagreement, and so on.

—. _____

_____

—. _____

_____

—. _____

_____

DIAGNOSTIC SUGGESTIONS

Axis I:

309.0	Adjustment Disorder With Depressed Mood
309.24	Adjustment Disorder With Anxiety
309.28	Adjustment Disorder With Mixed Anxiety and Depressed Mood
305.00	Alcohol Abuse
303.9	Alcohol Dependence
300.15	Dissociative Disorder NOS
300.4	Dysthymic Disorder
300.02	Generalized Anxiety Disorder
296.x	Major Depressive Disorder
300.21	Panic Disorder Without Agoraphobia
V61.1	Partner Relational Problem
V61.2	Parent–Child Relational Problem
_____	_____
_____	_____

Axis II: 301.82   Avoidant Personality Disorder
        301.6   Dependent Personality Disorder
        301.81   Narcissistic Personality Disorder
        301.9   Personality Disorder NOS

        _____   _____

        _____   _____

FAMILY BUSINESS CONFLICTS

BEHAVIORAL DEFINITIONS

1. The children and/or spouse are angry and jealous because of the time and energy required by the family business.
2. The children and/or spouse are angry and resentful about having to dedicate their own time to the family business.
3. Conflict arises between two or more family members vying for control of the family business.
4. The parents continue to interfere with the operation of the family business after handing over the reins to the children.
5. Conflict arises between the spouses of siblings who are involved with the family business.
6. Conflict arises over a parent's new spouse's role in the family business.
7. Resentment surfaces over variations within the family in power, compensation, or privileges associated with the business.
8. Family members employed in the family business feel anger and resentment toward family members who derive financial remuneration from the business but are not employed in it.
9. Some family members fail to consult with other family members about important business decisions.
10. Hidden anger and resentments are harbored by certain family members over business issues, which serves to erode the family relationships.
11. Family members engage in blaming each other for the lack of financial success of the family business.
12. Schisms in the family over business issues lead to the exclusion of certain members from holiday celebrations and special events.

—. _____
_____

—. _____
_____

—. _____
_____

LONG-TERM GOALS

1. Reduce or eliminate the amount of anger and jealousy regarding the amount of time the family business consumes from the working family members.
2. Reduce, eliminate, or restructure the amount of time and energy that is consumed by the family business.
3. Achieve agreement regarding who will run the family business or how the level of leadership might permit the sharing of power and responsibilities.
4. Achieve some guidelines for the boundaries, responsibilities, and roles of all family members in the business.
5. Settle all issues over the roles and ownership that non-family-of-origin members will have in the family business.
6. Achieve agreement about power, compensation, and privileges within the family business.
7. Establish ground rules regarding the process of making major corporate decisions.
8. Reduce feelings of anger and resentment associated with the business to eliminate the erosion of family relations.

—. _____
_____

—. _____
_____

—. _____
_____

SHORT-TERM OBJECTIVES

1. Verbalize any anger, jealousy, or resentments about the family business. (1)

2. Identify how the expression of anger or resentment has affected the dynamics of the family. (2)

3. Rank the goals and objectives for the company and compare this list with the original charter that was designed. (3)

4. Vote on who can best direct the business to achieve the goals identified. (4)

5. Retired or retiring members verbalize the emotional struggle with relinquishing control of the business. (5, 6, 12)

6. Verbalize agreement on the role of the spouses of family members during their tenure as employees of the family business. (7, 8, 12)

7. Identify relationship and role boundaries in the family business versus boundaries for non-business-related activities. (9, 10)

8. Family members agree on how much and when non-working family-of-origin members will receive financial benefit from the family business. (11, 12)

9. Verbalize a feeling of resolution and understanding

THERAPEUTIC INTERVENTIONS

1. Explore family members' thoughts and feelings generated by the issue of the family business.

2. Poll each family member about how he/she has expressed feelings and explore the conflicts that have resulted from expression and nonexpression of feelings.

3. Facilitate the construction of a hierarchy of goals and objectives for the family business and stipulate how they will be used to achieve the projections set forth for the business each year.

4. Assist family members in ranking the skills of each family member and his/her suitability for directing the company. Have family members vote on who should be in control.

5. Explore how some parents or older siblings may have difficulty letting go of the reins emotionally, even though they have done so formally. Facilitate the expression of struggling with a sense of the loss of power or control, lessened self-esteem, and/or a lack of planning for a postleadership position.

6. Secure some understanding from family members of the role of former leaders of the family business and develop

regarding all resentment
and anger associated with
family business issues.
(1, 2, 5, 13)

__. _____
     _____

__. _____
     _____

__. _____
     _____

specific rules of disengagement for them to follow.

7. Brainstorm about the way
   spouses of family members
   should be treated regarding
   power in the family business; facilitate an agreement about the role of
   non-family-of-origin members.

8. Assist family members in
   designing a formal mechanism for working through
   the conflict that exists over
   the role of spouses of family
   members within the business.

9. Explore with family members resentments regarding
   boundary issues in the family of origin. Facilitate the
   expression of emotions over
   restrictions imposed by
   boundaries.

10. Assist family members in
    developing a set of rules
    that govern interaction
    within the business versus
    non-business-related family
    interaction.

11. Solicit agreement with the
    concept that family-of-
    origin members are all
    equally eligible for some fi-
    nancial benefit from the
    family business, allowing
    for a differentiation be-
    tween contributing and
    noncontributing members.

12. Recommend utilizing a
    skilled family business con-
    sultant to help family mem-
    bers with issues of fairness,

succession, buy-sell agreements, and so on.

13. Use role-playing, empty
chair, and cognitive restructuring techniques to reduce
anger on the part of family
members.

—. _____
_____

—. _____
_____

—. _____
_____

DIAGNOSTIC SUGGESTIONS

Axis I: 309.4   Adjustment Disorder With Mixed Disturbance
of Emotions and Conduct
V61.1   Partner Relational Problem
V61.2   Parent–Child Relational Problem

_____   _____
_____   _____

Axis II: 301.0   Paranoid Personality Disorder
301.81   Narcissistic Personality Disorder
301.9   Personality Disorder NOS

_____   _____
_____   _____

FAMILY MEMBER SEPARATION

BEHAVIORAL DEFINITIONS

1. Family members are forced to temporarily separate from one another due to employment obligations, military duty, incarceration, illness, or the like.
2. Feelings arise of disengagement, insecurity, and difficulty in coping with the separation.
3. Conflict and turmoil ensue due to the redistribution of the balance of power in the family system.
4. Children regress emotionally and behaviorally due to the separation.
5. The family experiences difficulty in readjusting to the return of the absent family member(s), especially after a significant period of adjustment to the absence.
6. Conflict arises between those family members who react with relief versus those who react with grief over the separation.
7. <u>Child Reacts the loss of his father due to substance use and moves into mother's home.</u>
___. _____
   _____
___. _____
   _____

LONG-TERM GOALS

1. Family members accept the fact that loss may occur at any time in many different ways and prepare themselves for how to deal with the situation should it arise.

2. Develop skills for working together to cope with the interim time of absence.
3. Reorder the balance of power between remaining family members in order to compensate for the absence of the other family member(s).
4. Children learn improved ways to cope with the absence of a family member and locate viable nurturing substitutes until the absent family member returns.
5. Welcome the absent family member(s) back into the home and make a positive transition to the change.

—. _____
   _____
—. _____
   _____
—. _____
   _____

SHORT-TERM OBJECTIVES

1. Departing family member describes feelings about the absence and how it may affect the family. (1)

2. Departing family member verbalizes mechanisms that he/she will use to cope with the separation. (2)

3. Agree on ways to communicate with each other during the absence. (3)

4. Identify how the absence will affect or has affected each family member. (4)

5. Children verbalize coping skills for dealing with the absence of a parent. (5, 6, 7)

6. Parents verbalize how they will cope with the absence of the family member. (5, 6, 7)

THERAPEUTIC INTERVENTIONS

1. Bring family member who will be leaving into a predeparture family session and gather his/her perceptions of how separation will affect the family as a whole.

2. The family member who is departing will talk about ways in which he/she plans to cope with the separation until his/her return.

3. Brainstorm ways in which family members can stay in touch with each other (video, e-mail, etc.).

4. Explore how the loss will impact or has impacted each family member.

5. Determine whether the absence is likely to be short-

7. List ways that family members can help each other cope with and adjust to the absence. (8)

8. Identify conflicts that arise in light of the absent family member's departure. (9)

9. Report a resolution of conflicts that have resulted from the family member's absence. (10)

10. Identify changes in roles, power, and alliances that have resulted from the family member's absence. (11)

11. Agree to a change in roles and responsibilities within the family structure. (8, 12, 13)

12. Acknowledge a child's regressive behaviors and how they pertain to the way the child is coping with the situation. (14, 15)

13. Grieving child utilizes memory-preserving techniques to cope with the loss of the absent family member. (16)

14. Grieving child increases activity level with the family generally and with the remaining parent to strengthen the dependency bond. (17, 18)

15. Acknowledge the conflict that develops as a result of some family members experiencing relief that the absent family member has departed. (10, 19)

term, long-term, or permanent and, depending on the length of the loss, introduce various coping skills (e.g., finding a surrogate parent through a relative or friend) for the separation period.

6. Open a line of discussion about how each family member is attempting to deal with the loss.

7. Discuss how and why the various internal coping skills differ among family members.

8. Teach family members how to support each other in the use of coping skills and in the redistribution of the roles in the household.

9. Assist family members in identifying conflicts over the absence by tracing when they surfaced and relate their development to the absent family member.

10. Help family members work through their issues of conflict resulting from the family member's absence and learn to respect each other's perceptions and viewpoints. Aim for some form of compromise regarding the conflicts that are being produced.

11. Assist the family in identifying changes in specific roles, balance of power, alliances, and caretakers that have emerged during the absence.

16. Verbalize ways to deal with the return of the absent family member and adjust to the person's reintroduction into the family. (20, 21)

—. _____
_____

—. _____
_____

—. _____
_____

12. Teach that the redistribution of roles is a necessary mechanism for adjustment to the new situation (see *101 Interventions in Family Therapy* [Nelson and Trepper]).

13. Introduce techniques (e.g., cognitive restructuring, weighing the alternatives, and challenging the evidence) that reinforce alteration in roles and expectations and restructuring of perception (see *Case Studies in Couples and Family Therapy* [Dattilio]).

14. Educate the family about how regressive behaviors in children are common during periods of stress, crisis, or loss (see *Helping Children Cope with Separation and Loss* [Jewett]).

15. Instruct family members on how not to berate children for the regressive behaviors, but rather to use methods of comfort, nurturance, and role-modeling of desirable, more productive behaviors.

16. Encourage children to use imaging techniques or to periodically view videos or photos of the absent family member. Have the children keep in their possession different mementos of or personal items belonging to the absent member.

17. Support the grieving children by developing activi-

ties (e.g., reading books together, playing together,
going for a walk or to a
movie together, watching
children's video together)
that strengthen the bond
with the remaining parent
or family members as a
means of coping with the
absence.

18. Review activities (e.g., self-
constructed board games,
sculptural metaphors) that
promote family cohesive-
ness and engagement (see
*101 More Interventions in
Family Therapy* [Nelson
and Trepper]).

19. Investigate with the entire
family why certain mem-
bers have experienced relief
as a result of the other family member's absence, ex-
ploring possible issues of
jealousy, physical/sexual
abuse, and so on.

20. Explore the issue of
anger/resentment toward
the absent family member
for returning to the family
unit and review construc-
tive methods for venting
this anger/resentment (e.g.,
assign readings such as *The
Dance of Anger* [Lerner],
When Anger Hurts [McKay,
Rogers, and McKay], or
Anger Workout Book
[Weisenberger]).

21. Discuss the effect that the
reintroduction of the absent
member will have on the
changed family.

—. _____
   _____
   _____
—. _____
   _____
—. _____
   _____

DIAGNOSTIC SUGGESTIONS

Axis I: 309.0   Adjustment Disorder With Depressed Mood
                309.24   Adjustment Disorder With Anxiety
                309.28   Adjustment Disorder With Mixed Anxiety and
                         Depressed Mood
                309.3   Adjustment Disorder With Disturbance of
                         Conduct
                309.4   Adjustment Disorder With Mixed Disturbance
                         of Emotions and Conduct
                309.9   Adjustment Disorder Unspecified
                309.21   Separation Anxiety Disorder
                300.4   Dysthymic Disorder
                300.02   Generalized Anxiety Disorder
                312.9   Disruptive Behavior Disorder NOS
                307.21   Transient Tic Disorder
                313.81   Oppositional Defiant Disorder
                787.6   Encopresis
                307.6   Enuresis
                313.23   Selective Uretism
                313.89   Reactive Detachment Disorder

                _____   _____

                _____   _____

Axis II: 301.6   Dependent Personality Disorder
                301.0   Paranoid Personality Disorder
                301.20   Schizoid Personality Disorder
                301.82   Avoidant Personality Disorder
                301.9   Personality Disorder NOS

                _____   _____

                _____   _____

FAMILY-OF-ORIGIN INTERFERENCE

BEHAVIORAL DEFINITIONS

1. The spouse's parents express unsolicited opinions and judgments about behavior or decisions of the couple in an apparent attempt to control the spouse.
2. The grandparents attempt to impose their beliefs about how the parents should raise the grandchildren.
3. The parents' siblings interfere with issues regarding raising the children.
4. The couple argues over the perception that one spouse's family of origin is overstepping their boundaries.
5. The children begin to act out emotionally/behaviorally as a result of extended family interference.
6. Dissension occurs within the family of origin due to a confrontation over extended family interference.

—. _____

_____

—. _____

_____

—. _____

_____

LONG-TERM GOALS

1. The parents' family-of-origin members accept boundaries and terminate the practice of directly imposing their beliefs and values onto their children's immediate family.

2. The parents make clear to all members of their families of origin that they have a specific set of rules and regulations by which they govern their children and wish no outside interference.
3. Marital conflict regarding a spouse's family-of-origin interference with family issues is reduced.
4. Children learn alternative ways of expressing the tension that builds in the family due to the parents' family-of-origin interference.
5. Family-of-origin members understand that their interference can be a very destructive force when not invited or welcomed and, therefore, they refrain from offering opinions, judgments, or directives.

—. _____

_____

_____

—. _____

_____

—. _____

_____

SHORT-TERM OBJECTIVES

1. Each family member outlines the family-of-origin interference problem. (1)
2. Each family member expresses feelings that have been generated by the interference issue. (2, 3)
3. Parents cooperate with training in assertiveness and problem solving. (4, 5)
4. Parents express support for each other in dealing with the interference issue. (6)
5. Parents confront interfering members of the family of origin. (7, 8)

THERAPEUTIC INTERVENTIONS

1. Explore issues related to extended family interference, getting the perspective of each family member.
2. Facilitate family members' expression of feelings to each other to promote understanding and empathy.
3. Utilize techniques such as thought stopping, cognitive restructuring, and anger management to reduce the level of tension between family members over the issue of extended family interference in their lives.
4. Educate parents about how to deal effectively with in-

6. Parents tell family-of-origin members how they can make suggestions to them in an appropriate fashion. (9)

7. Each parent curtails his/her anger at the spouse and rechannels any resentment maintained for the spouse's family-of-origin members. (3, 10)

8. Children verbalize an understanding that parents, not extended family members, are in control. (11)

9. Parents identify personal issues that promote family-of-origin interference. (12)

10. Parents tacitly suggest to interfering members of the family of origin that they need to address their own issues that cause them to interfere. (13, 14)

11. Children assert themselves with those who interfere by directing them to their parents. (15)

12. Increase the frequency of enjoyable family unit activities. (16)

13. Children reduce their acting-out behaviors that result from the external interference by extended family. (16, 17)

14. Parents verbalize a sense of balance and achieve a resolution of their marital conflict. (18, 19)

terfering family-of-origin members through training in assertiveness, communication, and problem-solving strategies. Also, assign readings such as *Toxic Parents* (Forward).

5. Use role-playing, modeling, and behavior rehearsal to teach parents how to approach difficult family-of-origin members and set boundaries on their interference.

6. Reinforce the parents' need to unite and be supportive of each other in maintaining a stance with their respective family-of-origin members.

7. Assign the parents as a unit to set boundaries on interfering family members.

8. If the family-of-origin members will agree to come into a specially held family session with the therapist, then address the interference directly (see *Family-of-Origin Therapy: An Intergenerational Approach* [Framo]).

9. Assist parents in developing acceptable ways that extended family members can offer suggestions to them when invited.

10. Teach spouses not to hold each other responsible for the other's family-of-origin interference.

—. _____
   _____
   _____
—. _____
   _____
—. _____
   _____

11. Explore any confusion that has occurred in the children, reaffirming the parents' sense of power and control in the situation.

12. Address with each parent any residual individual issues that may be perpetuating family interference (e.g., unresolved guilt feelings, a history of having always been controlled by or dependent on his/her family of origin).

13. Support the parents in being assertive enough to confront their respective family-of-origin members about getting counseling for themselves. Use role-playing, letter-writing techniques, and so on.

14. Offer to the interfering members of the family of origin the option of family-of-origin sessions or individual/family therapy elsewhere.

15. Utilize assertiveness training, role-playing, and modeling to teach children how to direct interfering people to their parents.

16. Encourage family communication and group activities to increase cohesiveness, tighten the family bond, and close gaps that may be facilitating external interference.

17. Confront children's acting-out behavior, assisting par-

ents in setting limits and interpreting the children's behavior as a reflection of their confusion generated by outside interference in family dynamics.

18. Explore why and how the interference has had such a significant effect on the marital relationship and suggest methods for rebalancing the relationship. Also address issues of loyalty to parents and utilize problem-solving techniques.

19. Refer parents to couples therapy, particularly if the relational problems are more extensive.

—. _____
   _____

—. _____
   _____

—. _____
   _____

DIAGNOSTIC SUGGESTIONS

Axis I:	309.4	Adjustment Disorder With Mixed Disturbance of Emotions and Conduct
	_____	_____
	_____	_____
Axis II:	301.83	Borderline Personality Disorder
	301.5	Histrionic Personality Disorder
	301.6	Dependent Personality Disorder
	301.9	Personality Disorder NOS
	_____	_____
	_____	_____

FINANCIAL CHANGES

BEHAVIORAL DEFINITIONS

1. A drastic decrease in family income occurs through either one or both parents' loss of employment or some other type of financial crisis (major illness, bills, etc.).
2. Family members feel the pinch of less money and argue over the amount of money spent on miscellaneous items and extras.
3. Children and/or spouse are critical of the breadwinning parent for the financial change or crisis (e.g., as being the result of alcohol or substance abuse).
4. Family arguments occur over the amount of money to be saved and how much is spent.
5. Other members exert pressure on certain family members to always shop for the lowest possible prices.
6. Family arguments arise over the children's desire to earn income for themselves without having to account to their parents for the expenditure of their own money.
7. The family is unable to pay bills for fixed expenses and must relocate, cancel commitments, face bill collectors, cancel phone service, and so on.

—. _____
   _____
—. _____
   _____
—. _____
   _____

LONG-TERM GOALS

1. Agree on a plan for coping with the financial change and compensate for the loss of income.
2. Reduce the arguments over the decrease in financial resources and improve coping skills for a reduced standard of living.
3. Develop open communication of feelings of resentment over the perceived reasons for the financial change.
4. Develop some structured, detailed financial plans for budgeting the income that does exist.
5. Agree on how to shop for certain items, given the change in financial resources.
6. Agree on the rules that will govern the children in earning outside income and the way that money will be spent (how much will be placed in savings, etc.).
7. Develop a plan for income supplementation and reassignment of family/home duties.
8. Terminate parental maladaptive behaviors (e.g., substance abuse, gambling, compulsive shopping) that contribute to financial crisis.

__. _____
   _____
__. _____
   _____
__. _____
   _____

SHORT-TERM OBJECTIVES

1. Verbalize anger, frustration, and resentment pertaining to financial stress. (1, 2, 3)

2. Identify how and why arguments develop over finances. (3)

3. List alternatives to the verbal expression of frustration within the family. (4)

4. Family members agree to work on improving commu-

THERAPEUTIC INTERVENTIONS

1. Facilitate an atmosphere in which family members can freely express emotions about the financial situation.

2. Focus specifically on eliciting feelings and beliefs about the restrictions caused by the financial situation.

nication skills and learning alternative ways to express themselves more productively. (3, 4, 5)

5. Acknowledge and seek treatment for any compulsive or addictive behaviors that interfere with family income. (6)

6. Identify the differences in spending priorities that exist between family members. (7)

7. List the future income, saving, and spending expectations. (8)

8. Set financial goals that are plausible and make realistic budgetary decisions jointly without undue reactions to family pressure. (9)

9. Practice showing patience with each other when expressing various financial plans and expense-saving strategies. (10)

10. Agree on the steps that will be taken to cope with the financial problem. (11, 12)

11. Implement a mutual agreement on how decisions are made regarding allocation of money in the family. (13)

12. Acknowledge that a mental illness or personality disorder is interfering with financial disposition within the family. (14)

13. Identify any unrealistic ideas held by the children or spouse regarding what

3. Explore the nature of anger expression over financial strictures, emphasizing how conflicts and arguments only exacerbate the situation.

4. Brainstorm alternatives that can be used to ventilate frustration (e.g., express aggression via sports, develop an exercise routine, or keep a feelings journal).

5. Train family members in communication skills via structured techniques (e.g., Speaker/Listener Strategies in *Relationship Enhancement* [Guerney]).

6. Help the family to confront individual family members' issues that may be contributing or causing the financial problems (e.g., substance abuse, gambling, or compulsive shopping); refer them for treatment.

7. Assist family members in identifying their priorities regarding financial expenditures and discuss how they arrived at their values.

8. Have family members share their individual (or joint) expectations regarding future income, expenses, and savings; discuss how realistic their expectations are.

9. Brainstorm various avenues for financial planning that will involve family cooperation and a reduction in conflict (e.g., consultations with financial advisors; use of

they personally earn and how it will be spent. (15)

14. Identify alternative ways that income can be increased. (16)

—. _____
   _____

—. _____
   _____

—. _____
   _____

computer software for budgeting income and recording expenditures).

10. Encourage the use of communication skills and anger/frustration management skills to cope with other family members' ideas that violate expectations.

11. Explore the need for consolidating loans, declaring bankruptcy, applying for welfare, and so on. If financial planning is deemed necessary, refer the family to a professional planner (see *Consumer Reports,* January 1998, for a review of financial planning services, or *Family Economics Review,* published by the U.S. Department of Agriculture).

12. Assist family members in identifying specific coping skills needed because of the change in financial situation (e.g., living with less, spending more wisely, borrowing items, or bartering).

13. Reinforce changes in money management that reflect compromise, responsibility, planning, perseverance, and respectful cooperation.

14. Assess whether a mental illness or personality disorder (e.g., bipolar disorder or narcissistic personality) is interfering with responsible financial planning; refer for individual treatment as necessary.

15. Develop an agreed-upon plan for income earned by the children (and spouse) and how it will be spent.

16. Assist the family in identifying how other sources of income can be developed.

___. _____
    _____

___. _____
    _____

___. _____
    _____

DIAGNOSTIC SUGGESTIONS

Axis I:	309.24	Adjustment Disorder With Anxiety
	309.0	Adjustment Disorder With Depressed Mood
	309.28	Adjustment Disorder With Mixed Anxiety and Depressed Mood
	303.9	Alcohol Dependence
	305.00	Alcohol Abuse
	304.30	Cannabis Dependence
	296.0x	Bipolar I Disorder, Single Manic Episode
	V62.2	Occupational Problem
	296.2x	Major Depressive Disorder, Single Episode
	311	Depressive Disorder NOS
	_____	_____
	_____	_____
Axis II:	301.7	Antisocial Personality Disorder
	301.4	Obsessive-Compulsive Personality Disorder
	301.81	Narcissistic Personality Disorder
	_____	_____
	_____	_____

GEOGRAPHIC RELOCATION

BEHAVIORAL DEFINITIONS

1. One or both parents are forced to relocate due to transfer to another geographic area to maintain employment.
2. One or both parents want to relocate due to climate, family connections, job opportunity, or a perceived better way of life.
3. Spouse and/or family members do not want to relocate because they are very comfortable in the present home and environment.
4. Dissension and opposition arise over the notion of the family relocating.
5. Spouse and/or children protest with demands that the breadwinner find another job locally instead of agreeing to relocate.
6. Children threaten noncompliance and acting-out behaviors (e.g., runaway behaviors, assault threats, false allegations of abuse, demands to live with a friend, threats of not doing well academically) in reaction to relocation.
7. Several months after relocation, various family members feel that they cannot adjust to the new location.
8. Feelings of grief, anger, and depression arise related to the issue of relocation.

—. _____

_____

—. _____

_____

—. _____

_____

LONG-TERM GOALS

1. Resolve negative feelings associated with relocation and accept without hostility the necessity for the change.
2. All family members treat each other with respect and fairness during the course of this conflict and its resolution.
3. Increase and improve the communication between family members and the level of empathy for each other's position.
4. Family members terminate hurtful verbal attacks on and behaviors toward each other.
5. Accept that the probability of relocation is a family problem that must be worked out as a unit and is not an individual problem.
6. Develop coping skills for better adjustment to the move.

__. _____
_____
__. _____
_____
__. _____
_____

SHORT-TERM OBJECTIVES	THERAPEUTIC INTERVENTIONS
1. Describe the specific conflict between family members regarding relocation. (1, 2, 3)	1. Explore each family member's thoughts and feelings regarding the possible relocation.
2. Make an extensive list of the pros and cons of moving. (1, 4)	2. Promote discussion by the spouse or family members who are reluctant to relocate. If this is a marital issue, deal with the problem in couples therapy, apart from family therapy, considering financial reality and power and control issues.
3. Identify alternatives to solving the relocation conflict. (5)	
4. Identify the impact on the family unit of the spouse's or children's threatening noncompliant behaviors in response to being mandated to relocate. (6)	3. Address the interfamilial dynamics regarding conflict in general and focus on how the family normally deals

5. Parents express understanding for the feelings behind children's threats or actual running away from home, but implement firm limits on such behavior. (7, 8, 9)

6. Children express feelings of powerlessness regarding the decision to move. (10)

7. Children terminate stealing, violence, or other delinquent behaviors. (7, 8, 9, 11)

8. Children verbalize an accusation of physical/sexual abuse against one or both parents as a means to get themselves removed from the home. (12, 13, 14)

9. Children express anger verbally and respectfully, without threat of or actual violence toward parents. (15, 16)

10. Identify losses related to relocation and express grief feelings. (17, 18)

11. Identify ways of developing replacements for the losses once the move is complete. (19)

12. Children propose a viable plan for residing with a friend or an extended family member as an alternative to relocating with the family of origin. (20)

13. Parents affirm their role as authority figures who must make decisions in the best interest of the family as a unit. (21)

with disagreements. Attempt to prevent the family from dividing, forming schisms and subgroup alliances. Deal with the conflict as a unit, utilizing a systemic approach.

4. Have family members brainstorm about possible advantages and disadvantages of moving.

5. Ask the family to identify three alternative resolutions to the relocation conflict and to strongly consider the possibility of implementing aspects of all three alternatives.

6. Address the individual, noncompliant, rebellious behaviors of each family member as they emerge. Discuss the impact of these specific behaviors on other family members and effective ways in which they can be modified.

7. Assist parents in responding to children's acting out by setting limits (response cost, grounding, etc.) and discuss reasons for the children's acting out as a part of the expression of feelings.

8. In a separate conjoint session with the parents, suggest appropriate behavioral responses to each child's acting-out behavior (e.g., loss of privileges, selected chores, or community service).

___. _____

_____

___. _____

_____

___. _____

_____

9. Discuss disciplinary measures with the parents and alternative recourse (e.g., removal of privileges or temporary removal from the home) for not tolerating such behavior.

10. Facilitate the children's expressions of feelings of powerlessness and/or frustration with parents or other family members over the issue of relocation.

11. Facilitate the family in separating the children's anger and involvement in criminal behavior. Utilize techniques such as family sculpting and reverse role-play to address feelings and behavior separately and how they affect the overall family.

12. Explore the issue of children's accusations of physical or sexual abuse in both family therapy and with parents alone. Address issues of power and control/resentment.

13. Refer the family to protective services or another social service agency, working in concert with them to resolve the accusations of physical or sexual abuse and to determine the veracity of the children's allegations.

14. Consider the temporary removal of the children if the possibility exists that physi-

cal or sexual abuse has occurred.

15. Address the children's
anger and teach controlled
expression of this anger to
prevent violence or threats
toward any family member.

16. Offer the children alternatives (sports, music, use of a
punching bag, etc.) for expressing their anger and
resentment/frustration.

17. Assist family members in
identifying losses associated
with relocation.

18. Facilitate the expression of
all family members' grief
feelings to promote mutual
understanding and empa-
thy.

19. Validate real losses and
challenge family members
to focus on utilizing new
horizons to expand their
ideas, friendships, and experiences.

20. Address the issue of children residing with a friend
or an extended family member. Discuss the pros and
cons of such an alternative.
Also address how such a decision would affect the general dynamics of the family.

21. Reinforce the structure of
the family with parents as
architects with the role of
executives who have ulti-
mate authority to make the
final decision about what
the family will do.

—.＿ ＿＿＿＿＿＿＿＿＿＿＿
 ＿＿＿＿＿＿＿＿＿＿＿

—.＿ ＿＿＿＿＿＿＿＿＿＿＿
 ＿＿＿＿＿＿＿＿＿＿＿

—.＿ ＿＿＿＿＿＿＿＿＿＿＿
 ＿＿＿＿＿＿＿＿＿＿＿

DIAGNOSTIC SUGGESTIONS

Axis I: 309.4   Adjustment Disorder With Mixed Disturbance
                        of Emotions and Conduct
             313.81   Oppositional Defiant Disorder
             312.9   Disruptive Behavior Disorder NOS
             V61.1   Partner Relational Problem
             V61.2   Parent–Child Relational Problem
             _____   _____

             _____   _____

Axis II: 301.9   Personality Disorder NOS
             V61.1   Partner Relational Problem
             _____   _____

             _____   _____

INCEST SURVIVOR

BEHAVIORAL DEFINITIONS

1. Verbal demands for sexual interactions are made to a family member by another immediate or extended family member (i.e., parent, sibling, relative).
2. Refusal of verbal demands for sexual interaction is met by psychological or physical threat to fulfill sexual demands, causing the victim to submit to ongoing abuse and secrecy.
3. The sexually abused family member is reluctant to share the trauma of the abuse with anyone for fear of blame, rejection, retaliation, and so on.
4. The sexually abused family member struggles with guilt, shame, anger, resentment, depression, and isolation as a result of the abuse.
5. Family members are confused by the change in emotions and behavior (agitation, avoidance, depression, withdrawal, etc.) of the sexually abused family member and suspect that abuse may be occurring or has occurred in the past.
6. Family members learn of the sexual abuse sustained by the victim and experience a range of emotions, including rage, guilt, depression, denial, and sorrow.
7. The sexually abused family member begins to act out sexually (e.g., abusing family members or individual outside of the immediate family), causing problems in the family.
8. Family members pressure the victim of sexual abuse not to report the abuse to the authorities.
9. Family members take responsibility for reporting the sexual abuse to authorities, thus causing the abused victim to feel guilty.
10. The sexual abuse victim is temporarily removed from the home by court-appointed authorities, causing stress and strain to the family.

11. The sexual abuse victim threatens to expose the abuse to relatives, neighbors, friends, or others.

—. _____

_____

—. _____

_____

—. _____

_____

LONG-TERM GOALS

1. Family members become educated about the trauma of sexual abuse and learn the effects of various types of sexual abuse (e.g., forcible rape versus being exposed to pornography).
2. Family members learn how to comfort the sexual abuse victim and help the victim to express himself/herself and to slowly deal with the effects of the abuse.
3. Family members work through their guilt and shame, as well as shock and anger, toward the perpetrator.
4. The family helps the sexual abuse victim with the decision about how to report the situation to the authorities and/or press charges and helps the victim deal with the negative side effects of this decision.
5. The family learns to cope with the sexual abuse victim's own expression of acting-out behaviors as a result of the abuse.
6. The family develops ways to protect each other from future sexual abuse.
7. The family bands together to insist that the perpetrator stop the abusive behavior immediately, get therapeutic help, or move out.

—. _____

_____

—. _____

_____

—. _____

_____

SHORT-TERM OBJECTIVES

1. Sexual abuse victim talks openly about the sustained abuse. (1, 2, 3, 4)
2. Sexual abuse victim attends a support group. (5)
3. Family members verbalize an increased understanding of the dynamics of sexual abuse and its effects. (6, 7)
4. Family members protect the victim from the perpetrator and from any ongoing abuse. (8)
5. Sexual abuse victim affirms being comfortable with reporting the abuse. (8, 9, 10)
6. Family members verbalize an awareness of what to expect from the effects of the abuse, both in the victim as well as in the family as a whole. (11)
7. Family members list ways to respond supportively to the victim as symptoms of abuse evolve. (12, 13)
8. Family members verbalize their own emotional and behavioral reactions to the abuse. (14, 15, 16)
9. Verbalize the conflict that has developed between family members in reaction to the abuse. (17, 18)
10. Family members identify methods of support for the victim. (12, 13, 19)

THERAPEUTIC INTERVENTIONS

1. Actively build the level of trust with the sexual abuse victim in individual sessions through consistent eye contact, active listening, unconditional positive regard, and warm acceptance to help increase his/her ability to identify and express feelings.
2. Explore, encourage, and support the sexual abuse victim in verbally expressing and clarifying his/her feelings associated with the abuse.
3. Encourage family members to offer verbal and, possibly, physical support to the sexually abused family member.
4. Use indirect methods of describing the abuse and its effects (i.e., play therapy, artwork, psychodrama, or questionnaires/inventories such as the Modified Post-traumatic Symptom Scale [Resick, Falsetti, Resnick, and Kilpatrick] or the Sexual Assault Symptom Scale [Ruch, Gartell, Amedeo, and Coyne]).
5. Refer the sexual abuse victim to a community-based support group.
6. Recommend that the family read books on sexual abuse and how it affects the victim (e.g., *Repressed Memories* [Fredrickson] or

11. Utilize relaxation and positive self-talk to decrease anxiety. (20, 21, 22)

12. Family members refrain from informally confronting the perpetrator of the abuse, and schedule a time to do it therapeutically and/or in a legal setting. (23)

13. Agree to the best ways to legally and appropriately handle the perpetrator in the best interest of all family members, being especially sensitive to the feelings of the victim. (23, 24, 25)

14. Nonabused family members express their anger and frustration at a slower pace of processing the abuse but also verbalize sensitivity to the victim's feelings. (25, 26)

15. Follow through with contact with the legal authorities. (27)

16. Family members verbalize an understanding of the potential acting-out behaviors that may manifest in the victim of incest. (28, 29)

17. Family members verbalize an understanding that the victim's sexual acting out may occur as a result of both the abuse as well as other aspects that have to do with individual or family problems. (30, 31)

18. Family members decide as a group on the most appropriate time and place to listen

Betrayal of Innocence [Forward and Buck]).

7. Educate the family and the victim about the posttraumatic effects of incest (flashbacks, external cues, etc.) and how these effects may vary in their display. (See "Child Sexual Abuse" [Deblinger and Hope-Heflin].)

8. Discuss or brainstorm ways in which the family can protect the victim from being alone with or having contact with the perpetrator.

9. Assist the victim in resolving his/her fear of reporting the abuse due to fear of the perpetrator being criminally prosecuted. Address the tendency for victims to retract their statements.

10. Help the family deal with the victim's fear of retaliation by the perpetrator for reporting the abuse and the victim's inclination toward retraction.

11. Educate family members about the victims and perpetrators of incest and why incest happens, how it starts, and so on. Focus specifically on the effects on the victim.

12. Brainstorm about both individual and family group methods for responding to symptoms in the victim as they appear.

to the perpetrator's request for forgiveness. (32, 33)

19. Perpetrator accepts responsibility for his/her sexual abuse victim. (34)

20. Perpetrator offers apology and seeks forgiveness. (35)

21. The family as a whole sets a goal of healing from the sustained abuse and moving on. (36, 37)

—. _____
   _____

—. _____
   _____

—. _____
   _____

13. Caution the nonabused family members not to over-anticipate symptoms in the victim to the point of seeing what is not there and/or inducing it.

14. Explore how the incidence of abuse has emotionally affected the nonabused family members and how they have been expressing these feelings about it.

15. Brainstorm about and suggest various coping skills (e.g., venting, psychodrama, reverse role-play) for dealing with emotions such as anger, guilt, and despair.

16. Encourage the victim to become part of the healing process for the other family members by showing support for their pain and anger.

17. Address conflict that emerges within the family over the abuse (e.g., blaming one another for not protecting the victim; resentment by siblings that the victim is getting too much attention).

18. Utilize strategies such as conflict resolution, behavioral contracts, and cognitive restructuring to help family members resolve the issues that separate them.

19. Assist family members in identifying the best method of supporting the victim in dealing with his/her vulner-

ability (e.g., supportive listening, empathetic understanding, or determining comfort zones).

20. Teach the victim and the family deep muscle relaxation techniques.

21. Assist all family members in identifying dysfunctional negative automatic thoughts that generate anxiety.

22. Teach all family members to replace negative self-talk with positive, realistic messages that promote confidence and calm.

23. Help the family understand how dealing with the perpetrator in an appropriate legal and/or therapeutic manner is better than confronting the perpetrator informally.

24. Refer the family to the victims' rights and support group that is usually associated with the local district attorney's office or police station.

25. Help nonabused family members see past their own emotions and develop a feel for the pace of the victim (too much too quickly, which can have a negative effect on the victim; fear of testifying; etc.).

26. Allow for the ventilation of the nonabused family members' emotions and frustrations, particularly over the

seemingly slow pace of the prosecution.

27. Refer the victim and his/her family to the local authorities (police abuse unit, district attorney's office, etc.), while being sensitive to the feelings of the victim.

28. Explore for sexual acting out as a response by the victim to the abuse.

29. Teach the family the connection between the sexual acting out by the victim and the sexual abuse, urging calm limit setting and no overreaction.

30. Help family members sift through the aspects of the victim's sexual acting out that may be due to preexisting individual or family issues (i.e., lack of attention, low self-esteem, need for additional comfort, or anger toward men/women).

31. Separate specific aspects of the sexual acting-out issue that can be dealt with familially as well as what needs to be addressed in individual or group therapy for the victim.

32. Explore the victim's and family members' readiness for accepting an apology from the perpetrator.

33. Outline with the family the changes they would like to see in the perpetrator and whether they are willing to

support him/her through rehabilitation.

34. Provide a family forum for
the perpetrator to be confronted with his/her responsibility for the abuse,
allowing the victim the priority in expressing feelings.

35. Provide a family forum for
the perpetrator to ask for
forgiveness of the victim
and the family, allowing the
victim to respond as fully as
possible or even to delay responding until a later time.

36. Brainstorm methods for
going forward and healing
from the effects of the
abuse. Utilize such tech-
niques as rituals, taking
advantage of various com-
munity support programs,
and accepting an apology
from the perpetrator.

37. Reinforce the agreement between family members not
to revisit the trauma too
often once healing has
begun.

___. _____
     _____

___. _____
     _____

___. _____
     _____

DIAGNOSTIC SUGGESTIONS

Axis I:	309.81	Posttraumatic Stress Disorder
	308.3	Acute Stress Disorder
	309.0	Adjustment Disorder With Depressed Mood
	309.24	Adjustment Disorder With Anxiety
	309.28	Adjustment Disorder With Mixed Anxiety and Depressed Mood
	309.3	Adjustment Disorder With Disturbance of Conduct
	309.4	Adjustment Disorder With Mixed Disturbance of Emotions and Conduct
	312.9	Disruptive Behavior Disorder NOS
	313.81	Oppositional Defiant Disorder
	V61.21	Physical Abuse of Child
	V61.21	Sexual Abuse of Child
	995.5	Physical Abuse of Child (Victim)
	995.5	Sexual Abuse of Child (Victim)
	307.42	Primary Insomnia
	300.6	Depersonalization Disorder
	300.15	Dissociative Disorder NOS
	296.2x	Major Depressive Disorder, Single Episode
	296.3x	Major Depressive Disorder, Recurrent
	_____	_____
	_____	_____
Axis II:	799.9	Diagnosis Deferred
	V71.09	No Diagnosis
	_____	_____
	_____	_____

INFIDELITY

BEHAVIORAL DEFINITIONS

1. One or both parents engage in sexual behavior (coitus, oral sex, etc.) with an extramarital partner that violates the marital relationship.
2. One or both parents share intimate feelings or thoughts with an extramarital partner and maintain secrecy that violates the explicit or implicit expectations of the marital relationship (e.g., sending messages, e-mails, or gifts that carry a tone of romance; overtly or covertly expressing romantic attraction).
3. The children discover the extramarital involvement by one parent prior to the other parent's becoming aware of this himself/herself.
4. The nonoffending parent becomes aware of his/her spouse's involvement with an extramarital partner and confides in the children either prior or subsequent to confronting the spouse.
5. The offending parent secretly shares with the children his/her feelings for a nonspousal partner.

—. _____
   _____
—. _____
   _____
—. _____
   _____

LONG-TERM GOALS

1. Parents confront each other and agree to submit to couples therapy to address the infidelity issue as well as the problems with the relationship.

2. Parents arrive at an agreement about how to inform the children only if they suspect or know that the children are aware of the infidelity.
3. Children feel understood regarding the emotional impact of the infidelity on them.
4. Resolve how a marital separation will be introduced to the children and understand the impact that it will have on them.
5. Children resolve their feelings of guilt about knowing of the secret infidelity of one parent and struggling with how to divulge it to the other parent.
6. Children resolve their feelings about the parent inappropriately confiding in them about the affair.

—. _____
   _____
   _____

—. _____
   _____
   _____

—. _____
   _____

SHORT-TERM OBJECTIVES

1. Parents commit to relationship therapy and address the deterioration in the marriage as well as the impact of the extramarital saffair. (1)
2. Parents agree to separation therapy. (2)
3. Children identify the emotional impact that infidelity has had on them. (3, 4)
4. Unfaithful partner expresses understanding regarding the impact of his/her actions on the family and apologize for the hurt caused. (4)

THERAPEUTIC INTERVENTIONS

1. Refer parents to conjoint couples therapy without involvement of the children.
2. Discuss with the children their feelings about the option of the parents separating and address the impact and coping skills required. Also, discuss living arrangements for all parties involved with some potential time line.
3. Conduct an open-ended discussion about the children's feelings of anger, frustration, and betrayal of trust toward the offending par-

5. Children disclose and resolve their feelings of guilt, anger, frustration, disappointment, fear, and loyalty conflict that result from knowing secret infidelity information. (5)

6. Parents acknowledge the need for boundaries between themselves and the children and for using good judgment about the information to share with the children. (6)

7. Children verbalize that they are not responsible for their parents' behavioral choices. (7)

8. Parents and children agree on how to respond to others who hear about and react to the news of the infidelity. (8)

___. _____
   _____
___. _____
   _____
___. _____
   _____

ent. Utilize assertiveness training and confrontational skills, encourage letter writing, and so on.

4. Use exercises for anger mediation and rituals (e.g., cognitive mediation or *After the Affair* [Spring]) to deal with lack of trust and feelings of abandonment. Attempt to solicit an apology from the offending parent to the nonoffending parent and/or children. Indicate that forgiveness may take time but is necessary to move beyond the affair.

5. Address the issues of the children's guilt, anger, frustration, and disappointment, and the awkwardness around the bind of loyalty whether to tell the other parent of the infidelity.

6. Discuss the appropriateness of boundaries, as well as the negative results of enmeshment with and parentification of the child.

7. Support the children in understanding that they carry no responsibility for either parent's behavior and should not be held accountable, nor should they feel the need to fix the situation.

8. Address with the family how to cope with word of the infidelity reaching extended family members and the community (e.g., other children in the neighborhood and in school). Provide

supportive listening and
coping skills. Also recommend readings such as *Private Lies* (Pittman).

—. _____

      _____

—. _____

      _____

—. _____

      _____

DIAGNOSTIC SUGGESTIONS

Axis I: 309.0   Adjustment Disorder With Depressed Mood
            309.24   Adjustment Disorder With Anxiety
            309.28   Adjustment Disorder With Mixed Anxiety and
                       Depressed Mood
            296.xx   Bipolar I Disorder
            301.13   Cyclothymic Disorder
            296.xx   Major Depressive Disorder
            V61.1   Partner Relational Problem
            V61.2   Parent–Child Relational Problem

            _____   _____

            _____   _____

Axis II: 301.7   Antisocial Personality Disorder
            301.6   Dependent Personality Disorder
            301.81   Narcissistic Personality Disorder

            _____   _____

            _____   _____

INHERITANCE DISPUTES BETWEEN SIBLINGS

BEHAVIORAL DEFINITIONS

1. A significant sum of money and/or assets are willed to the children by grandparent(s), parent(s), or other relative(s).
2. Allocations of inheritance funds are perceived by one or several siblings to be unfair or imbalanced, precipitating conflict between family members.
3. Disputes arise between family members over how to equally divide money or assets among siblings.
4. Old feelings of favoritism spark resentment and negative feelings between siblings and toward the deceased.
5. Siblings are suspicious of one another with regard to having influenced the deceased while they were alive to bias the will in their favor, causing the distribution to be unfair.
6. Distribution of the inheritance was based on the quality of the relationship between offspring and the parent(s) prior to death.
7. Siblings refuse to speak with each other, which makes for difficult times during family gatherings, holidays, and special events.

__. _____
   _____
__. _____
   _____
   _____
__. _____
   _____

LONG-TERM GOALS

1. Family members reach a level of understanding and/or acceptance of the will and its asset distribution.
2. Resolve misperceptions of siblings regarding the fairness of distribution of an inheritance.
3. Resolve family members' conflicts that stem from the perceived unfair distribution of an inheritance.
4. Agree to a redistribution of inheritance assets that is acceptable to all.
5. Resolve any disputes regarding favoritism toward certain siblings by the deceased.
6. Quell suspiciousness on the part of the siblings for each other.
7. Accept the fact that the distribution of an inheritance may be related to the quality of the recipient's relationship to the deceased prior to death.
8. Siblings agree not to use noncommunication or shunning of one another to express their feelings of discontent or resentment.

—. _____

_____

—. _____

_____

—. _____

_____

SHORT-TERM OBJECTIVES

1. Outline the facts of the will's dispersement of assets. (1)

2. Identify how the differences in the distribution of the inheritance have affected each sibling. (2, 3)

3. Identify ways in which the inheritance might have been distributed more fairly. (4, 5)

THERAPEUTIC INTERVENTIONS

1. Collect the facts regarding asset distribution from legal documents and/or from input from various family members.

2. Brainstorm ideas of how the deceased may have arrived at his/her decision to distribute assets in the manner that he/she did. Address the emotional impact that

4. Identify how the inheritance meets financial and emotional needs. (6)

5. Define the relationship with the deceased parent. (7)

6. Agree to relinquish certain assets in a more equitable distribution of the inheritance. (8, 9)

7. Resolve feelings of suspicion regarding one or more siblings having influenced the deceased to favor them in the will. (10, 11)

8. Identify and implement alternative methods of dealing with anger, frustration, and disappointment. (12, 13)

—. _____
   _____

—. _____
   _____

—. _____
   _____

this has had on each family member.

3. Discuss specific resentments that have surfaced between siblings by holding face-to-face confrontations. Utilize exercises such as sitting opposite each other, holding hands, looking directly into each other's eyes, and softly, respectfully saying what they think and feel.

4. Have siblings rewrite the will of the deceased as they would have liked it to read. Have them discuss the effects of this exercise with each other.

5. Discuss what it means for siblings to accept the conditions of the will the way it was written and how this will affect their relationship. Explore whether they are open to redistributing the inheritance among themselves.

6. Explore what the inheritance means to each family member and how it fulfills their individual needs financially and emotionally. Discuss the need for each sibling to gain the parents' love, attention, and acceptance.

7. Facilitate the confiding of siblings in one another regarding their relationship with the deceased and how this affected their self-esteem.

8. Recommend mediational strategies that include redivision of allocations, healing of previous wounds, and providing a sense of comfort to one another.

9. Assist siblings in negotiating a more equitable formula for distribution of the inheritance.

10. Assist the siblings that are suspicious in reevaluating their perceived evidence that supports their belief, and challenge them with any new, contrary information that is uncovered during the family meeting.

11. Assess whether the suspicious family member may be suffering from any additional psychopathology (paranoia, depression, delusion, etc.). Refer this family member for psychological testing or a clinical evaluation if this is the case.

12. Facilitate a brainstorming session in which siblings consider alternative methods (e.g., assertiveness, "I" messages to express feelings, active listening to promote communication) rather than silence to deal with their feelings.

13. Facilitate role-playing of the communication strategies that emanate from the brainstorming; encourage implementation *in vivo*.

DIAGNOSTIC SUGGESTIONS

Axis I: 309.0   Adjustment Disorder With Depressed Mood

309.28   Adjustment Disorder With Mixed Anxiety and Depressed Mood

296.x   Major Depressive Disorder

_____   _____

_____   _____

Axis II: 301.6   Dependent Personality Disorder

301.50   Histrionic Personality Disorder

301.81   Narcissistic Personality Disorder

301.0   Paranoid Personality Disorder

301.7   Antisocial Personality Disorder

_____   _____

_____   _____

INTERRACIAL FAMILY PROBLEMS

BEHAVIORAL DEFINITIONS

1. Children of interracial marriage experience conflict in their environment due to the rejection by peers, society, and so on.
2. Parents experience backlash from children who resent their mixed race and feel the need to punish their parents for having exposed them to a difficult life.
3. Parents display some of their own hidden racial prejudices, creating marital conflict, which inadvertently affects the children.
4. Children who are discontent with their mixed heritage attempt to cope by downplaying or even denying their "undesirable" race (ignoring cultural aspects, superficial changes in physical image such as dying hair, etc.).
5. Children are rejected by extended family members who are opposed to the parents' interracial partnership.

__. _____
   _____
__. _____
   _____
__. _____
   _____

LONG-TERM GOALS

1. Children of interracial marriage learn to effectively cope with the stress of being mixed-race.
2. Parents recognize and address the children's resentment and find a way to supportively help the children work through their anger, resentment, and frustration for the mixed-race situation.

3. Parents acknowledge any personally harbored racial prejudices and take responsibility for not allowing them to effect the psychological welfare of the children.
4. Children who are discontent with their heritage learn to accept themselves as mixed-race without loss of self-esteem.
5. Parents and family members confront rejecting grandparents and/or extended family members about their insensitivity toward innocent children, leading to more acceptance and kindness toward the children.

__. _____
   _____
__. _____
   _____
__. _____
   _____

SHORT-TERM OBJECTIVES

1. Children describe situations in which they have felt rejection and the feelings that resulted from those experiences. (1, 2)

2. Parents verbalize their feelings of pain associated with their children being rejected or harassed. (1, 2)

3. Children read about the struggles of other individuals of mixed heritage. (3)

4. Children and/or parents attend a support group for mixed-race families. (4)

5. Children express feelings of anger and resentment toward parents for being the cause of the mixed-race heritage. (5, 6)

THERAPEUTIC INTERVENTIONS

1. Explore the nature of the rejection children have experienced due to their biracial heritage.

2. Explore the children's and parents' feelings that were generated by having experienced racial prejudice.

3. Introduce mixed-race children to literature about great individuals (e.g., Frederick Douglass) who have struggled through interracial challenges.

4. Refer children and/or parents to mixed-race support groups in the community.

5. Empathize with and show respect for children who have to endure social prejudice.

6. Parents verbalize acceptance of their children's resentment and acknowledge their anger as real and justified. (6, 7)

7. Parents explain the history of their relationship and their desire to have children in spite of social prejudices. (8, 9)

8. Parents admit to their own hidden prejudices and acknowledge a need to change their belief system. (10)

9. Children verbalize acceptance of who they are and abandon methods of trying to change or deny their race or culture. (11, 12, 13)

10. Children develop a set of friends and peers within their own race. (4, 14)

11. Verbalize the feelings surrounding extended family member's prejudice-based rejection of children. (15, 16)

12. Children verbalize possible causes for grandparents' rejection that have nothing to do with the child. (17)

13. Parents confront and attempt to resolve extended family members' rejection. (18)

14. Extended family members verbalize acceptance of biracial children. (18, 19)

6. Facilitate a session whereby children are able to ventilate their feelings without recrimination or fear of retaliation from parents.

7. Use role-playing and role reversal to help parents connect with their children's sense of danger and resentment.

8. Have parents explain their reasons and decisions for marrying and having children in an environment hostile to interracial relationships and children of mixed heritage.

9. Have parents share with the children their specific struggles with being victims of prejudice as a young couple during their courtship and how they coped with it.

10. Have parents explore the sources of their prejudices against a particular race and how they were developed and sustained.

11. Help children search behind the superficial rejection of their race and identify the real reason for their desire to be different (low self-esteem, desire for power and control, fear of prejudicial rejection, etc.).

12. Explore methods for children to positively identify with their particular race and assist them in creating a list of individuals of their race whom they can look up

—. _____
    _____
    _____
—. _____
    _____
—. _____
    _____

to (scientists, astronauts, religious leaders, politicians, sports figures, movie stars, etc.).

13. Have children freely express their fantasies of the race they would prefer to be if they could change and why. Have them make a list of the pros and cons of such a change.

14. Assist the family in developing a list of avenues of social exchange and interaction with members of various races through either community or church activities.

15. Explore the feelings that result from grandparents' or other extended family members' prejudice-based rejection of children.

16. Propose a course of individual treatment for family members who are struggling with the rejection expressed by the grandparents and/or extended family members.

17. Lead the family in an exploration of what may lurk behind the grandparents' rejection of their own grandchildren (jealousy, need to overcontrol, etc.) and help the children to understand this.

18. Encourage the parent from the rejecting family-of-origin to establish a family-of-origin meeting to discuss

the issue of inappropriate rejection (see *Family-of-Origin Therapy: An Intergenerational Approach* Framo).

19. Propose a rebonding session with rejecting grandparents and/or extended family members and biracial children in an attempt to heal the wounds of the rejection. Accomplish this via the use of family-of-origin or multigenerational meetings.

___. _____

_____

___. _____

_____

___. _____

_____

DIAGNOSTIC SUGGESTIONS

Axis I:	V61.1	Partner Relational Problems
	V61.2	Parent–Child Relational Problems
	_____	_____
	_____	_____
Axis II:	301.81	Narcissistic Personality Disorder
	301.0	Paranoid Personality Disorder
	_____	_____
	_____	_____

INTOLERANCE/DEFENSIVENESS

BEHAVIORAL DEFINITIONS

1. Development of tension and conflict over some family members' attitudes of self-righteousness and convictions that their opinions are superior to those of other family members.
2. Refusal to keep an open mind about considering other family members' opinions.
3. Irritability on the part of certain family members toward others' habits, actions, and/or the expression of their feelings and opinions.
4. Expression of denial on the part of some family members when confronted about their intolerance.
5. Ultimatum for change issued by one or more family members against another, placing the other members of the family in an awkward position of having to choose sides.

___. _____
   _____
___. _____
   _____
___. _____
   _____

LONG-TERM GOALS

1. Eliminate tension and conflict in the family, along with attitudes of self-righteousness and superiority over others.
2. Become more open-minded and tolerant of one another.
3. Use less critical methods for expressing displeasure over other family members' habits, actions, and so on.

4. Develop improved skills in conflict resolution and mediation techniques.

5. Work toward harmony and affirmation among all family members in a way that is realistic and achievable.

—. _____

_____

—. _____

_____

—. _____

_____

SHORT-TERM OBJECTIVES

1. Define the nature and intensity of family conflict. (1, 2, 3)

2. Each family member defines the nature of his/her positive and negative qualities. (4, 5, 6)

3. Each family member defines the likes and dislikes that he/she has for one another and for the functioning of the family as a unit. (7, 8, 9)

4. Compare family-of-origin intolerance to current attitudes. (10)

5. Cite examples of intolerance within the family and the feelings associated with being the object of that rejection. (11, 12)

6. Implement empathy development techniques to increase open-mindedness and sensitivity to others' feelings. (13, 14)

THERAPEUTIC INTERVENTIONS

1. Conduct an assessment of the level of conflict and relationship satisfaction via interview and/or use of an inventory (e.g., Conflict Tactics Scale [Strauss and Gelles] or Family Awareness Scale [Kolevzon and Green; cited in Green, Kolevzon, and Vosler]).

2. Give feedback on the assessment results and categorize the conflict areas (e.g., reasoning, verbal aggression and violence/family structure, autonomy, and family expression).

3. Have family members replace conflict terms that they don't understand with their own terms that they can relate to (e.g., change the term "defensive" to the phrase "copping an attitude").

7. Cite examples of irritability among family members, what triggers the irritability, and its impact on others. (15, 16)

8. List alternate behaviors to irritability that promote family harmony. (17, 18, 19)

9. Implement adaptive conflict resolution techniques. (20, 21, 22)

10. Each family member acknowledges the use of denial of intolerance and agree to take responsibility for his/her own behavior. (23, 24, 25, 26)

11. Terminate the use of ultimatums as a means of expressing frustration with other family members. (27, 28, 29, 30)

12. List ways that power and control can be distributed within the family. (31, 32)

13. Verbalize an understanding that some frustration with one another is expected but that this should not result in anger, rejection, or ultimatums as a means of control. (33, 34, 35)

__. _____
   _____

__. _____
   _____

__. _____
   _____

4. Assess the current strengths and needs in the family relationships via interview and/or the use of an inventory (e.g., Index of Family Relationships in *The Walmyr Assessment Scales Scoring Manual* [Hudson] or Kansas Family Life Satisfaction Scale [Schumm, Jurich, and Bollman]).

5. Help each family member get in touch with his/her strong points as a family member and compare and contrast them with the weaknesses.

6. Probe how each family member's weaknesses developed or what they may be based on.

7. Assess the development of family dynamics via interview and/or use of an inventory (e.g., Family-of-Origin Scale [Hovestadt, Anderson, Percy, Cochran, and Fine] or Family of Origin Questionnaire [Stuart]).

8. Have family members make an overall assessment of what they do/do not like about how the family functions, qualities that are desirable/undesirable, historical high points/low points, and what they would change if they could.

9. Request that each family member be honest about his/her feelings toward the others, admitting to possible jealousy and envy.

10. Trace intolerance, criticism, and judgmental attitudes within the parents' families of origin and compare these to what is witnessed within the current family dynamics.

11. Ask each family member to cite examples of when their ideas were rejected, criticized, or ignored by other members with closed minds; explore the feelings related to this rejection.

12. Poll each family member in order to determine what it would take for each of them to keep an open mind toward the others and how it would feel to live in an atmosphere of acceptance.

13. Use role-playing to teach family members to keep open minds. Ask one member to talk to other members to get them to see a different side of a rather neutral issue. Use role reversal to highlight the feelings of hurt and frustration associated with being rejected.

14. Recommend a homework assignment for them to apply the role-playing technique of trying to get other family members to respect their points of view with a real situation at home and then discuss the results in a follow-up session.

15. Explore irritability in the family and discuss how

each family member expresses his/her irritability and what triggers it.

16. Explore the impact of the expression of irritability on each family member and assess whether or not irritability may be used to manipulate or control others.

17. If it is determined that irritability is used to control or manipulate other family members, teach how this is destructive and suggest some alternative behaviors (assertiveness training, rehearsal of positive statements, etc.).

18. Brainstorm some alternative methods for expressing anger and frustration ("I" messages, letter writing, time-out before sharing feelings, etc.). Encourage family members to be as creative and as accepting as possible.

19. Suggest the use of techniques (e.g., meditation, deep breathing, journaling, or thought restructuring) to reduce tension and the frequency of irritable responses.

20. Ask the family to work through an issue of actual conflict while in session; observe the process and point out ineffective strategies used (talking when others are talking, misinterpreting statements, cutting each other off, etc.).

21. Propose alternative strategies to those maladaptive ones used in the family's conflict resolution interaction (use of reflective listening, clarification, gaining closure, etc.). Suggest readings such as *The Eight Essential Steps to Conflict Resolution* (Weeks) or *Getting What You Want: How to Reach Agreement and Resolve Conflict Every Time* (Anderson).

22. Use modeling and role-playing to teach successful and effective conflict resolution strategies (e.g., stage an argument and coach each family member on how to respond; role-play examples of the effective and noneffective ways to interact).

23. Be quite direct with family members who engage in denial of their intolerance. Attempt to facilitate confrontation by other family members.

24. Attempt to point out to the family how denial can be a primitive form of defense and suggest that it might be used because of an underlying helplessness or feeling of vulnerability.

25. If it comes to the surface that vulnerability does underlie denial in family members, then allow the expression of their vulnerability.

26. Assess for the presence of blaming behaviors that are based in denial of taking personal responsibility (see Blame in this *Planner*).

27. Educate the family about the notion that once family members have reached a point of issuing ultimatums as a means of controlling others, problem solving has become stalled.

28. Probe the level of frustration in the family member issuing the ultimatum.

29. Develop a behavioral contract that stipulates that family members will not issue ultimatums to one another; define in concrete terms what ultimatum behaviors are to be avoided.

30. Suggest a family meeting when family members are feeling so desperate as to want to issue an ultimatum to get things to change to their satisfaction.

31. Address whether the issuing of an ultimatum may be a means of exerting power or calling attention to oneself. Open a discussion on who has power and control in the family and how it is governed.

32. Brainstorm ways in which power and control can be restructured within the family. Use strategies such as give-and-take exercises, in which family members al-

ternate times when they take the lead in planning an activity or directing a major task in the household that needs to be accomplished. Discuss how it feels to be in command and also to be on the receiving end. Also discuss how each family members' respective skills may dictate to him/her in taking the lead role. Another strategy is to use the UnGame (Zakich).

33. Prepare the family for the fact that there will be times in the future when they become frustrated with each other and to accept this as common to all families rather than lashing out in intolerance.

34. Consider having family members learn the need to love and accept the other members' irritating behavior as a means of coping with it.

35. Discuss the use of coping strategies (e.g., engaging in self-talk and perceptual reconstruction of what it means to give in and accept each other's shortcomings) for building family members' respective tolerances. Recommend the book *Simple Courtesies* (Gallant).

—. _____
   _____
—. _____
   _____
—. _____
   _____

DIAGNOSTIC SUGGESTIONS

Axis I: 309.0   Adjustment Disorder With Depressed Mood
309.24   Adjustment Disorder With Anxiety
309.28   Adjustment Disorder With Mixed Anxiety and
         Depressed Mood
305.00   Alcohol Abuse
303.90   Alcohol Dependence
300.4   Dysthymic Disorder
296.x   Major Depressive Disorder
V61.1   Partner Relational Problem
V61.20   Parent–Child Relational Problem

_____   _____
_____   _____

Axis II: 301.7   Antisocial Personality Disorder
301.83   Borderline Personality Disorder
301.4   Obsessive-Compulsive Personality Disorder
301.81   Narcissistic Personality Disorder

_____   _____
_____   _____

JEALOUSY/INSECURITY

BEHAVIORAL DEFINITIONS

1. Existence of tension and conflict due to jealousy and insecurity within the family context.
2. Arguments among family members over the amount of time spent with each other.
3. Accusations by family members regarding parental favoritism and the lack of a display of interest and concern for certain family members.
4. Certain family members overcontrol other family members, which causes resentment.
5. Dependent behaviors that are based in the need for attention.
6. Acting out on the part of the children, which may involve delinquent or incorrigible behaviors.
7. Insatiable jealousy that results in physical destruction when expressing rage.

—. _____

_____

—. _____

_____

—. _____

_____

LONG-TERM GOALS

1. Eliminate tension and conflict over issues involving jealousy and/or insecurity.
2. Reduce frustration regarding lack of time spent with one another.

3. Eliminate blaming of each other regarding favoritism.
4. Acquire an alternate means of dealing with the need to be in control.
5. Reduce dependent behaviors and acquire more independent behaviors.
6. Children eliminate delinquent and acting-out behaviors.

__. _____

   _____

__. _____

   _____

__. _____

   _____

SHORT-TERM OBJECTIVES

THERAPEUTIC INTERVENTIONS

1. Identify the jealousy and insecurity in the family and their origins. (1, 2, 3)

2. Identify and replace irrational, dysfunctional thoughts that trigger jealousy. (4, 5, 6)

3. Identify any evidence of jealousy and insecurity being modeled by adults and imitated by children. (7)

4. List and specifically describe the jealous behaviors that need to change. (8, 9)

5. Detail how jealous/insecure behaviors have affected each family member emotionally. (10)

6. Identify alternative reactions that can replace episodes of jealousy or insecurity. (9, 11, 12)

1. Have family members discuss their feelings that relate to jealousy and insecurity by having them cite specific examples of times when jealousy arose.

2. Compare and contrast the perception of the jealous family member with those of the nonjealous family members when the same event is interpreted very differently.

3. Have family members cite specific conflicts by verbal description or by having them role-play the scene in session.

4. Explore for irrational thoughts that may typically accompany jealousy and educate the family about how jealousy is related to inse-

7. Acknowledge the presence of favoritism within family relationships. (13, 14)

8. Verbalize an understanding of the destructive, negative effects of favoritism on the family unit. (15, 16)

9. Identify the use of subtle or overt overcontrolling behaviors among family members. (17, 18, 19)

10. Terminate aggressive or immature acting out that may result from jealous feelings and identify replacement behaviors that are more constructive. (20, 21)

11. Accept referral to adjunctive treatment outside of family therapy for anger management. (22, 23)

12. Identify dependent behaviors and how they are enabled within the family system. (24, 25, 26)

13. Dependent family member implements assertiveness and other independent behaviors. (27, 28)

14. Identify delinquent or incorrigible behaviors on the part of the children. (29)

15. Parents institute behavior contracting to reduce delinquent and/or aggressive behaviors in the family. (30, 31)

16. Acting-out children give their perspective on the family dynamics and their feelings in reaction to them. (32)

curity and possessiveness. Suggest to family members that they educate themselves by reading material on the topic (e.g., *The Psychology of Jealousy and Envy* [Salovey] and *Jealousy* [Friday]).

5. Brainstorm more rational self-talk, which can replace irrational thoughts that trigger jealousy.

6. Educate the family about the Rational Emotive Behavior Therapy model of restructuring thoughts and how the A-B-C-D theory (Ellis and Becker) may be applied to jealousy and insecurity in the family.

7. Assess whether jealousy and/or insecurity in children may be the result of modeling by older family members.

8. Have all family members compose individual lists of jealous and insecure behaviors expressed in the family.

9. Facilitate the development of a list of alternative, healthy behaviors the family would like to see in place of jealousy.

10. Facilitate the open expression of how each family member has been affected by the dynamics of jealousy and insecurity in the family.

11. Trace in specific detail how jealous and insecure thoughts lead to emotional

17. Parents implement more intense treatment measures for children who are acting out. (33, 34)

18. Jealous or insecure family member cooperates with an evaluation for the presence of an emotional, personality, or cognitive disorder. (35, 36, 37, 38)

19. Give support and encouragement to family member receiving treatment for emotional disorder. (39)

—. _____
   _____

—. _____
   _____

—. _____
   _____

deterioration and destructive behavior.

12. Recommend ways in which family members can intervene when jealous rage arises and rely on alternative reactions (time-out procedures, deep breathing for behavior control, etc.).

13. Search the family dynamics for coalitions or favoritism displayed by one family member toward another/others.

14. Confront the presence of favoritism that exists and determine reasons for its development.

15. Help family members understand how favoritism is an unhealthy dynamic and point out its devastating effects.

16. Use role reversal techniques to teach how it feels to be on the receiving end of exclusion and favoritism; note feelings of rejection, resentment, and guilt.

17. Define overcontrolling behaviors for the family (i.e., when one family member wants to dictate other family members' personal choices) and assist in identifying their existence in the family.

18. Help the family see why overcontrolling behaviors developed and how they provide only a false sense of security.

19. Address any fears that family members may have about relinquishing over-controlling behaviors.

20. Solicit agreement that the family will not tolerate any aggressive, assaultive behaviors. Use behavioral contracting with clear ramifications for what will occur if the agreement is broken.

21. Brainstorm alternative ways to express feelings of jealousy or insecurity without being aggressive.

22. Consider adjunctive treatment for individual family members who cannot control their anger or aggressive behaviors (group therapy, medication, etc.).

23. Help family members be supportive and encouraging to the family member who requires outside treatment.

24. Trace the origin of dependent, insecure behaviors and how they have emerged within the family.

25. Explore how family members may be enabling the dependent behaviors and identify specific enabling patterns.

26. Teach how the dependent behaviors interfere with the family's functioning (e.g., one family member constantly needing to rely on other family members, restricting their mobility and

independence, and thwarting their personal growth).

27. Encourage the dependent family member to practice independent-type behaviors (assertiveness, "I" messages, self-affirmation, etc.).

28. Reinforce family support for the acquisition of the new independent behaviors by the dependent member.

29. Explore for incidents of delinquent or incorrigible behavior with the family and discuss how they may be a means for children to act out the fairness imbalance in the family.

30. Redirect parents toward pulling together to confront the child's incorrigible behavior and to reinforce more appropriate, desirable behaviors.

31. Help parents devise a behavior contract against delinquent or incorrigible behavior.

32. Facilitate the delinquent child in giving free expression to his/her perception of and reactions to difficulties in the family.

33. Develop an alternative plan of individual treatment for the child if delinquent behaviors continue.

34. Explore alternative living arrangements (e.g., group home, residential treatment, foster home) for the

child if acting out continues or escalates.

35. Educate the family about the difference between jealous/insecure behaviors and symptoms of mental illness (paranoia, major depression, bipolar disorder, etc.).

36. Use assessment techniques (e.g., the Minnesota Multiphasic Personality Inventory-2 [Hathaway and McKinley]) to determine if emotional, personality, or cognitive disorder is present.

37. Refer the jealous, insecure family member for a consultation with either a clinical psychologist or psychiatrist.

38. Devise a follow-up plan for working with the family while the ill family member is either hospitalized or in outpatient follow-up.

39. If the use of medication and/or hospitalization is necessary, help the family find ways that they can provide encouragement and support to the mentally ill family member.

__. _____
_____

__. _____
_____

__. _____
_____

DIAGNOSTIC SUGGESTIONS

Axis I:	309.0	Adjustment Disorder With Depressed Mood
	309.24	Adjustment Disorder With Anxiety
	309.28	Adjustment Disorder With Mixed Anxiety and Depressed Mood
	309.4	Adjustment Disorder With Mixed Disturbance of Emotions and Conduct
	309.3	Adjustment Disorder With Disturbance of Conduct
	296.5x	Bipolar I Disorder
	300.4	Dysthymic Disorder
	296.x	Major Depressive Disorder
	V61.1	Partner Relational Problem
	V61.1	Physical Abuse of Adult
	995.81	Physical Abuse of Adult (Victim)
	____	_____
	____	_____
Axis II:	301.7	Antisocial Personality Disorder
	301.83	Borderline Personality Disorder
	301.81	Narcissistic Personality Disorder
	301.0	Paranoid Personality Disorder
	____	_____
	____	_____

LIFE-THREATENING/CHRONIC ILLNESS

BEHAVIORAL DEFINITIONS

1. Family member diagnosed with a life-threatening or chronic illness (e.g., AIDS, severe coronary disease, brain tumor, schizophrenia).
2. Slow but progressive deterioration throughout course of illness.
3. Tremendous time and attention devoted to the ill family member, detracting from time for other family members.
4. Healthy family members' guilt over their own state of good health.
5. Development of tension and strain over the uncertainty surrounding the course of the illness and impending death.
6. Healthy family members in serious denial over the severity of the other family member's illness.
7. Worry, fatigue, anger, and resentment in healthy family members because of ill family member's condition.
8. Increased financial stress due to the expenses and/or the loss of income related to the illness.
9. Social isolation as a result of the illness.
10. Conflict over decisions about what is medically best for ill family member versus what is best for the family (e.g., home hemodialysis can mobilize ill family member, but place greater demands on family).

__. _____
     _____

__. _____
     _____

__. _____
     _____

LONG-TERM GOALS

1. Become educated regarding what is to be expected during the course of the illness.
2. Learn to avoid boundary problems, enmeshment, and overinvolvement with the illness.
3. Healthy family members overcome their guilt and tendency to self-blame due to their own state of good health.
4. Prepare for unexpected downturns in the illness and potential relapse or sudden death.
5. Learn to face the reality of the medical situation.
6. Learn stress management techniques.
7. Find an outside support system that can help to offset the financial burden caused by the illness.
8. Make family decisions that are balanced and in the best interests of both the ill family member and the family as a whole.

___. _____

_____

___. _____

_____

___. _____

_____

SHORT-TERM OBJECTIVES

1. Verbalize the symptoms, treatment, and course of the illness. (1, 2, 3)

2. Share how the illness has impacted family members and how they relate to the ill family member. (4, 5, 9)

3. Identify which phase of the life cycle the family is in and the impact the illness has had on this stage. (6)

4. Identify how a parent's incapacitation has affected

THERAPEUTIC INTERVENTIONS

1. Refer family members to written material, support groups, lectures, and the treating physician/specialist to learn about the symptoms, treatment, and course of the other family member's illness.

2. Suggest that family members share new medical information with each other during family meetings.

3. Encourage family members to become involved with

the mode of caretaking and leadership. (7, 8)

5. Ill family member verbalizes any feelings of isolation resulting from the illness and the causes for these feelings. (5, 9)

6. Identify ways to overcome the ill family member's isolation. (10)

7. List the chores associated with the illness and agree about their assignment and the need for outside assistance. (11)

8. Identify ways to avoid polarization or enmeshment as responses to the family crisis. (12, 13)

9. Identify the strengths of the family. (14)

10. Reduce expressions of guilt and blame toward each other for the illness and its impact on the family. (15)

11. Utilize problem-solving strategies to cope with the medical crisis. (16, 21)

12. List sources of social/emotional support outside the family. (17)

13. Each family member assesses his/her individual contribution to the stress within the family as a result of the illness and how each will change to increase family harmony. (18)

14. Identify how family conflicts could contribute to the worsening of the ill family member's condition. (19)

other families through networking with those who have endured a similar illness (i.e., a support group).

4. Facilitate family members' sharing of thoughts and feelings associated with the illness; include the ill family member for his/her feedback as well.

5. Allow for the ventilation of emotions (e.g., anger, guilt, blame, fear, or frustration) related to the illness of the family member and explore how these feelings affect the relationship with the ill family member.

6. Educate the family on how they will progress through various stages (shock, denial, grief, etc.). Help them to identify the stage they are presently in and allow for the expression of the impact of the illness on this stage of family development. Also recommend the book *Beliefs: The Heart of Healing in Families and Illness* (Wright, Watson, and Bell).

7. Explore how the illness of a parent has affected caretaking and leadership in the family.

8. Help the family to reassign a leader in the family, soliciting input from the ill family member. Utilize a democratic family vote in order to take pressure off of the ill family member.

15. Utilize stress reduction and conflict resolution techniques to reduce tension within the family. (20)

16. Agree to decisions that are in the best interest of all family members involved as they relate to the ill family member. (21)

17. Acknowledge becoming overly protective of one another as a result of the impact of the chronic/life-threatening illness. (22, 23)

—. _____
   _____
—. _____
   _____
—. _____
   _____

9. Explore the ill family member's sense of isolation from the rest of the family and identify the factors that are contributing to these feelings.

10. Brainstorm ways to reduce the ill family member's sense of being excluded from the rest of the family (e.g., think of things that the ill family member can do for healthy family members).

11. Discuss the assignment of chores related to the illness and weigh the benefits of hiring or enlisting outside help to lessen the amount of time absorbed by the illness.

12. Educate the family on the importance of boundaries and how families can become either polarized or enmeshed when faced with a crisis. Focus on techniques for disengagement (see *Families and Family Therapy* [Minuchin]) or depolarization.

13. Help family members to recognize their beliefs and find resources that may help them to prevent the illness from dominating their lives. Recommend reading *Beliefs: The Heart of Healing in Families and Illness* (Wright, Watson, and Bell).

14. Assist the family in identifying and building on their strengths (e.g., playing table games together; developing a family hobby such

as coin collecting) rather than bemoaning and being overwhelmed by their deficits (e.g., complaining of not having enough money; criticizing each other for not doing a fair share of work).

15. Encourage family members to take their focus off of guilt and blame and to acknowledge their own individual and joint responsibilities to deal with the crisis.

16. Teach the family negotiation skills and problem-solving strategies (e.g., family forum meetings, "I" message communication, role reversal empathy enhancement) to be applied to the family's response to coping with the illness.

17. Assist the family in identifying outside sources of social support (e.g., hospice, church, extended family, and friends).

18. Ask each family member to assess how he/she has contributed to the family conflict surrounding the illness and then what he/she will do differently to contribute to harmony.

19. Ask the family to identify how tensions due to negative reactions or conflicts have exacerbated or inhibited the improvement of the condition of the ill family member.

20. Suggest measures and/or techniques for stress reduction (e.g., relaxation training, respite care, exercise, or programmed family recreation) and conflict resolution (e.g., family forum meetings, "I" message communication, role reversal empathy enhancement) between family members.

21. Provide family members with a method for decision making (e.g., weighing the pros and cons) and role-play its implementation.

22. Help family members to become aware of the fact that overprotectiveness is not unusual when one family member is seriously ill and teach the need to exercise some independence between members to aid in promoting less intensity and conflict.

23. Provide family members with attentive behaviors (e.g., verbal expression of need for support) to use in place of overprotectiveness.

__. _____

_____

__. _____

_____

__. _____

_____

DIAGNOSTIC SUGGESTIONS

Axis I:	296.2x	Major Depressive Disorder, Single Episode
	300.4	Dysthymic Disorder
	309.0	Adjustment Disorder With Depressed Mood
	309.24	Adjustment Disorder With Anxiety
	309.28	Adjustment Disorder With Mixed Anxiety and Depressed Mood
	308.30	Acute Stress Disorder
	309.21	Separation Anxiety Disorder
	300.02	Generalized Anxiety Disorder
	300.00	Anxiety Disorder NOS
	313.89	Reactive Attachment Disorder of Early Childhood
	————	————————————————
	————	————————————————
Axis II:	301.6	Dependent Personality Disorder
	301.83	Borderline Personality Disorder
	301.5	Histrionic Personality Disorder
	————	————————————————
	————	————————————————

MULTIPLE-BIRTH DILEMMAS

BEHAVIORAL DEFINITIONS

1. Parents experience a pregnancy that yields multiple newborns (triplets, quadruplets, and higher-order multiples), causing them and other family members to become emotionally and physically overwhelmed.
2. The family is burdened with added work stress, increased food and supply expenses, as well as sleepless nights.
3. Parents are plagued by potential infant mortality, neurological defects, eye or lung disorders, and developmental abnormalities.
4. Parents experience clinical depression as a result of the added burden of multiple-birth children.
5. The need to obtain larger living quarters is paramount and an immediate burden on the family.

LONG-TERM GOALS

1. Secure financial, emotional, and child care support from extended family and friends to accommodate the immediate situation until they can develop a longer-term arrangement.
2. Utilize stress management techniques to deal with the burden and obligations of the abrupt increase in family members.

3. Participate in a support group to provide comfort and encouragement for dealing with infant mortality.
4. Resolve feelings of depression.
5. Relocate to a new home or remodel the family's existing dwelling in order to accommodate the multiple births.
6. Add paid or volunteer domestic help to alleviate the overwhelming child care needs.

—. _____

_____

—. _____

_____

—. _____

_____

SHORT-TERM OBJECTIVES

1. Verbalize feelings of anxiety and fatigue related to the addition of multiple-birth children. (1)
2. List options available for child care and emotional support. (2)
3. Parents express positive thoughts regarding present and future situation. (3)
4. Parents and family express grief about infant mortality associated with multiple birth. (4, 5)
5. Utilize methods of learned optimism to deal with stress of medical problems. (6)
6. Family members share responsibilities associated with medical care of infants. (7)

THERAPEUTIC INTERVENTIONS

1. Provide a system for venting the family members' initial shock and fear of not being able to handle the extra burden.
2. Brainstorm and list options available to the family regarding child care and emotional support.
3. Assist parents in identifying negative self-talk associated with the responsibility of multiple-birth children; replace with positive, realistic automatic thoughts.
4. Help family members deal with the death of infant(s) through bereavement counseling. Also, assign parents such readings as *Necessary Losses* (Viorst) and, for chil-

7. Preexisting children verbalize their concerns and fears associated with the dramatic change in family dynamics. (8)

8. Parents and preexisting children spend structured time together. (9)

9. Parents develop a financial plan to help with the burden of increased expenses. (10, 11)

10. Identify emotional needs and the extended family and friends who can provide support. (12, 13)

11. Parents and children implement behavioral and cognitive stress reduction techniques. (3, 9, 14)

12. Parents report a reduction in their level of depression. (15, 16, 17)

13. Parents decide to either relocate or have an addition built onto the home in order to accommodate the new infants. (18)

__. _____
_____
__. _____
_____
__. _____
_____

dren, *The Fall of Freddy the Leaf* (Buscalglia).

5. Suggest rituals for the family to follow to grieve the death of the infant(s) and to focus on the surviving infants as a blessing.

6. Teach the family methods of learned optimism (see *Learned Optimism* [Seligman]) for dealing with the stress of the medical problems.

7. Assist the family in scheduling all members to share in attending to the medical necessities of the infants (feeding, changing diapers, assisting in-home nurses, attending to appointments, giving medications, etc.).

8. Allow for preexisting children of the family to vent their feelings and concerns about the instant addition of new offspring and their fear of being ignored and neglected.

9. Solicit parents' reassurance of preexisting children that they will not be ignored; schedule some structured individual attention from a parent for each child.

10. Brainstorm with family members about how they can solicit extra financial support and/or reduce/contain overhead costs to improve the family's financial situation.

11. Reinforce the notion of the family's bond and how everyone needs to work together in a cohesive fashion to contend with the financial situation and the overload of responsibility.

12. Assist the family in identifying and defining what type of emotional support the family needs in order to survive the current situation.

13. Identify specific extended family members and friends on whom the family can rely for emotional support.

14. Teach techniques for stress management and stress inoculation (e.g., cognitive restructuring, progressive muscle relaxation, lighthearted recreational family activities, exercise).

15. Using cognitive behavior therapy, medication, or a combination of both, assist parents in reducing depression.

16. Refer the parent for depression treatment on an outpatient or even on an inpatient basis, depending on the severity of the depression.

17. Provide supportive family therapy to the nondepressed family members.

18. Teach the family to utilize a decision-making paradigm to review their living space options and select the best decision to suit their needs.

__.   _____
       _____
__.   _____
       _____
__.   _____
       _____

DIAGNOSTIC SUGGESTIONS

Axis I: 309.0   Adjustment Disorder With Depressed Mood
              309.28   Adjustment Disorder With Mixed Anxiety and
                         Depressed Mood
              300.4   Dysthymic Disorder
              V61.20   Parent–Child Relational Problem
              V61.0   Postpartum Depression
              _____   _____
              _____   _____

PHYSICAL/VERBAL/
PSYCHOLOGICAL ABUSE

BEHAVIORAL DEFINITIONS

1. Physical pain or injury that is inflicted on family members intentionally by one or more family members.
2. Family members being called insulting names (e.g., fat, stupid, ugly).
3. Intentional threat of physical pain or injury (i.e., verbal threat, damaging of personal items).
4. Critical comments being made about family members' mental states (e.g., "you're crazy," "you need a shrink").
5. Fear, apprehension, and intimidation felt by some or all family members.
6. Ignoring of or refusal to talk to other family members for days ("silent treatment").
7. Failure by family members to warn other family members of situations, incidents, or events in which they have knowledge of potential physical harm that may befall the others (e.g., knowing of a planned physical assault against a sibling by another sibling or an individual outside the immediate family).
8. Domination or excessive control over one or more family members.

__. _____
   _____
__. _____
   _____
__. _____
   _____

LONG-TERM GOALS

1. Family members discontinue all use of physical aggression and verbal and psychological abuse, and identify viable alternatives (other forms of verbal exchange, etc.).
2. Replace hostile, threatening, and critical comments with respectful communication that builds self-esteem and positive relationships with one another.
3. Nonabusive family members protect identified victims (using avoidance techniques, alternative shelter or respite, etc.).
4. Identify the underlying dynamics in the family that may be promoting tension and abusive behavior.
5. Discontinue alcohol or drug abuse that serves as precipitant of violence.

—. _____

_____

—. _____

_____

—. _____

_____

SHORT-TERM OBJECTIVES

1. Identify and acknowledge the existence of physical, verbal, or psychological abuse. (1, 2, 3, 8)

2. Implement a plan that guarantees the protection of abused family members. (4, 5, 6, 7, 8)

3. The physically abusive family member signs a nonviolence, nonintimidation contract as well as a contract agreeing to attend treatment. (3, 5, 6, 11)

THERAPEUTIC INTERVENTIONS

1. Initiate individual therapy, family therapy, or both in order to address the issues of the abuse. Operationally identify abusive comments and behaviors.

2. Explore the dynamics of the family that facilitate the abusive behavior. Also, address the victimization of nonabusive family members and the immediate plan for family safety (e.g., relocation of nonabusive family members).

4. Identify the destructive results of physical abuse on the family. (9)

5. Family members reach an agreement on what constitutes psychological and verbal abuse. (10)

6. Accept referrals to treatment and self-help groups. (11)

7. Identify the signs of escalating anger. (12, 13, 14, 15)

8. Family members agree not to use incidences discussed during the course of treatment as weapons outside of the sessions. (16)

9. Family members agree to use time-out procedures in the therapy session and at home if the circumstances become volatile. (17, 18)

10. Abusive family member states the emotional results of his/her abuse on the victim and the family. (9, 19, 20)

11. Identify the role that substance use plays in the physically or verbally abusive family patterns. (21)

12. Terminate the use of mood-altering substances. (22)

13. Family members evaluate their own patterns of thoughts and actions and identify how they contribute to any maladaptive patterns of verbal/physical abuse. (23)

3. Recommend individual therapy with a separate therapist for the abusive family member, focusing on anger issues and impulse control.

4. Assist the family in developing a plan that ensures the safety of abused members (call police, escape to safe environment, etc.) if abuse continues to be a threat.

5. Assist family members in constructing a written contract assuring that no abusive behavior will be tolerated and that it will be readily pointed out by the abuse victim.

6. Assist family members in defining what constitutes violation of the nonabuse contract and what steps will be taken to ensure safety (abuser vacates the situation; victims seek alternative shelter, call police, etc.).

7. Develop a list of resources in the community (shelters, friends, extended family members, etc.) for escape from abuse.

8. Fulfill legally mandated requirement for reporting the abuse of a minor by contacting the appropriate protective agency.

9. Educate all family members about the emotional destructiveness and illegality of even the slightest inci-

14. Parents identify the negative impact the abuse within their families of origin had on them. (24, 25)

15. Abusive family member accepts responsibility for abusive behavior and agrees to a nonblame contract for acts of abuse. (26, 27)

16. Abusive family member apologizes for abusive behavior, identifying the behavior and taking full responsibility for it. (28)

17. Victims hold abusive family member responsible for the abuse while accepting an apology for the abuse without excuse. (29)

18. List ways to build each other's self-esteem. (30)

19. Abusive family member constructs a plan that provides several alternatives to abusive behavior when anger is triggered. (31, 32, 33, 34, 35)

20. Abusive family member reports instances where feelings of anger were expressed in a controlled, assertive, respectful manner. (31, 34, 36)

21. Victims identify experiences in childhood that taught tolerance for and excuse of abusive behavior. (37)

22. Victims identify a pattern of self-blame for the abusive behavior by other family members. (38)

dences of physical abuse and why such abuse should not be tolerated.

10. Aid the family in defining what constitutes psychological and verbal abuse in specific behavioral/emotional terms; focus on the subtle, more tacitly implied verbal and psychological abuse and the vulnerability of the victims.

11. Refer victims to a victims support group and the abuser to an offenders treatment program.

12. Aid family in identifying early cues of potential violence.

13. Inform/educate the family members about the various levels of frustration and anger, and those cognitions, emotions, and behaviors that are associated with escalation toward abusive outbursts.

14. Teach the family to differentiate between volatile emotions and those that may appear to be volatile. Also, discuss family anger patterns in general.

15. Role-play exercises of heated situations and work on identifying the cues that indicate that the situation may spiral out of control (e.g., family members becoming quiet or seething, voices being raised).

23. Victims report instances when aggressive or abusive behavior occurred and they did not verbalize being at fault for it. (29, 38, 39)

24. Abusive family member identifies instances in childhood when he/she was a victim of abuse and the feelings of pain, helplessness, and rage this generated. (24, 25, 40, 41)

25. Abusive family member verbalizes feelings of inadequacy, failure, and fear that fuel the anger. (13, 40, 41, 42)

26. Abusive family member verbalizes an understanding of the need for a process of forgiveness of others and self to begin to reduce anger. (43, 44)

27. Family members identify negative communication patterns that facilitate abuse. (45)

28. Family members implement positive communication skills. (46)

29. Family members identify and implement alternative means of venting their anger and aggression. (47)

—. _____
  _____

—. _____
  _____

—. _____
  _____

16. Solicit agreement between family members to not use in-session material against each other when outside of the treatment session.

17. Teach the use of time-out procedures (*Anger Workout Book* [Weisenberger]) to reduce the intensity of anger.

18. Teach the importance of maintaining structure and boundaries, particularly during emotionally charged discussions and/or exchange. Help family members make the connection that verbal and psychological abuse often lead to physical abuse.

19. Use role reversal techniques, in which the abusive family member assumes the role of the victim, in order to learn the emotional impact of abuse.

20. Assist abusive family member in listing 10 negative effects of his/her abuse on the victim and the family unit (e.g., modeling disrespect and violence for children; lowering self-esteem of victim; loss of own self-respect; conflict with other family members over abusive practices).

21. Assess for the presence of substance abuse in each family member and examine how it may be contributing to the dysfunction in the family.

22. Refer substance-abusing family members to Alcoholics Anonymous and to chemical dependence treatment and solicit a pledge to terminate the use of mood-altering substances.

23. Explore thought patterns and behavior that may be encouraging each family member in an abusive exchange (jealousy, prejudice, etc.).

24. Examine family-of-origin abuse issues with parents to identify the effects of any verbal/physical abuse sustained by them during their upbringing; include an examination of any learned enabling behaviors on the part of the nonabusive spouse. Point out the repeating cycle of abuse.

25. Review with aggressive family member(s) the family-of-origin experiences that reinforced physical and verbal abuse as acceptable ways of expressing anger/frustration.

26. Support and encourage family members in confronting the abuser without excusing his/her behavior or allowing the abuser to externalize blame.

27. Family therapist models the process of accepting the responsibility for individual behavior without excuses or externalizing blame.

28. Confront abusive family member about not taking responsibility for the abuse and not expressing remorse and sensitivity.

29. Confront the victims' pattern of taking responsibility for abusive family member's behavioral decisions and reinforce the victims for holding abusive family member responsible for the abusive behavior.

30. Review the evidence that supports the association between physical and psychological aggression and poor self-esteem/depression on the part of the abuser. Have family members list specific ways for them to build self-esteem in each other.

31. Differentiate for family members between nonassertive, assertive, and aggressive communication.

32. Establish the function of the family member's abuse and identify nonabusive means to accomplish such goals.

33. Process the abusive family member's angry feelings or angry outbursts that have recently occurred and review available alternative behaviors.

34. Suggest that the abusive family member write a list of several alternative behaviors to abuse when anger is experienced (e.g.,

taking a time-out; contacting a support system; taking a walk; writing out feelings; reviewing a list of the negative consequences of violence).

35. Have the abusive family member read the following books: *Of Course You're Angry* (Rosellini and Worden), *The Angry Book* (Rubin), *Anger Workout Book* (Weisenberger), or *The Verbally Abusive Relationship* (Evans).

36. Reinforce assertiveness behaviors in session and family members' reports of successful assertiveness between sessions.

37. Review with victims previous experiences that modeled physical or verbal abuse as behavior that is to be expected, excused, and tolerated.

38. Help victims identify a pattern of blaming themselves for another family member's abusive behavior and teach that everyone is personally responsible for behavioral decisions.

39. Have victims cite instances in which abusive behavior occurred and they did not take responsibility for it; provide emotional support to victims for holding the abusive family member responsible for abusive behavior.

40. Have abusive family member list hurtful life experiences that have led to his/her abusive acting-out behavior.

41. Empathize with and clarify feelings of hurt and anger tied to past traumas.

42. Make the connection between the abuser's past feelings of rage when abused and current uncontrolled anger leading to the abuse of others.

43. Discuss the need for forgiveness of abuse from the past and the process of letting go of anger and resentment associated with that past abuse.

44. Request that the abusive family member read the book *Forgive and Forget* (Smedes) or *Forgiveness: A Bold Choice for a Peaceful Heart* (Casarjian).

45. Make the family aware of dysfunctional communication patterns that co-occur with and increase the likelihood of physical abuse (e.g., vocalized attributions of family members' blame of fault for problems; fast reciprocation of family members' anger; lack of empathy; contempt for or lack of respect for family members; defensiveness; withdrawal; coercive control/entitlement). Suggest that the family read *Verbal*

Abuse Survivors Speak Out
(Evans).

46. Use role-playing and behavioral rehearsal techniques to teach positive communication skills (e.g., problem identification, "I" statements, listening skills, problem-solving skills, behavioral contracting) and assign practice.

47. Teach the use of displacement techniques to ventilate anger (punching bag, jogging, bowling, kickboxing, etc.); caution the clients against seeing these activities as practice for aggression but rather as energy-draining activities to reduce tension.

___. _____

_____

___. _____

_____

___. _____

_____

DIAGNOSTIC SUGGESTIONS

Axis I:	309.0	Adjustment Disorder With Depressed Mood
	309.24	Adjustment Disorder With Anxiety
	309.28	Adjustment Disorder With Mixed Anxiety and Depressed Mood
	309.4	Adjustment Disorder With Mixed Disturbance of Emotions and Conduct
	309.3	Adjustment Disorder With Disturbance of Conduct
	305.00	Alcohol Abuse
	303.90	Alcohol Dependence

	300.4	Dysthymic Disorder
	296.x	Major Depressive Disorder
	V61.1	Partner Relational Problem
	V61.1	Physical Abuse of Adult
	V61.2	Parent–Child Relational Problem
	995.81	Physical Abuse of Adult (Victim)
	995.5	Physical Abuse of Child (Victim)
	V61.21	Physical Abuse of Child
	_____	_____
	_____	_____
Axis II:	301.7	Antisocial Personality Disorder
	301.83	Borderline Personality Disorder
	301.6	Dependent Personality Disorder
	_____	_____
	_____	_____

RELIGIOUS/SPIRITUAL CONFLICTS

BEHAVIORAL DEFINITIONS

1. Conflict between parents erupts over differently espoused creeds (e.g., father is Jewish, mother is Catholic).
2. Religious conflicts affect decisions about rearing children in a particular faith.
3. Adolescent child decides to reject parents' religious faith/beliefs and refuses to attend services.
4. Parents conflict over disciplining children due to their respective religious faiths or spiritual beliefs (e.g., the use of physical versus nonphysical chastisement).
5. Family becomes lax in their faith practices and feels the loss of spirituality in their lives.

—. _____

_____

—. _____

_____

—. _____

_____

LONG-TERM GOALS

1. Family members resolve interfaith conflicts.
2. Parents and family members reach an accord about how children will be raised according to a chosen faith.
3. Family members decide at what age children are permitted to choose how they wish to worship and whether they attend services.
4. Reach agreement regarding how children will be reared that is in harmony with religious beliefs and wishes.

5. Attend church or synagogue services and engage in other faith practices on a regular basis.

—. _____

_____

—. _____

_____

—. _____

_____

SHORT-TERM OBJECTIVES

1. Parents verbalize the role that religion played in their upbringing and the beliefs that they brought to the marriage from their family of origin. (1)

2. Parents state current spiritual beliefs. (2)

3. Parents review their thoughts and perceived agreements regarding an interdenominational marriage and their earlier discussions on raising children. (3, 4, 5)

4. Identify the impact the different religions have had on the marriage and later on the children. (6, 7)

5. Pinpoint the specific problem that exists about the differing religious beliefs and/or practices. (8)

6. Identify how the two religions strengthen the family and how they contribute to conflict. (9)

THERAPEUTIC INTERVENTIONS

1. Explore parents' histories of religious training, belief, and practice from families of origin to the present.

2. Ask each parent to articulate his/her current spiritual beliefs and faith practices that he/she finds meaningful.

3. Have parents discuss what their expectations were once they decided to enter into an interdenominational marriage; explore any agreements regarding religious practices that were understood or explicit.

4. Have parents explore, in the presence of children, how preexisting agreements regarding religious practices and/or children's training fell by the wayside and led to the present conflict.

5. Explore any previously unverbalized misgivings about religious training of the children.

7. Each family member acknowledges respect for each parent's religious beliefs and practices. (10)

8. Family members vent their frustration, resentment, and confusion about the religious conflict. (11)

9. Identify the problems that differing religions cause with child rearing. (12, 13)

10. Children express what they like and dislike about their parents' respective religious beliefs and practices. (14)

11. Parents agree on the religious education and practice for the children. (15)

12. Family members express the need for flexibility in accepting different beliefs. (16, 17)

13. Family members list ways they will support the religious changes made. (18)

14. Adolescent children attend special seminars through each denomination's congregation that deal with an adolescent's life in an interdenominational family. (19)

15. Children delay pressing for religious autonomy until reaching an age agreed to by parents. (20)

16. Family members increase religious practice behaviors that strengthen their faith and increase their spirituality. (21, 22)

6. Assist parents in identifying the effect their different spiritual beliefs and practices have had on their relationship and on the children.

7. Explore any conflicts between a spouse and his/her in-laws over the issue of religious belief and practice.

8. Assist parents in identifying the specific conflict that exists between them regarding religious belief and/or practice; explore each spouse's belief system in terms of its view of the other spouse's belief system. Suggest books such as *Holy Hatred* (Haught) or *Firestorm: Preventing and Overcoming Church Conflicts* (Susek and Kennedy).

9. Brainstorm with the family members to construct a list in which each family member cites pros and cons of the impact of two religions on the family.

10. Help family members construct a list of reasons to respect each parent's religious beliefs and practices; develop a contract to display respect for the freedom to exercise choice of belief.

11. Facilitate an open expression of feelings regarding the conflict over religious beliefs and practices; focus on children's confusion, frustration, and loyalty conflicts.

—. _____

_____

—. _____

_____

—. _____

_____

12. Highlight areas of conflict such as pressure for children to conform to one or the other religion, grandparents' disappointment about certain milestones not reached, (e.g., Confirmation for Catholics, Bar/Bat Mitzvahs for Jews).

13. Explore any lifestyle strictures that each parent's religious beliefs would impose on the children (e.g., not engaging in some forms of entertainment, dress code, foods eaten); resolve parental conflicts over these issues.

14. Ask the children to state their thoughts about desirable and undesirable characteristics of the parents' religious beliefs and practices.

15. Assist parents in expressing their desires regarding religious education for the children and what aspects of both religions they would like to see adopted; solicit agreement about education and practice.

16. Explore how family members could participate in practices of both religions and how a degree of flexibility may aid in conflict resolution.

17. Highlight core beliefs of each parent and how these may be respected and shared by all family members.

18. Discuss ways in which family members can support the agreements reached over religious training issues.

19. Have family members search through both parents' denominations to locate teen programs addressing the issue of interdenominational families.

20. Assist parents in reaching an agreement about when children can make independent decisions regarding participation in religious practices.

21. Brainstorm about the denomination-related activities that the family can become involved in to help them avoid drifting away from their religion.

22. Encourage the family to engage in some recommitment exercises (e.g., meet with their religious leader privately; read meditational literature together) that promote the adherence to and practice of their religious beliefs.

__. _____
   _____

__. _____
   _____

__. _____
   _____

DIAGNOSTIC SUGGESTIONS

Axis I: V61.1   Partner Relational Problem
               V61.2   Parent–Child Relational Problem
               _____   _____
               _____   _____

Axis II:
               _____   _____
               _____   _____

SEPARATION/DIVORCE

BEHAVIORAL DEFINITIONS

1. Marital difficulties lead to disagreements and arguments, causing ongoing erosion of the marital and family relationship.
2. Partners are alienated from each other, which places tension on the family unit.
3. Talk of separation sparks fears and concern among various family members, causing them to compensate in various ways (e.g., parentification or overindulgence).
4. Parents decide to separate, giving rise to questions about which family members remain in the home and which leave.
5. Children are in a loyalty conflict over being separated from one parent and perhaps from their siblings.
6. Parents decide to separate and/or divorce, but remain under the same roof, contributing to coldness and estrangement in the home.
7. Financial difficulties arise as the result of operating two separate households and this restricts family members' amenities.
8. Symptoms of anxiety, depression, or acting-out behaviors (substance use, poor school performance, etc.) develop in family members.
9. New family members, in the form of stepparents, stepchildren, and stepsiblings, must be accommodated.
10. Child management problems develop as a result of single parenting and lack of support from ex-spouse.
11. Children assume some responsibility and guilt for the marital failure.

—. _____
    _____
    _____
—. _____
    _____
    _____
—. _____
    _____

LONG-TERM GOALS

1. Work through fears and learn to cope with the separation/divorce harmoniously.
2. Parents continue to nurture the children and reassure them that they are loved and are not responsible for the marital discord.
3. Develop living arrangements that are flexible and meet everyone's needs.
4. Develop rules and guidelines for living under the same roof despite a legal separation and/or divorce.
5. Reach a fair and reasonable financial settlement that places the needs of the children as a high priority.
6. Cope with new additions to the family as the result of remarriage or cohabitation and cooperate in supporting each other.
7. Parents agree to cooperate in issues of parenting and reduce the amount of conflict between them.
8. Children accept the breakup of their parents' relationship as being independent of anything they have said or done.

—. _____
    _____
—. _____
    _____
—. _____
    _____

SHORT-TERM OBJECTIVES	THERAPEUTIC INTERVENTIONS
1. Parents verbalize their assessment of the marriage relationship. (1, 2)	1. Explore the nature and intensity of the marriage conflict.

2. Parents state whether they are amenable to couples therapy. (2, 3, 4)

3. Children state their perception of the nature and intensity of the parents' conflict. (5, 6)

4. Parents reduce the frequency of arguments and simultaneously engage in activities that promote cohesiveness within the family unit. (7, 8, 9)

5. Each family member openly shares his/her fears regarding the separation and/or divorce. (10, 11, 12)

6. Each family member describes his/her role in the family and how it has been impacted by the separation/divorce. (13, 14, 15, 16, 17)

7. Family members assume new roles as a reasonable adaptation to the situation. (15, 17)

8. Parents verbalize a desire to be sensitive to the children's feelings and needs in reaction to the separation/divorce. (18, 19)

9. Parents list the benefits of keeping the children in the original home as opposed to relocating them. (20, 21)

10. Children express any experience of being placed in a double bind and struggling with their loyalty toward parents. (22, 23, 24)

2. Assess whether there is motivation on the part of both spouses to attempt to resolve their conflicts.

3. Refer the parents to a couples therapist or some other type of relationship treatment (e.g., marriage encounter). Suggest that the therapist consider reading *Cognitive Therapy with Couples* (Dattilio and Padesky).

4. Recommend selected readings on conflict resolution in marriage for the couple to review (e.g., Fighting for Your Marriage [Markman, Stanley, and Blumberg] or Why Marriages Succeed and Fail [Gottman]).

5. Poll the other family members and assess their perceptions of the marital difficulties. Try to determine whether or not they have an accurate picture of what is happening with the marriage. With children ages 10 and over, use direct dialogue or the Thinking, Feeling, and Doing Game (Gardner). With younger children, use drawings and play activity.

6. Facilitate the children in expressing their feelings about the marriage conflict; suggest that they write a story about the family or draw pictures to depict the dynamics.

11. Parents and children agree to maintain appropriate roles and boundaries. (25, 26)

12. Define the financial difficulties that have arisen due to the divorce and its negative impact. (27, 28, 29, 30)

13. Define the acting out occurring with the child/adolescent and how it is impacting the family. (31, 32, 33)

14. Children express their feelings and beliefs regarding interacting with a parent's dating partner and his/her children. (34, 35)

15. Identify the conflicts that result from attempting to blend children from two families. (36, 37)

16. Biological parents meet and agree to an approach to parenting together. (38, 39)

17. Blended family parents report a plan for reducing their disagreements regarding stepparenting issues. (40, 41, 42)

18. Children express resolution of any guilt over their parents' separation/divorce. (43, 44, 45)

19. Parents terminate blaming the spouse for the dissolution of the marriage. (46)

20. Children report successful social encounters in which they had to respond to questions about their parents' relationship. (47, 48)

7. Suggest that the parents contain the ugliness of their marital problems (arguments, disagreements, etc.) and disengage from their battle to stay engaged with their children.

8. Assist the family in planning activities that draw on family interaction with less reliance on the need for a strong marriage (e.g., preparing meals together or family chores).

9. Encourage the use of structured family meetings to focus on the children's needs with less focus on the parents' issues.

10. Open up discussion about family members' fears and concerns regarding the marital breakup, walking them through the most dreaded outcome as if it were indeed to occur. Suggest reading books such as *Mom's House, Dad's House* (Ricci) and *Dinosaurs Divorce* (Brown and Brown).

11. Suggest specific coping mechanisms for dealing with the defined fears and concerns (living with one parent and visiting the other on weekends, having less money to live on, etc.) such as open communication between the parents regarding the children, everyone pledging to sacrifice together financially, or

21. Children attend a support group for children of parents who are separating/divorcing. (48)

—. _____
   _____

—. _____
   _____

—. _____
   _____

holding periodic family meetings to exchange views.

12. Help the family members to identify support systems in the community as part of a coping mechanism (extended family, church groups, school services, etc.).

13. Facilitate family members in describing their roles in the family in light of the marital difficulties. Use analogies or family sculpting techniques to accentuate these roles and discuss how they impact each family member.

14. Assess for family members who attempt to cope by using overcompensatory strategies (e.g., a child taking the role of the caretaker; a parent overindulging a child with material items).

15. Suggest some exercises for role change or substitution by assigning different roles and having family members elaborate on how the roles feel.

16. Explore issues of balance of power, alliances, and caretakers that have emerged in the wake of the separation/divorce.

17. Introduce techniques (e.g., cognitive restructuring, challenging the evidence) that reinforce alteration in roles, expectations, and restructuring of perception (see *Case Studies in Cou-*

ples and Family Therapy: Systemic and Cognitive Perspectives [Dattilio]).

18. Suggest that parents read *How It Feels When Parents Divorce* (Krementz), or *Why Are We Getting Divorced?* (Mayle and Robbins).

19. Discuss what parents have learned about children's reactions to the separation/divorce and how this affects their perception of and sensitivity to their own family situation.

20. Brainstorm ways to avoid moving the children (e.g., having both parents rent an apartment outside of the home that each can use when he/she is spending time with the children; parents rotate in and out of the house while children remain; one parent rent a home very near the children to allow easy access and frequent visits).

21. Reinforce the need for parents to work together in order to avoid placing the children in the position of having to choose which parent they want to live with. Suggest that parents read *The Good Divorce* (Ahrons).

22. Facilitate a mode of expression for children to convey how they feel about issues of loyalty and having to choose. Consider using structured games (e.g., the UnGame [Zakich]).

23. Have family members list one-word adjectives that best describe how they feel.

24. Suggest that families engage in creative exercises for children and adolescents to better understand the feelings about their parents' separation/divorce (e.g., for adolescents, use *Teens Are Nondivorceable* [Bonkowski], and for children, use *Children Are Nondivorceable* [Bonkowski]).

25. Emphasize the need to maintain boundaries within the family and between family members. Address specific examples with children who attempt to become caretakers and parents who share intimate details with children, leaning on them for emotional support.

26. Recommend that parents read *Boundaries: Where You End and I Begin* (Katherine).

27. Facilitate an atmosphere in which family members can express emotions freely over the financial restrictions imposed by the separation/divorce.

28. Focus specifically on feelings and beliefs about how the loss of certain amenities will impact each family member. Allow for the release of anger and resentment.

29. Highlight specific coping skills needed due to the change in financial situation (e.g., living with less, spending more wisely, borrowing items, or bartering; see Financial Changes in this *Planner*).

30. Brainstorm how other sources of family income might be generated (e.g., part-time jobs, garage sales, or breeding pets).

31. Facilitate discussion for family members to outline the problematic behavior of children who are acting out in reaction to this family crisis.

32. Allow each family member to express how he/she is being affected by the children's acting-out behavior.

33. If the children's specific behavioral problems appear to be more than what can be addressed in family therapy, then refer them for individual or group therapy.

34. Allow for the children's ventilation of anger and resentment over having to meet and share with a parent's new mate and their children.

35. Establish a neutral zone in the family sessions for children to express themselves without fear of retaliation.

36. Have family members specifically define the conflict that occurs as a result

of the blending of two family systems. Use such techniques as Metaphors from *Problem-Solving Therapy* (Haley) or Family Sculpting from *The New People Making* (Satir) to facilitate the expression of emotion.

37. Assist the family in planning group activities involving children from both partners in an attempt to strengthen this bond (*101 Interventions in Family Therapy* and *101 More Interventions in Family Therapy* [Nelson and Trepper]); process the outcome of these activities.

38. Invite the biological parent/ ex-spouse into a conjoint session with the other biological parent in order to discuss differences in parenting philosophies, strategies, and misperceptions. Suggest the use of a unified parenting program (e.g., Parent Effectiveness Training [Gordon], Parents and Adolescents from "Behavioral Family Therapy" [Forgatch and Patterson], or *1-2-3 Magic* [Phelan]).

39. Hold a separate conjoint meeting with the biological parents to address any resentments or feelings that may be feeding the children's acting-out behaviors.

40. Conduct a separate conjoint meeting with parents of the blended family and address

personal insecurities, feelings of loss of power, and needs to demonstrate favoritism. Suggest alternative methods for dealing with these issues and explore how the spouse can be supportive during the change (see "Blended Family Problems" in *The Couples Psychotherapy Treatment Planner* [O'Leary, Heyman, and Jongsma]).

41. Use role exchange and role alternatives for reducing parenting conflicts. Have family members consider the advantages and disadvantages of behavior changes and deal with the emotional fear that accompanies change.

42. Address the potential manipulation of the children against a single parent or in playing one parent against the other for power and territorial advantages.

43. Explain to family members how common it is for children to blame themselves for the parents' separation/ divorce, but point out that the decisions are clearly in the hands of the parents and the conflicts are theirs alone.

44. Have parents actively accept responsibility for the demise of their marriage and reinforce the termina-

tion of the children blaming themselves.

45. Help the children engage in exercises that may reduce guilt and blame (e.g., monitoring statements of self-blame and telling themselves that it's okay to not assume the responsibility for the divorce).

46. Encourage the parents to stop blaming each other and accept responsibility for their own behavior.

47. Role-play various social contexts with the children and help them process situations that they may encounter socially that relate to questions about the parents' separation/divorce.

48. Refer the children to support groups for children of divorce in school or through the local church or community.

—. _____
_____
—. _____
_____
—. _____
_____

DIAGNOSTIC SUGGESTIONS

Axis I:	309.0	Adjustment Disorder With Depressed Mood
	309.24	Adjustment Disorder With Anxiety
	309.28	Adjustment Disorder With Mixed Anxiety and Depressed Mood

	309.4	Adjustment Disorder With Mixed Disturbance of Emotions and Conduct
	309.3	Adjustment Disorder With Disturbance of Conduct
	309.21	Separation Anxiety Disorder
	300.4	Dysthymic Disorder
	300.02	Generalized Anxiety Disorder
	313.81	Oppositional Defiant Disorder
	787.6	Encopresis
	307.6	Enuresis
	313.23	Selective Mutism
	_____	_____
	_____	_____
Axis II:	301.6	Dependent Personality Disorder
	301.0	Paranoid Personality Disorder
	301.20	Schizoid Personality Disorder
	301.82	Avoidant Personality Disorder
	_____	_____
	_____	_____

SEXUAL ORIENTATION CONFLICTS

BEHAVIORAL DEFINITIONS

1. A family member divulges that he/she is homosexual.
2. The announcement of the family member's homosexuality results in mixed emotions, rejection, and conflict with other family members.
3. The homosexual family member is ostracized, alienated, or mistreated by the other family members.
4. Parents blame themselves for the "abnormality" or "deviancy" of the child's sexual orientation.
5. Parents externalize blame onto each other about their child's sexual preferences, causing heated arguments.
6. Family members reveal homophobic fears that they will be negatively affected by the other family member's sexual orientation.
7. Family members fear social reprisal or rejection and avoid discussing the homosexuality issue outside the family.
8. Family members have different views regarding homosexuality, causing major family schisms.
9. Family members reject the homosexual family member's friends or sexual partner.

__. _____
   _____
__. _____
   _____
__. _____
   _____

LONG-TERM GOALS

1. Family members acknowledge and accept the family member's homosexual orientation.
2. Family members consider alternative responses to rejection of the family member and work through conflict issues that they have with the homosexual orientation.
3. Parents discontinue blaming themselves and each other for their child's sexual orientation and work together on a plan of acceptance.
4. Family members overcome their own homophobic fears, as well as fears of societal rejection.
5. Family members respectfully accept differing views of homosexuality without alienating one another.

—. _____

_____

—. _____

_____

—. _____

_____

SHORT-TERM OBJECTIVES

1. Discuss the homosexuality revelation history and its impact. (1, 2)
2. Verbalize beliefs regarding the origins of sexual orientation. (3, 4, 5)
3. Each family member articulates his/her moral values regarding homosexual practice. (6, 7, 8, 9)
4. Eliminate statements and actions that convey rejection and judgment of the homosexual family member. (10, 11)

THERAPEUTIC INTERVENTIONS

1. Open a forum for discussion regarding how the homosexual preference of a family member became known.
2. Allow for the ventilation of feelings regarding how the family member's sexual orientation is affecting everyone in the immediate family.
3. Open a discussion of family members' views surrounding the issue of heredity versus choice in determining a person's sexual orientation.

5. Express feelings of anger, outrage, alienation, or rejection as a result of the family member's disclosure of his/her sexual orientation. (12, 13, 14, 15, 19)

6. Become more educated by reading about the issue of sexuality. (16, 17)

7. Parents terminate blaming themselves or each other regarding their child's sexual orientation. (18, 19, 20)

8. Family members express fears of "contagion" regarding sexual preferences. (21)

9. Family members confront fears of social reprisal or rejection and develop ways to deal with it other than lying or avoidance. (22, 23, 24)

10. Family members verbalize fears about social rejection. (25, 26)

11. Family members attend a support group for families and friends of homosexuals. (27)

12. Verbalize understanding and acceptance of differing views regarding homosexuality, while embracing each other as loved family members. (28, 29, 30, 31)

13. Demonstrate acceptance of the homosexual family member's choice of a same-sex partner. (32, 33, 34)

14. Family members engage in social activities to build cohesiveness. (35)

4. Talk about how each individual is influenced by family members, peers, and the media during their upbringing, and how this affects sexuality.

5. Discuss some of the research on heredity and sexuality and how sexual preference may be genetically influenced.

6. Have family members express their moral values regarding sexual orientation and how their individual values may differ from those held by others in the family.

7. Help the family members understand how they arrived at their moral values regarding sexual orientation.

8. Help the family develop clarity regarding their religious and moral beliefs and whether or not homosexual behavior violates their religious beliefs.

9. Assess any conflict that exists between family members regarding their differing moral beliefs about sexual orientation.

10. If family members believe that the individual member's homosexual orientation violates their religious beliefs, then brainstorm ways individuals can address this (e.g., speak with their clergy; read literature with a different religious

—. _____
   _____
—. _____
   _____
—. _____
   _____

view; speak to clergy who are more accepting of homosexual behavior).

11. Allow for a discussion of individual freedom to choose sexual practices and each individual family member's accountability for his/her own life choices without being subject to judgment from others.

12. Encourage family members to express their feelings in a manner that promotes release but is respectful of the gay/lesbian family member (e.g., use role-playing, modeling, or assertiveness training).

13. Suggest modes of expression through journal writing, artwork, or other modes that deviate from blunt expression.

14. Explore the family members' emotions and look for homophobic fears or insecurity.

15. Assess whether family members' emotions are based on rational or irrational beliefs. Correct thoughts based on erroneous information.

16. Suggest that the family members read literature in the area of human sexuality, such as *The Family Guide to Sex and Relationships* (Walker) and *A Place at the Table* (Bawer).

17. Discuss with the family what they have read about

sexuality and how this affects their feelings and beliefs.

18. Allow parents to elaborate on why they blame themselves for their child's sexual orientation. Look for instances of guilt or, possibly, fears about their own sexuality.

19. If unresolvable, significant, personal issues of guilt, anxiety, anger, rejection, or depression surface during the family session, suggest the possibility of meeting privately or refer the family member for individual therapy.

20. If parents are blaming each other, interpret externalizing the blame as a defense for their own irrational guilt, fear, disappointment, or worry.

21. Explore family members' fears about their own sexual orientation, referring to educational materials (e.g., *Loving Someone Gay* [Clark]) or specific lectures on the topic in the community.

22. Review with family members what their specific fears are regarding societal reaction to homosexual orientation. Have them rank the fears they consider to be realistic and those they consider unrealistic.

23. Have family members role-play social events that deal

with responding to questions about family members' marital status, sexual orientation, and so on; provide alternative, nondefensive responses.

24. Have family members provide each other with feedback on the role-play.

25. Allow family members to ventilate feelings regarding societal rejection, how this affects them, and the importance to them of social acceptance.

26. Help family members determine whether or not they are indeed experiencing social alienation from others because a member is gay/lesbian and how to cope with this.

27. Recommend that family members attend a support group such as Parents, Families, and Friends of Lesbians and Gays (PFLAG).

28. Brainstorm with family members about commonalities in their beliefs regarding homosexuality and where points of difference exist.

29. Use role-reversal techniques to allow family members to articulate and support the others' opinions so that they can consider some of the opposing views.

30. Encourage cohesiveness within the family and weigh

the costs of remaining divided versus forming more of a bond based on tolerance and acceptance.

31. Review ways that family members can be more supportive of each other (e.g., increasing respectful communication; reinforcing the idea that despite differing sexual orientations, they are still family).

32. Explore what is tolerable and what is not regarding a family member bringing home a same-sex partner (for a visit, for an overnight stay, sleeping together, etc.).

33. Discuss ways to build tolerance for a same-sex partner of a family member and look beyond what might be superficial issues (disregard the individual's clothes and concentrate on the person; appreciate positive character traits, etc.).

34. Have family members make a list of the positive and negative aspects of the family member's same-sex partner and the assets he/she brings to the family.

35. Review activities that the family can engage in that might reinforce family cohesiveness (see Family Activity Disputes in this *Planner*).

—. _____
_____
—. _____
_____
—. _____
_____

DIAGNOSTIC SUGGESTIONS

Axis I: 300.4   Dysthymic Disorder
302.6   Gender Identity Disorder NOS
302.85   Gender Identify Disorder in Adolescents
309.0   Adjustment Disorder With Depressed Mood
309.28   Adjustment Disorder With Mixed Anxiety and
Depressed Mood
309.24   Adjustment Disorder With Anxiety
_____   _____
_____   _____

Axis II: 301.82   Avoidant Personality Disorder
301.6   Dependent Personality Disorder
301.20   Schizoid Personality Disorder
_____   _____
_____   _____

TRAUMATIC LIFE EVENTS

BEHAVIORAL DEFINITIONS

1. A major event has occurred (natural disaster, crime victimization, employment loss, etc.), causing disruption and instability in the family.
2. Family dynamics become more disrupted to the point where specific roles of family members are changed (e.g., one of the children has become parentified), causing an imbalance within.
3. A sense of disengagement occurs with family members, causing feelings of alienation.
4. Feelings of helplessness and hopelessness develop in one or more family members.

—. _____
   _____
—. _____
   _____
—. _____
   _____

LONG-TERM GOALS

1. Face the major event and accept the changes that it has brought, developing new methods for coping.
2. Resolve serious family conflicts and symptoms produced by the trauma or event.
3. Pull together and develop ways to function more cohesively in the face of the major life event.
4. Reestablish healthy and appropriate family role assignments.

—. _____
    _____
    _____

—. _____
    _____
    _____

—. _____
    _____

SHORT-TERM OBJECTIVES

1. Identify the specific traumatic event that has affected the family. (1)

2. Describe the impact the trauma has had on individuals and the family unit. (2)

3. Describe the manner of coping with the event. (3)

4. Describe emotional, cognitive, and behavioral symptoms that have developed since the trauma. (4, 5, 6)

5. Verbalize alternate interpretations of the crisis and list changes that must occur in coping. (7, 8, 9, 10)

6. Implement more adaptive strategies to cope with the trauma. (11, 12)

7. Admit and terminate denial, and identify alternative coping strategies. (13, 14, 15)

8. Each family member identifies his/her own stage of development in reaction to the current situation. (16, 17, 18)

THERAPEUTIC INTERVENTIONS

1. Allow each family member to explain the traumatic event in his/her own words.

2. Facilitate the expression of family members' feelings and begin to discuss the differences in perception of the event and how it has affected each of them differently (e.g., construct lists of changes, make drawings, or write journals or poems).

3. Assess the family's coping with the incidents, using instruments such as The Adolescent-Family Inventories of Life Events and Changes and Family Inventories of Life Events and Changes, in *Family Assessment Inventories for Research and Practice* (McCubbin and Thompson). For smaller children, use picture stories, drawings, or play assessment techniques.

4. Prompt each family member to describe any emotional, cognitive, or behavioral changes that

9. Identify conflicts that have arisen due to various styles of coping and stage of development. (19, 20, 21, 22)

10. Identify role changes that have resulted from the crisis and describe how to restore balance to the dynamics of the family. (23, 24)

11. Engage in group activities as a family unit to build cohesiveness. (25, 26)

12. Identify fears that cause resistance to family unity and cohesiveness. (27, 28)

13. Identify short- and long-term changes that must be achieved in order to resolve conflict and better cope with the crisis. (29, 30, 31)

14. Implement behavioral and cognitive strategies for inoculating against future stress regarding life-changing events. (32)

15. Attend community support groups to aid in crisis management. (33)

16. Verbalize acceptance of the fact that sometimes a situation is out of their control and they must simply cope effectively with it. (34, 35)

__. _____
   _____

__. _____
   _____

__. _____
   _____

have resulted from the trauma.

5. If the event was a major catastrophe (earthquake, assault/murder, robbery, etc.), then address the situation within the framework of a posttraumatic stress reaction; assess for symptoms related to posttraumatic stress disorder or an acute stress reaction.

6. If stress reactions are severe, consider referral of family members for individual treatment (psychologist, psychiatrist, etc.) and maintain collateral involvement with the treating professional.

7. Enlighten the family on how various families cope differently in the face of crisis. Explain how the pre-existing condition of the family predisposes them to deal with such events in a particular way.

8. Facilitate a discussion around what may need to change in the manner of the family's coping with the traumatic event.

9. Brainstorm with family members about how they might begin to introduce change in coping behavior in the face of the current event.

10. Suggest exercises that may help facilitate viewing the trauma differently and re-

acting to it more adaptively (e.g., have them rewrite the story, describing how they could have coped with the situation in a more adaptive fashion).

11. Use role-playing or modeling to teach new ways to react to unexpected, traumatic incidents (e.g., seeing challenges versus defeats, working together to overcome obstacles, relying on spiritual resources).

12. Help each family member adjust to a style of coping that fits best for him/her by using individual strengths as an advantage for self and the family unit.

13. Facilitate family members in admitting to their own denial as a defensive coping strategy in the face of trauma. Use confrontative techniques or metaphors to help draw this out.

14. Have each family member identify alternative behaviors to counteract denial.

15. Facilitate family members' support/reinforcement of each other in overcoming denial and family reality adaptively.

16. Assess the level of adaptive functioning that exists with the family members by using an interview or an inventory (e.g., Stages of Change Questionnaire in *Health Psychology* [Prochaska, et al.]).

17. Share the results of the assessment and lead the family in a discussion of their responses to the results.

18. Explain how their family differs from others and how their stage of development dictates how they cope with and survive traumatic crisis.

19. Have family members describe the conflicts that exist within the family as a result of the crisis and the perceptions that contributed to them.

20. Teach the use of conflict resolution techniques in order to reduce tension in the family. Refer to *Changing Families* (Fassler, Lash, and Ivers). Also, see Adolescent/Parent Conflicts and Child/Parent Conflicts in this *Planner*.

21. Look for any underlying dynamics that may be contributing to the conflict that results from the crisis (jealousy, favoritism, etc.).

22. Bring to light the underlying dynamics that contribute to conflict and have the family work toward resolution.

23. Assist in defining the roles of each family member and discuss how they have come to be (e.g., how a particular child became parentified).

24. Discuss the effects of the crisis on family member roles and how a redefining

of roles may contribute to the lessening of family pressures and tension.

25. Consider using some cohesion-building strategies (e.g., group or family activities with a goal of working together on a particular task).

26. Reinforce the notion that, by engaging in more rewarding family activities, family members will improve the quality of the overall interaction and sense of cohesiveness.

27. Address the issue of any underlying fears (e.g., "If I get too close to you, you will try to control me or I'll lose my autonomy") that might exist regarding intimacy or cohesiveness.

28. Help family members dispel fears of cohesiveness by facing them and considering alternative behaviors (e.g., "I can still be part of the family unit and maintain my autonomy and personal uniqueness") to aid in restructuring their belief systems.

29. Have family members use the Miracle Question in *Clues: Investigating Solutions in Brief Therapy* (DeShazer) by posing the question, "If all of you were to awaken tomorrow and, by way of a miracle, the conflict between you disappeared, how would you know it was gone?"

30. Discuss the Miracle Question responses in order to define the changes that must occur in the family to resolve conflict.

31. Brainstorm with family members to generate a list of behaviors that will facilitate, as well as those that will hinder, conflict resolution and crisis coping.

32. Teach specific stress inoculation techniques (deep breathing, progressive muscle relaxation, cognitive restructuring, etc.) as crisis coping strategies. See "Family Therapy" in *Practicing Cognitive Therapy: A Guide to Interventions* (Dattilio) or *Cognitive Behavior Modification* (Meichenbaum).

33. Help family members identify external support systems in the community to help them to cohesively respond to the crisis.

34. When dealing with problems outside of their control, instruct family members to avoid trying to solve the external problem, but instead to support each other and decide how they can best react to the unchangeable problem.

35. Have family members imagine themselves in the near future coping successfully and share their thoughts about how they will handle the transition regarding the life-changing event.

—. _____
    _____
    _____
—. _____
    _____
    _____
—. _____
    _____

DIAGNOSTIC SUGGESTIONS

Axis I: 309.24   Adjustment Disorder With Anxiety
              309.0   Adjustment Disorder With Depressed Mood
              309.28   Adjustment Disorder With Mixed Anxiety and
                       Depressed Mood
              296.x   Major Depressive Disorder
              V61.1   Partner Relational Problem
              V61.2   Parent–Child Relational Problem
              _____   _____

              _____   _____

Axis II: 301.5   Histrionic Personality Disorder
              301.82   Avoidant Personality Disorder
              301.6   Dependent Personality Disorder
              _____   _____

              _____   _____

UNWANTED/UNPLANNED PREGNANCY

BEHAVIORAL DEFINITIONS

1. A teenage, unmarried family member is pregnant and decides that she wishes to keep and raise the child, contrary to her parents' and other family members' wishes.
2. Tension mounts over the disadvantages of keeping a child out of wedlock or when the mother is so young as opposed to considering abortion or releasing the child for adoption.
3. A moral dilemma arises over the issues of considering abortion or releasing the child for adoption.
4. A parent is unexpectedly pregnant and experiences ambivalence about whether to keep the child, abort, or adopt the child out, because of the parent's age, economic constraints, medical/health problems, and so on.
5. Significant marital and/or family strife develops as a result of keeping the child in the family.
6. Family members become estranged over the issue of the pregnancy and ignore it, choosing not to confront it.
7. Parents who were contemplating divorce now discover they are expecting another child, placing pressure on them to attempt a reconciliation.

—. _____

_____

—. _____

_____

—. _____

_____

LONG-TERM GOALS

1. Arrive at a united decision about how to respond to the unexpected/ unwanted pregnancy.
2. Terminate self-blame and/or blame of others for the pregnancy.
3. Strengthen marital and/or family relationships by working through the dilemma.
4. Reunite estranged family members who have become alienated as a result of the pregnancy.
5. Parents consider pros and cons of reconciliation and whether or not to seek marital therapy for themselves.

—. _____

_____

—. _____

_____

—. _____

_____

SHORT-TERM OBJECTIVES

1. Identify feelings about the pregnancy and attempt to express them constructively. (1, 2, 3)
2. List the alternative courses of action that are available. (4, 5)
3. Pregnant child reviews the options and arrive at a tentative decision. (6, 7)
4. Parents verbalize acceptance of their daughter's right to decide how to react to her pregnancy. (8, 9, 10)
5. Verbalize expectations regarding the future based on the current response plan. (11, 12)

THERAPEUTIC INTERVENTIONS

1. Open a forum for the expression of the emotions of the family members (e.g., fear and guilt on the part of pregnant child, embarrassment and anger on the part of siblings, shame and anger on the part of the parents).
2. Reassure family members that these emotions are normal and real and can be used in the decision-making process.
3. Help family members bring their emotions to a stable level through venting, defining, and bonding and the reassurance of solutions.

6. Identify ways to be supportive of the pregnant child. (13, 14)

7. Express respect for the right of the pregnant child to make the decision for abortion, even if it is contrary to the beliefs of others in the family. (15, 16)

8. Spouse expresses his ambivalence about how to respond to the wife's unexpected pregnancy. (17, 18, 19, 20, 21)

9. Each family member expresses his/her feelings about the addition of a baby to the family. (22, 23)

10. Parent who was contemplating separation or divorce verbalize how this unexpected pregnancy affects that decision. (24)

11. Parents agree to further conjoint counseling. (25, 26)

__. _____
_____

__. _____
_____

__. _____
_____

4. Help the family identify the situation as a crisis and that their initial emotional reaction may be clouding their use of sound judgment.

5. Help the family to define the alternative responses to the pregnancy and reassure them that they have time to consider options.

6. Review with the pregnant child the options of adoption, abortion, or raising the baby and recommend readings (e.g., *In Good Conscience* [Runkle], *Should I Have This Baby* [Jones]).

7. Recommend individual sessions with the pregnant child to evaluate whether her decision is reactionary, influenced by others, or soundly thought through.

8. Encourage the family to be supportive of the pregnant child, to recognize her struggle and fear, and to acknowledge her right to choose a response.

9. Review the concept of each individual's right to make life decisions and also that this does not need to reflect the other family members' moral beliefs or feelings.

10. Explore the parents' feelings of disappointment, loss of control, and fear for the child's and the unborn baby's futures.

11. Promote family discussion on what their expectations for the future are regarding the option selected.

12. Refer the family to other families who may have been in similar situations (e.g., through an unwed mothers' group, adoption agencies, acquaintances).

13. Discuss coping strategies for living with each other after the decision has been made. Talk about appropriate versus inappropriate expressions of anger, fear, frustration, resentment, and guilt.

14. Discuss with family members ways in which to be supportive of one another (e.g., allowing time for venting anger, fear, or sadness); teach reflective listening skills.

15. Meet conjointly with the parents to establish and define what their feelings are regarding abortion and then evaluate how this may be addressed in the course of family therapy.

16. Highlight the need for other family members to respect the rights of the pregnant individual despite any contrary feelings. Also help them recognize that they do not have to own the final choice.

17. If the spouses feel open to discussing the wife's unex-

pected pregnancy with other family members, then review the pros and cons of the response alternatives, remaining sensitive to the anger of the other family members.

18. Explore the parents' ambivalence regarding the unexpected pregnancy, assisting them in clarifying the multiple factors and feelings they see as relevant.

19. If the age or health of the pregnant parent is an issue, support the family in gathering all relevant medical information.

20. Recommend that parents read *Should I Keep My Baby?* (Zimmerman) to help them explore the issue of an unexpected pregnancy.

21. Hold a separate conjoint interview with parents to discuss their feelings about the wife's unexpected pregnancy and any unconscious motives that may contribute to the wife's pregnancy.

22. Explore what the addition of a baby means to each family member and how it will impact their lives. Look for underlying feelings of resentment or jealousy in each family member, confronting any distortions or myths that may be fostering these feelings.

23. Consider the use of some nondirective techniques

such as metaphors (e.g., an addition to the family is like adding extra baggage to an already overloaded cart) to reduce the tension within the family and address the estrangement over the decision to keep the child. Discuss alternative ways of expressing feelings of resentment or discontent with the decision.

24. Discuss the impact that the other children have on the decision regarding whether to continue the marriage relationship. Also have parents consider how their decision will impact the other children.

25. Help the couple consider interim steps (e.g., separating within the household; traveling to the same location in separate vehicles; engaging in activities that give space in the relationship) prior to the decision to announce a separation and/or divorce to the family.

26. Review some of the alternatives to separating and/or refer the couple for conjoint counseling.

___. _____

_____

___. _____

_____

___. _____

_____

DIAGNOSTIC SUGGESTIONS

Axis I:

309.0	Adjustment Disorder With Depressed Mood
309.24	Adjustment Disorder With Anxiety
309.28	Adjustment Disorder With Mixed Anxiety and Depressed Mood
309.4	Adjustment Disorder With Mixed Disturbance of Emotions and Conduct
309.3	Adjustment Disorder With Disturbance of Conduct
300.4	Dysthymic Disorder
296.x	Major Depressive Disorder
V61.1	Partner Relational Problem
V61.2	Parent–Child Relational Problem
308.3	Acute Stress Disorder
_____	_____
_____	_____

Axis II:

301.6	Dependent Personality Disorder
301.83	Borderline Personality Disorder
301.4	Obsessive-Compulsive Personality Disorder
301.81	Narcissistic Personality Disorder
_____	_____
_____	_____

Appendix A

BIBLIOTHERAPY SUGGESTIONS

Note: Most of the inventories and questionnaires on families can be found in their entirety in the following work:

Fischer, J., and K. Corcoran, eds. (1994). *Measures for Clinical Practice: A Sourcebook.* Vol. 1: *Couples, Families, and Children.* New York: Free Press.

Activity/Family Imbalance

Zakich, R. (1995). The UnGame—Family Version. Las Vegas, NV: Taicor, Inc.

Adolescent/Parent Conflicts

Bluestein, J. E. (1993). *Parents, Teens and Boundaries: How to Draw the Line.* Pompano Beach, FL: Health Communications.

Goldberg-Freeman, C. (1996). *Living with a Work in Progress: A Parents Guide to Surviving Adolescence.* Columbus, OH: National Middle School Association.

Guerney, B. (1977). *Relationship Enhancement.* San Francisco: Jossey-Bass.

Markman, H. J., S. Stanley, and S. L. Blumberg (1994). *Fighting for Your Marriage.* San Francisco: Jossey-Bass.

Orvin, G. (1995). *Understanding the Adolescent.* Washington, DC: American Psychiatric Association Press.

Patterson, G. R., and M. Forgatch (1987). *Parents and Adolescents: Living Together.* Vol. 1: *The Basics.* Vol. 2: *Family Problem Solving.* Eugene, OR: Castalia.

York, P., D. York, and T. Wachtel (1983). *Tough Love.* New York: Bantam Books.

Adoption Issues

Deveraux, L. L., and A. J. Hammerman (1998). *Infertility and Identity.* San Francisco: Jossey-Bass.

Gilman, L. (1998). *The Adoption Resource Book.* 4th ed. New York: Harper Perennial.

Glazer, E. S. (1998). *The Long-Awaited Stork.* 2d ed. San Francisco: Jossey-Bass.

Krementz, J. (1997). *How It Feels to Be Adopted.* New York: Alfred A. Knopf.

Alcohol Abuse

Alberti, R. E., and M. L. Emmons (1997). *Your Perfect Right.* San Luis Obispo, CA: Impact Publishers.

Bradshaw, J. (1998). *Bradshaw on the Family.* Deerfield Beach, FL: Health Connection.

Markman, H. J., S. Stanley, and S. L. Blumberg (1994). *Fighting for Your Marriage.* San Francisco: Jossey-Bass.

Miller, W. R., and R. F. Muñoz (1982). *How to Control Your Drinking.* Rev. ed. Albuquerque, NM: University of New Mexico Press.

National Institute on Alcohol Abuse and Alcoholism (1996). *Alcoholism: Getting the Facts* (NIH publication 96-4153). Rockville, MD: Author. (301) 443-3680. www.niaaa.nih.gov.

National Institute on Alcohol Abuse and Alcoholism (1996). *How to Cut Down on Your Drinking* (NIH pamphlet 96-3770). Rockville, MD: Author. (301) 443-3680. www.niaaa.nih.gov.

Anger Management

Alberti, R. E., and M. L. Emmons (1997). *Your Perfect Right.* San Luis Obispo, CA: Impact Publishers.

Carlson, R. (1998). *Don't Sweat the Small Stuff with Your Family.* New York: Hyperion.

Carter, L., and F. Minirth (1993). *The Anger Workbook.* Nashville, TN: Thomas Nelson Publishers.

Weisenberger, P. (1993). *Anger Workout Book.* New York: Quill.

Anxiety

Barlow, D. H., and M. Craske (1994). *Mastering Your Anxiety and Panic—Patient's Workbook.* San Antonio, TX: Psychologial Corporation.

Benson, H. (1975). *The Relaxation Response.* New York: Avon.

Bourne, E. J. (1990). *The Anxiety and Phobia Workbook.* New York: Rawson.

Craske, M. G., D. H. Barlow, and T. A. O'Leary (1992). *Mastery of Your Anxiety and Worry.* San Antonio, TX: Psychological Corporation.

Greist, J., J. Jefferson, and I. Marks (1986). *Anxiety and Its Treatment: Help Is Available.* Washington, DC: American Psychiatric Association Press.

Wilson, R. (1986). *Don't Panic: Taking Control of Anxiety Attacks.* New York: Rawson.

Blame

Beattie, M. (1990). *The Language of Letting Go.* San Francisco: Harper.
Carson, C. (1998). *Forgiveness: The Healing Gift We Give Ourselves.* Nashville, TN: Carlson.
Lukeman, A., and G. Lukeman (1996). *Beyond Blame: Reclaiming the Power You Give to Others.* New York: North Star.

Blended Family Problems

Bray, J. H., and J. Kelly (1998). *Step-Families.* New York: Broadway Books.
Forgatch, M., and G. R. Patterson (1987). *Parents and Adolescents: Living Together.* Vol. 2: *Family Problem Solving.* Eugene, OR: Castalia.
Miller, S., and P. A. Miller (1997). *Core Communications, Skills and Processes.* Littleton, CO: Interpersonal Communications Programs.

Child/Parent Conflicts

Clark, L. (1991). *SOS! Help for Parents: A Practical Guide for Handling Common Everyday Behavior Problems.* Bowling Green, KY: Parents Press.
Joslin, K. R. (1994). *Positive Parenting from A to Z.* New York: Fawcett.

Communication

Alberti, R. E., and M. L. Emmons (1997). *Your Perfect Right.* San Luis Obispo, CA: Impact Publishers.
Carter, L., and F. Minirth (1993). *The Anger Workbook.* Nashville, TN: Thomas Nelson Publishers.
Chapman, J. (1991). *Journaling for Joy.* Hollywood, CA: New Castle Books.
Fassler, D., M. Lash, and S. Ivers (1988). *Changing Families.* Burlington, VT: Waterfront Books.
Markman, H. J., S. Stanley, and S. L. Blumberg (1994). *Fighting for Your Marriage.* San Francisco: Jossey-Bass.
Miller, S., and P. A. Miller (1997). *Core Communications, Skills and Processes.* Littleton, CO: Interpersonal Communications Programs.
Weisenberger, P. (1993). *Anger Workout Book.* New York: Quill.

Compulsive Behaviors

Catalano, E. M., and N. Sonenberg (1993). *Consuming Passions: Help for Compulsive Shoppers.* Oakland, CA: New Harbinger.
Horvath, A. T., and R. K. Hester (1999). *Sex, Drugs, Gambling and Chocolate: A Workbook for Overcoming Addictions.* Atascadero, CA: Impact Publishers.

Markman, H. J., S. Stanley, and S. L. Blumberg (1994). *Fighting for Your Marriage.* San Francisco: Jossey-Bass.

McEnvoy, A. (1991). *Compulsive Gamblers and Their Families.* Holmes Beach, FL: Learning Publications.

Wegscheider-Cruse, S. (1989). *Another Chance: Hope and Health for the Alcoholic Family.* 2d ed. Palo Alto, CA: Science and Behavior Books.

Young, K. S. (1998). *Caught in the Net: How to Recognize the Signs of Internet Addiction—and a Winning Strategy for Recovery.* Somerset, NJ: John Wiley & Sons.

Death of a Child

Buscaglia, L. F. (1983). *The Fall of Freddie the Leaf.* New York: Holt Rinehart & Winston.

Finkbeiner, A. K. (1996). After the Death of a Child. Baltimore, MD: Johns Hopkins.

Sanders, C. M. (1992). *How to Survive the Loss of a Child.* Rocklin, CA: Prima Publishing.

Wholey, D. (1992). *When the Worst That Can Happen Already Has.* New York: Berkley Books.

Death of a Parent

Akner, L. F. (1993). *How to Survive the Loss of a Parent.* New York: William Morrow.

Buscaglia, L. F. (1983). *The Fall of Freddie the Leaf.* New York: Holt Rinehart & Winston.

Davies, P. (1998). *Grief: Climb Toward Understanding.* San Luis Obispo, CA: Sunnybank Publishers.

Gilbirt, R. B., and D. D. Sims (1999). *Finding Your Way after Your Parent Dies.* Boulder, CO: Ave Maria Press.

Nuland, S. B. (1993). *How We Die.* New York: Vintage Books.

Sanders, C. M. (1992). *How to Survive the Loss of a Child.* Rocklin, CA: Prima Publishing.

Volkan, V. V., and E. Zintl (1993). *Life after Loss.* New York: Collier Books.

Wholey, D. (1992). *When the Worst That Can Happen Already Has.* New York: Berkley Books.

Dependency Issues

Beattie, M. (1997). *Beyond Codependency.* San Francisco: Harper.

Beattie, M. (1987). *Codependent No More: How to Stop Controlling Others and Start Caring for Yourself.* San Francisco: Harper.

Beattie, M. (1990). *The Language of Letting Go.* San Francisco: Harper.

Burns, D. D. (1993). *Ten Days to Self-Esteem.* New York: Quill/William Morrow.

Depression in Family Members

Burns, D. D. (1989). *The Feeling Good Handbook: Using the New Mood Therapy in Everyday Life.* New York: William Morrow.

Burns, D. D. (1980). *Feeling Good: The New Mood Therapy.* New York: Signet.

Greenberger, D., and C. A. Padesky (1995). *Mind over Mood.* New York: Guilford Press.

McKay, M., and P. Fanning (1987). *Self-Esteem.* Oakland, CA: New Harbinger.

Slaby, A., and F. Garfinkel (1994). *No One Saw My Pain: Why Teens Kill Themselves.* New York: W. W. Norton.

Disengagement/Loss of Family Cohesion

Markman, H. J., S. Stanley, and S. L. Blumberg (1994). *Fighting for Your Marriage.* San Francisco: Jossey-Bass.

Eating Disorders

Claude-Pierre, P. (1999). *The Secret Language of Eating Disorders: The Revolutionary New Approach.* New York: Vintage Books.

National Institute of Mental Health (1994). *Eating Disorders* (NIMH brochure 94-3477). Bethesda, MD: Author. www.nimh.nih.gov/publist/puborder.htm.

Pipher, M. B. (1995). *Reviving Ophelia.* New York: Ballantine Books.

Extrafamilial Sexual Abuse

Dattilio, F. M. (1994). "Families in Crisis." In F. M. Dattilio and A. Freeman, eds., *Cognitive-Behavioral Strategies in Crisis Intervention* (pp. 278–301). New York: Guilford Press.

Forward, S., and C. Buck (1988). *Betrayal of Innocence.* New York: Penguin Books.

Ruch, L. O., J. W. Gartell, S. R. Amedeo, and B. I. Coyne (1991). "The Sexual Assault Symptom Scale: Measuring Self-Reported Sexual Assault Trauma in the Emergency Room."

Psychological Assessment, 1: 3–8.

Family Member Separation

Jewett, C. (1982). *Helping Children Cope with Separation and Loss.* Cambridge, MA: Harvard University Press.

Lerner, H. (1985). *The Dance of Anger.* New York: Harper Row.

McKay, M., P. D. Rogers, and J. McKay (1989). *When Anger Hurts: Quieting the Storm Within.* Oakland, CA: New Harbinger.

Weisenberger, P. (1993). *Anger Workout Book.* New York: Quill.

Family-of-Origin Interference

Forward, S. (1989). *Toxic Parents.* New York: Bantam Books.

Framo, J. L. (1992). *Family-of-Origin Therapy: An Intergenerational Approach.* New York: Brunner/Mazel.

Incest Survivor

Deblinger, E. and A. Hope-Heflin (1994). "Child Sexual Abuse." In F. M. Dattilio and A. Freeman, eds., *Cognitive-Behavioral Strategies in Crisis Intervention* (pp. 177–199). New York: Guilford Press.

Forward, S., and C. Buck (1988). *Betrayal of Innocence.* New York: Penguin Books.

Fredrickson, R. (1992). *Repressed Memories: A Journey to Recovery from Sexual Abuse.* New York: Fireside.

Infidelity

Pittman, F. (1989). *Private Lies: Infidelity and the Betrayal of Intimacy.* New York: W. W. Norton.

Spring, J. A. (1996). *After the Affair: Healing the Pain and Rebuilding Trust When a Partner Has Been Unfaithful.* New York: HarperCollins.

Interracial Family Problems

Douglass, F. (1995). *Narrative of the Life of Frederick Douglass.* New York: Dover.

Intolerance/Defensiveness

Anderson, K. (1994). *Getting What You Want: How to Reach Agreement and Resolve Conflict Every Time.* New York, NY: Plume.

Gallant, J. (1998). *Simple Courtesies.* Pleasantville, NY: Reader's Digest.

Weeks, D. (1994). *The Eight Essential Steps to Conflict Resolution.* East Rutherford, NJ: Putnum Publication Group.

Zakich, R. (1995). The UnGame—Family Version. Las Vegas, NV: Taicor, Inc.

Jealousy/Insecurity

Ellis, A., and I. Becker (1982). *A Guide to Personal Happiness.* North Hollywood, CA: Wilshire Books.

Friday, N. (1997). *Jealousy.* New York: M. Evans.

Salovey, P. (1991). *The Psychology of Jealousy and Envy.* New York: Guilford Press.

Life-Threatening/Chronic Illness

Minuchin, S. (1974). *Families and Family Therapy.* Cambridge, MA: Harvard University Press.

Wright, L. M., W. L. Watson, and J. M. Bell (1996). *Beliefs: The Heart of Healing in Families and Illness.* New York: Basic Books.

Multiple-Birth Dilemmas

Buscaglia, L. F. (1983). *The Fall of Freddie the Leaf.* New York: Holt Rinehart & Winston.

Seligman, M. E. P. (1998). *Learned Optimism.* New York: Pocket Books.

Viorst, J. (1997). *Necessary Losses.* New York: Simon & Schuster.

Physical/Verbal/Psychological Abuse

Casarjian, R. (1992). *Forgiveness: A Bold Choice for a Peaceful Heart.* New York: Bantam Books.

Evans, P. (1993). *Verbal Abuse Survivors Speak Out: On Relationship and Recovery.* Holbrook, MA: Adams.

Evans, P. (1996). *The Verbally Abusive Relationship: How to Recognize It and How to Respond.* Holbrook, MA: Adams.

Rosellini, G., and M. Worden (1986). *Of Course You're Angry.* San Francisco: Harper Hazelden.

Rubin, T. I. (1969). *The Angry Book.* New York: Macmillan.

Smedes, L. (1991). *Forgive and Forget: Healing the Hurts We Don't Deserve.* San Francisco: Harper.

Weisenberger, P. (1993). Anger Workout Book. New York: Quill.

Religious/Spiritual Conflicts

Haught, J. A. (1995). *Holy Hatred: Religious Conflicts of the 90s.* Chicago: Prometheus Books.

Susek, R., and D. J. Kennedy (1999). *Firestorm: Preventing and Overcoming Church Conflicts.* New York: Baker Book House.

Separation/Divorce

Ahrons, C. (1994). *The Good Divorce: Keeping Your Family Together When Your Marriage Comes Apart.* New York: Harper Perennial.

Bonkowski, S. (1990). *Children Are Nondivorceable.* Chicago: ACTA Publications.

Bonkowski, S. (1990). *Teens Are Nondivorceable.* Chicago: ACTA Publications.

Brown, L. K., and M. Brown (1998). *Dinosaurs Divorce: A Guide for Changing Families.* New York: DEMCO Media.

Gottman, J. (1994). *Why Marriages Succeed and Fail.* New York: Fireside.

Katherine, A. (1991). *Boundaries: Where You End and I Begin.* New York: Fireside.

Krementz, J. (1998). *How It Feels When Parents Divorce.* New York: Alfred A. Knopf.

Markman, H. J., S. Stanley, and S. L. Blumberg (1994). *Fighting for Your Marriage.* San Francisco: Jossey-Bass.

Mayle, P., and A. Robins (1998). *Why Are We Getting a Divorce.* New York: Harmony Books.

Ricci, I. (1997). *Mom's House, Dad's House: A Complete Guide for Parents Who Are Separated, Divorced, or Remarried.* New York: Fireside.

Zakich, R. (1995). The UnGame—Family Version. Las Vegas, NV: Taicor, Inc.

Sexual Orientation Conflicts

Bawer, B. (1993). *A Place at the Table.* New York: Touchtone Books.

Clark, D. (1997). *Loving Someone Gay.* Berkeley, CA: Celestial Arts.

Walker, R. (1996). *The Family Guide to Sex and Relationships.* New York: Macmillian.

Traumatic Life Events

Fassler, D., M. Lash, and S. Ivers (1988). *Changing Families.* Burlington, VT: Waterfront Books.

Unwanted/Unplanned Pregnancy

Jones, C. (1996). *Should I Have This Baby: What to Do When Your Pregnancy Is Unexpected.* Secaucus, NJ: Birch Lane Press.

Runkle, A. (1998). *In Good Conscience: A Practical, Emotional and Spiritual Guide to Deciding Whether to Have an Abortion.* San Francisco, CA: Jossey-Bass.

Zimmerman, M. (1997). *Should I Keep My Baby.* Minneapolis, MN: Bethany House.

Appendix B

INDEX OF DSM-IV CODES ASSOCIATED WITH PRESENTING PROBLEMS

Acute Stress Disorder   308.3
Death of a Child
Death of a Parent
Incest Survivor
Life-Threatening/Chronic Illness
Unwanted/Unplanned Pregnancy

**Adjustment Disorder
Unspecified**   309.9
Family Member Separation

**Adjustment Disorder
With Anxiety**   309.24
Activity/Family Imbalance
Adoption Issues
Anxiety
Blame
Communication
Death of a Child
Death of a Parent
Extrafamilial Sexual Abuse
Family Activity Disputes
Family Member Separation
Financial Changes
Incest Survivor
Infidelity
Intolerance/Defensiveness
Jealousy/Insecurity
Life-Threatening/Chronic Illness
Physical/Verbal/Psychological Abuse
Separation/Divorce
Sexual Orientation Conflicts
Traumatic Life Events
Unwanted/Unplanned Pregnancy

**Adjustment Disorder
With Depressed Mood**   309.0
Activity/Family Imbalance
Adoption Issues
Anger Management
Blame
Communication
Death of a Child
Death of a Parent
Depression in Family Members
Disengagement/Loss of Family
   Cohesion
Extrafamilial Sexual Abuse
Family Activity Disputes
Family Member Separation
Financial Changes
Incest Survivor
Infidelity
Inheritance Disputes between
   Siblings
Intolerance/Defensiveness
Jealousy/Insecurity
Life-Threatening/Chronic Illness
Multiple Birth Dilemmas
Physical/Verbal/Psychological Abuse
Separation/Divorce
Sexual Orientation Conflicts
Traumatic Life Events
Unwanted/Unplanned Pregnancy

**Adjustment Disorder
With Disturbance of Conduct**   309.3
Activity/Family Imbalance
Adolescent/Parent Conflicts

Anxiety Disorder NOS   300.00
  Anxiety
  Life-Threatening/Chronic Illness

**Attention-Deficit/
Hyperactivity Disorder,
Combined Type**   314.01
  Adolescent/Parent Conflicts
  Child/Parent Conflicts

**Avoidant Personality
Disorder**   301.82
  Alcohol Abuse
  Anxiety
  Dependency Issues
  Depression in Family Members
  Disengagement/Loss of Family
    Cohesion
  Family Activity Disputes
  Family Member Separation
  Separation/Divorce
  Sexual Orientation Conflicts
  Traumatic Life Events

Bereavement   V62.82
  Death of a Child
  Death of a Parent
  Depression in Family Members

Bipolar I Disorder   296.5x
  Activity/Family Imbalance
  Anger Management
  Communication
  Compulsive Behaviors
  Depression in Family Members
  Infidelity
  Jealousy/Insecurity

**Bipolar I Disorder,
Single Manic Episode**   296.0x
  Financial Changes

Bipolar II Disorder   296.89
  Activity/Family Imbalance
  Depression in Family Members

**Borderline Personality
Disorder**   301.83
  Adoption Issues
  Anger Management
  Blame
  Communication

  Compulsive Behaviors
  Death of a Child
  Death of a Parent
  Depression in Family Members
  Eating Disorder
  Extrafamilial Sexual Abuse
  Family-of-Origin Interference
  Intolerance/Defensiveness
  Jealousy/Insecurity
  Life-Threatening/Chronic Illness
  Physical/Verbal/Psychological Abuse
  Unwanted/Unplanned Pregnancy

Bulimia Nervosa   307.51
  Eating Disorder

Cannabis Dependence   304.30
  Financial Changes

**Conduct Disorder, Adolescent
Onset Type**   312.8
  Adolescent/Parent Conflicts
  Child/Parent Conflicts

Cyclothymic Disorder   301.13
  Activity/Family Imbalance
  Depression in Family Members
  Infidelity

**Dependent Personality
Disorder**   301.6
  Activity/Family Imbalance
  Adoption Issues
  Alcohol Abuse
  Anxiety
  Death of a Child
  Death of a Parent
  Dependency Issues
  Depression in Family Members
  Eating Disorder
  Family Activity Disputes
  Family Member Separation
  Family-of-Origin Interference
  Infidelity
  Inheritance Disputes between Siblings
  Life-Threatening/Chronic Illness
  Physical/Verbal/Psychological Abuse
  Separation/Divorce
  Sexual Orientation Conflicts
  Traumatic Life Events
  Unwanted/Unplanned Pregnancy

Blame
Communication
Dependency Issues
Disengagement/Loss of Family
   Cohesion
Eating Disorder
Family Activity Disputes
Infidelity
Inheritance Disputes between
   Siblings
Intolerance/Defensiveness
Jealousy/Insecurity
Physical/Verbal/Psychological Abuse
Traumatic Life Events
Unwanted/Unplanned Pregnancy

**Major Depressive Disorder,
Recurrent**   296.3x
   Death of a Child
   Death of a Parent
   Depression in Family Members
   Extrafamilial Sexual Abuse
   Incest Survivor

**Major Depressive Disorder,
Single Episode**   296.2x
   Activity/Family Imbalance
   Compulsive Behaviors
   Death of a Child
   Death of a Parent
   Depression in Family Members
   Extrafamilial Sexual Abuse
   Financial Changes
   Incest Survivor
   Life-Threatening/Chronic Illness

**Narcissistic Personality
Disorder**   301.81
   Activity/Family Imbalance
   Adoption Issues
   Anger Management
   Blame
   Communication
   Family Activity Disputes
   Family Business Conflicts
   Financial Changes
   Infidelity
   Inheritance Disputes between
      Siblings
   Interracial Family Problems

Intolerance/Defensiveness
Jealousy/Insecurity
Unwanted/Unplanned Pregnancy

Neglect of Child   V61.21
   Adolescent/Parent Conflicts
   Child/Parent Conflicts

Neglect of Child (Victim)   995.5
   Adolescent/Parent Conflicts
   Child/Parent Conflicts

No Diagnosis or Condition   V71.09
   Disengagement/Loss of Family
      Cohesion
   Incest Survivor

**Obsessive-Compulsive
Personality Disorder**   301.4
   Adoption Issues
   Compulsive Behaviors
   Eating Disorder
   Financial Changes
   Intolerance/Defensiveness
   Unwanted/Unplanned Pregnancy

**Obsessive-Compulsive
Disorder**   300.3
   Eating Disorder

Occupational Problem   V62.2
   Financial Changes

**Oppositional Defiant
Disorder**   313.81
   Adolescent/Parent Conflicts
   Child/Parent Conflicts
   Extrafamilial Sexual Abuse
   Family Member Separation
   Geographic Relocation
   Incest Survivor
   Separation/Divorce

**Panic Disorder
With Agoraphobia**   300.21
   Anxiety

**Panic Disorder Without
Agoraphobia**   300.01
   Anxiety
   Family Activity Disputes

Communication
Incest Survivor
Physical/Verbal/Psychological Abuse

Postpartum Depression   V61.0
Multiple Birth Dilemmas

**Posttraumatic Stress
Disorder**   309.81
Adoption Issues
Death of a Child
Extrafamilial Sexual Abuse
Incest Survivor

Primary Hypersomnia   307.44
Extrafamilial Sexual Abuse

Primary Insomnia   307.42
Extrafamilial Sexual Abuse
Incest Survivor

**Reactive Attachment
Disorder of Early Childhood** 313.89
Death of a Parent
Dependency Issues
Life-Threatening/Chronic Illness

**Reactive Detachment
Disorder**   313.89
Dependency Issues
Family Member Separation

Religious/Spiritual Problem V62.89
Death of a Child
Death of a Parent

Schizoaffective Disorder   295.70
Depression in Family Members

**Schizoid Personality
Disorder**   301.20
Disengagement/Loss of Family
    Cohesion
Extrafamilial Sexual Abuse
Family Member Separation
Separation/Divorce
Sexual Orientation Conflicts

Selective Mutism   313.23
Separation/Divorce

Selective Uretism   313.23
Family Member Separation

Separation Anxiety Disorder 309.21
Death of a Parent
Dependency Issues
Family Member Separation
Life-Threatening/Chronic Illness
Separation/Divorce

Sexual Abuse of Child   V61.21
Adolescent/Parent Conflicts
Child/Parent Conflicts
Extrafamilial Sexual Abuse
Incest Survivor

Sexual Abuse of Child (Victim) 995.5
Adolescent/Parent Conflicts
Child/Parent Conflicts
Extrafamilial Sexual Abuse
Incest Survivor

Sibling Relational Problem   V61.8
Blended Family Problems

Social Phobia   300.23
Anxiety

Specific Phobia   300.29
Anxiety

Transient Tic Disorder   307.21
Family Member Separation

REFERENCES

Budman, S. H., and A. S. Gurman (1988). *Theory and Practice of Brief Therapy.* New York: Guilford Press.

Consumer Reports (January 1995). "Does Therapy Help?" 734–739.

Crane, D. R. (1995). "Health Care Reform in the United States: Implications for Training and Practice in Marriage and Family Therapy." *Journal of Marital and Family Therapy,* 21(2): 115–125.

Kaufman, T. S., and H. Coale (1993). *The Combined Family: A Guide to Creating Successful Step-Relationships.* New York: Plenum Press.

Markman, H., S. Stanley, and S. L. Blumberg (1994). *Fighting for Your Marriage.* San Francisco: Jossey-Bass.

Novaco, R. (1975). *Anger Control: The Development and Evaluation of an Experimental Treatment.* Lexington, MA: D.C. Heath/Lexington Books.

O'Leary, K. D., R. E. Heyman, and A. E. Jongsma (1998). *The Couples Psychotherapy Treatment Planner.* New York: John Wiley & Sons.

Piercy, F. P., D. H. Sprenkle, J. L. Wetchler, and Associates. (1996). *The Family Therapy Sourcebook.* 2d ed. New York: Guilford Press.

Shore, M. F. (1996). "An Overview of Managed, Behavioral Healthcare." In M. F. Shore, ed., *Managed Care, the Private Sector and Medicaid, Mental Health and Substance Abuse Services.* San Francisco: Jossey-Bass.

BIBLIOGRAPHY

Achenbach, T. M. (1992). *Manual for the Child Behavior Checklist / 2–3 and 1992 Profile.* Burlington, VT: Department of Psychiatry, University of Vermont.

Ahrons, C. (1994). *The Good Divorce: Keeping Your Family Together When Your Marriage Comes Apart.* New York: Harper Perennial.

Akner, L. F. (1993). *How to Survive the Loss of a Parent.* New York: William Morrow.

Alberti, R. E., and M. L. Emmons (1997). *Your Perfect Right.* San Luis Obispo, CA: Impact Publishers.

American Psychiatric Association (1994). *Diagnostic and Statistical Manual of Mental Disorders.* 4th ed. Washington, DC: Author.

Anderson, K. (1994). *Getting What You Want: How to Reach Agreement and Resolve Conflict Every Time.* New York, NY: Plume.

Antonovsky, A., and T. Sourani (1988). "Family Sense of Coherence and Family Adaptation." *Journal of Marriage and Family Therapy,* 50: 79–92.

Barlow, D. H., and M. Craske (1994) *Mastering Your Anxiety and Panic—Patient's Workbook.* San Antonio, TX: Psychological Corporation.

Bawer, B. (1993). *A Place at the Table.* New York: Touchtone Books.

Beattie, M. (1997). *Beyond Codependency.* San Francisco: Harper.

Beattie, M. (1987). *Codependent No More: How to Stop Controlling Others and Start Caring for Yourself.* San Francisco: Harper.

Beattie, M. (1990). *The Language of Letting Go.* San Francisco: Harper.

Beck, A. T. (1989). *Beck Hopelessness Scale.* San Antonio, TX: Psychological Corporation.

Beck, A. T., A. Freeman, and associates (1990). *Cognitive Therapy of Personality Disorders.* New York: Guilford Press

Beck, A. T., and R. A. Steer (1990). *Beck Anxiety Inventory Manual.* San Antonio, TX: Psychological Corporation/Harcourt Brace Jovanovich.

Beck, A. T., and R. A. Steer (1987). *Manual for the Revised Beck Depression Inventory.* San Antonio, TX: Psychological Corporation.

Beck, J. S. (1995). *Cognitive Therapy: Basics and Beyond* (p. 202). New York: Guilford Press.

Benson, H. (1975). *The Relaxation Response.* New York: Avon.

Birchler, G. R. (1979). *The Inventory of Rewarding Activities.* Unpublished manuscript. San Diego, CA: Veterans Administration Medical Center and University of California Medical School.

Bluestein, J. E. (1993). *Parents, Teens and Boundaries: How to Draw the Line.* Pompano Beach, FL: Health Communications.

Bonkowski, S. (1990). *Children Are Nondivorceable.* Chicago: ACTA Publications.

Bonkowski, S. (1990). *Teens Are Nondivorceable.* Chicago: ACTA Publications.

Bourne, E. J. (1990). *The Anxiety and Phobia Workbook.* New York: Rawson.

Bradshaw, J. (1998). *Bradshaw on the Family.* Deerfield Beach, FL: Health Connection.

Bray, J. H., and J. Kelly (1998). *Step-Families.* New York: Broadway Books.

Brown, L. K., and M. Brown (1998). *Dinosaurs Divorce: A Guide for Changing Families.* New York: DEMCO Media.

Burns, D. D. (1989). *The Feeling Good Handbook: Using the New Mood Therapy in Everyday Life.* New York: William Morrow.

Burns, D. D. (1980). *Feeling Good: The New Mood Therapy.* New York: Signet.

Burns, D. D. (1993). *Ten Days to Self-Esteem.* New York: Quill/William Morrow.

Buscaglia, L. F. (1983). *The Fall of Freddie the Leaf.* New York: Holt Rinehart & Winston.

Carlson, R. (1998). *Don't Sweat the Small Stuff with Your Family.* New York: Hyperion.

Carson, C. (1998). *Forgiveness: The Healing Gift We Give Ourselves.* Nashville, TN: Carlson.

Carter, L., and F. Minirth (1993). *The Anger Workbook.* Nashville, TN: Thomas Nelson Publishers.

Casarjian, R. (1992). *Forgiveness: A Bold Choice for a Peaceful Heart.* New York: Bantam Books.

Catalano, E. M., and N. Sonenberg (1993). *Consuming Passions: Help for Compulsive Shoppers.* Oakland, CA: New Harbinger.

Chambless, D. L., G. C. Caputo, and P. Bright (1984). Assessment of Fear of Fear in Agoraphobia: The Body Sensations Questionnaire and the Agoraphobic Questionnaire. *Journal of Consulting and Clinical Psychology,* 52: 1090–1097.

Chapman, J. (1991). *Journaling for Joy.* Hollywood, CA: New Castle Books.

Clark, D. (1997). *Loving Someone Gay.* Berkeley, CA: Celestial Arts.

Clark, L. (1991). *SOS! Help for Parents: A Practical Guide for Handling Common Everyday Behavior Problems.* Bowling Green, KY: Parents Press.

Claude-Pierre, P. (1999). *The Secret Language of Eating Disorders: The Revolutionary New Approach.* New York: Vintage Books.

Conners, G. J., and S. A. Maisto (1988). "Alcohol Beliefs Scale." In M. Hersen and A. S. Bellack, eds., *Dictionary of Behavioral Assessment Techniques* (pp. 24–26) New York: Pergamon Press.

Constantine, L. (1978). "Family Sculpture and Relationship Wrapping Techniques." *Journal of Marriage and Family Counseling,* 4(2): 13–23.

Consumer Reports (January 1998). "Financial Fixers and Fakers." 31–35.

Covey, Stephen. (1997). *The Seven Habits of Highly Effective Families: Building a Beautiful Family Culture in a Turbulent World.* New York: Golden Books.

Craske, M., and D. Barlow (1992). *Mastering Your Anxiety and Worry: Patient's Workbook.* San Antonio, TX: Psychological Corporation.

Craske, M. G., D. H. Barlow, and T. A. O'Leary (1992). *Mastery of Your Anxiety and Worry.* San Antonio, TX: Psychological Corporation.

Dattilio, F. M., ed. (1998). *Case Studies in Couples and Family Therapy: Systemic and Cognitive Perspectives.* New York: Guilford Press.

Dattilio, F. M. (1994). "Families in Crisis." In F. M. Dattilio and A. Freeman, eds., *Cognitive-Behavioral Strategies in Crisis Intervention* (pp. 278–301). New York: Guilford Press.

Dattilio, F. M. (1997). "Family Therapy." In R. Leahy, ed., *Practicing Cognitive Therapy: A Guide to Interventions.* (pp. 409–450). New York: Jason Aronson.

Dattilio, F. M., and C. A. Padesky (1990). *Cognitive Therapy with Couples.* Sarasota, FL: Professional Resource Press.

Davies, P. (1998). *Grief: Climb Toward Understanding.* San Luis Obispo, CA: Sunnybank Publishers.

Deblinger, E., and Hope-Heflin, A. (1994). "Child Sexual Abuse." In F. M. Dattilio and A. Freeman, eds., *Cognitive-Behavioral Strategies in Crisis Intervention* (pp. 177–199). New York: Guilford Press.

DeShazer, S. (1988). *Clues: Investigating Solutions in Brief Therapy.* New York: W. W. Norton.

Deveraux, L. L., and A. J. Hammerman (1998). *Infertility and Identity.* San Francisco: Jossey-Bass.

Dinkmeyer, D., G. D. McKay, and D. Dinkmeyer (1997). *The Parents Handbook. STEP.* Westminster, MD: Random House.

Douglass, F. (1995). *Narrative of the Life of Frederick Douglass.* New York: Dover.

D'Zurilla, T. J., and A. Nezu (1992). "Development and Preliminary Evaluation of the Social Problem Solving Inventory (SPSI)." *Psychological Assessment,* 2: 156–163.

Ellis, A., and I. Becker (1982). *A Guide to Personal Happiness.* North Hollywood, CA: Wilshire Books.

Evans, P. (1993). *Verbal Abuse Survivors Speak Out: On Relationship and Recovery.* Holbrook, MA: Adams.

Evans, P. (1996). *The Verbally Abusive Relationship: How to Recognize It and How to Respond.* Holbrook, MA: Adams.

Fassler, D., M. Lash, and S. Ivers (1988). *Changing Families.* Burlington, VT: Waterfront Books.

Finkbeiner, A. K. (1996). *After the Death of a Child.* Baltimore, MD: Johns Hopkins.

Finkelhor, D., S. Araju, L. Baron, A. Browne, S. D. Peters, and G. E. Wyatt, eds. (1986). *A Sourcebook of Child Sexual Abuse.* Beverly Hills, CA: Sage.

Fischer, J., and K. Corcoran, eds. (1994). *Measures for Clinical Practice: A Sourcebook.* Vol. 1: *Couples, Families and Children.* New York: Free Press.

Forgatch, M., and G. M. Patterson (1998). "Behavioral family therapy." in F. M. Dattilio, ed., *Case Studies in Couple and Family Therapy: Systemic and Cognitive Perspectives.* New York: Guilford Press.

Forgatch, M., and G. R. Patterson (1987). *Parents and Adolescents: Living Together.* Vol. 1: *The Basics.* Vol. 2: *Family Problem Solving.* Eugene, OR: Castalia.

Forward, S. (1989). *Toxic Parents*. New York: Bantam Books.

Forward, S., and C. Buck (1988). *Betrayal of Innocence*. New York: Penguin Books.

Framo, J. L. (1992). *Family-of-Origin Therapy: An Integrational Approach*. New York: Brunner/Mazel.

Fredrickson, R. (1992). *Repressed Memories: A Journey to Recovery from Sexual Abuse*. New York: Fireside.

Friday, N. (1997). *Jealousy*. New York: M. Evans.

Friedrich, W. N. (1990). *Psychotherapy of Sexually Abused Children and Their Families*. New York: W. W. Norton.

Gallant, J. (1998). *Simple Courtesies*. Pleasantville, NY: Reader's Digest.

Gardner, R. A. (1973). *The Thinking, Feeling, and Doing Game: A Therapeutic Game for Children*. Cresskill, NJ: Creative Therapeutics.

Garner, D. M. (1991). Eating Disorder Inventory-2. Odessa, FL: Psychological Assessment Resources.

Gilbirt, R. B., and D. D. Sims (1999). *Finding Your Way after Your Parent Dies*. Boulder, CO: Ave Maria Press.

Gilman, L. (1998). *The Adoption Resource Book*. 4th ed. New York: Harper Perennial.

Glazer, E. S. (1998). *The Long-Awaited Stork*. 2d ed. San Francisco: Jossey-Bass.

Goldberg-Freeman, C. (1996). *Living with a Work in Progress: A Parents Guide to Surviving Adolescence*. Columbus, OH: National Middle School Association.

Goolishian, H. A., and H. Anderson (1987). "Language System and Therapy: An Evolving Idea." *Psychotherapy*, 24: 259–538.

Gordon, T. (1990). *PET: Parent Effectiveness Training*. Chicago: New American Library Trade.

Gottman, J. (1994). *Why Marriages Succeed and Fail*. New York: Fireside.

Green, R. G., M. S. Kolevzon, and N. R. Vosler (1985). "The Beavers-Timberlawn Model of Family Competence and the Circumplex Model of Family Adaptability and Cohesion: Separate but Equal? *Family Process*, 24: 385–398.

Greenberger, D., and C. A. Padesky (1995). *Mind over Mood*. New York: Guilford Press.

Greist, J., J. Jefferson, and I. Marks (1986). *Anxiety and Its Treatment: Help Is Available*. Washington, DC: American Psychiatric Association Press.

Guerney, B. (1977). *Relationship Enhancement*. San Francisco: Jossey-Bass.

Haley, J. (1976). *Problem-Solving Therapy*. New York: Harper Colophon.

Haley, J. (1987). *Problem-Solving Therapy*. 2d ed. San Francisco: Jossey-Bass.

Hathaway, S. R., and J. C. McKinley (1989). Minnesota Multiphasic Personality Inventory-2. Minneapolis, MN: University of Minnesota Press.

Haught, J. A. (1995). Holy Hatred: Religious Conflicts of the 90s. Chicago: Prometheus Books.

Heitler, S. (1990). *From Conflict to Resolution: Skills and Strategies for Individual, Couple and Family Therapy*. New York: W. W. Norton.

Herzberger, S. D., E. Chan, and J. Katz (1984). "The Development of an Assertiveness Self-Report Inventory." *Journal of Personality Assessment*, 48: 317–323.

Horvath, A. T., and R. K. Hester (1999). *Sex, Drugs, Gambling and Chocolate: A Workbook for Overcoming Addictions.* Atascadero, CA: Impact Publishers.

Hovestadt, A. J., W. T. Anderson, F. A. Piercy, S. W. Cochran, and M. Fine (1985). "Family-of-Origin Scale." *Journal of Marital and Family Therapy,* 11(3): 287–297.

Hudson, W. N. (1992). *The Walmyr Assessment Scales Scoring Manual.* Tempe, AZ: Walmyr Publishing.

Jewett, C. (1982). *Helping Children Cope with Separation and Loss.* Cambridge, MA: Harvard University Press.

Jones, C. (1996). *Should I Have This Baby: What to Do When Your Pregnancy Is Unexpected.* Secaucus, NJ: Birch Lane Press.

Joslin, K. R. (1994). *Positive Parenting from A to Z.* New York: Fawcett.

Kagan, D. M., and R. L. Squires (1985). "Measuring Non-Pathological and Compulsiveness." *Psychological Reports,* 57: 559–563.

Katherine, A. (1991). *Boundaries: Where You End and I Begin.* New York: Fireside.

Kaufman, T. S., and H. Coale (1993). *The Combined Family: A Guide to Creating Successful Step-Relationships.* New York: Plenum Press.

Kendall, P. C. (1990). *Coping Cat Workbook* (available from the author, Department of Clinical Psychology, Temple University, Philadelphia, PA 19122).

Kovacs, M. (1983). *The Children's Depression Inventory: A Self-Rated Depression Scale for School-Aged Youngsters.* New York: Multi-Health Systems.

Krementz, J. (1997). *How it Feels to Be Adopted.* New York: Alfred A. Knopf.

Krementz, J. (1998). *How It Feels When Parents Divorce.* New York: Alfred A. Knopf.

Kushner, H. S. (1997). *How Good Do We Have to Be?* New York: Little Brown.

Lerner, H. (1985). *The Dance of Anger.* New York: Harper Row.

Lukeman, A., and G. Lukeman (1996). *Beyond Blame: Reclaiming the Power You Give to Others.* New York: North Star.

Markman, H. J., S. Stanley, and S. L. Blumberg (1994). *Fighting for Your Marriage.* San Francisco: Jossey-Bass.

Mayle, P., and A. Robins (1998). *Why Are We Getting a Divorce.* New York: Harmony Books.

McCubbin, H. I., and A. I. Thompson, eds. (1991). *Family Assessment Inventories for Research and Practice.* Madison, WI: University of Wisconsin.

McEnvoy, A. (1991). *Compulsive Gamblers and Their Families.* Holmes Beach, FL: Learning Publications.

McKay, M., and P. Fanning (1987). *Self-Esteem.* Oakland, CA: New Harbinger.

McKay, M., P. D. Rogers, and J. McKay (1989). *When Anger Hurts: Quieting the Storm Within.* Oakland, CA: New Harbinger.

Meichenbaum, D. (1977). *Cognitive Behavior Modification.* New York: Plenum Press.

Miller, S. and P. A. Miller (1997). *Core Communications, Skills and Processes.* Littleton CO: Interpersonal Communications Programs.

Miller, W. R., and R. F. Muñoz (1982). *How to Control Your Drinking.* Rev. ed. Albuquerque, NM: University of New Mexico Press.

Minuchin, S. (1974). *Families and Family Therapy.* Cambridge, MA: Harvard University Press.

National Institute on Alcohol Abuse and Alcoholism (1996). *Alcoholism: Getting the Facts* (NIH publication 96-4153). Rockville, MD: Author. (301) 443-3860. www.niaaa.nih.gov.

National Institute on Alcohol Abuse and Alcoholism (1996). *How to Cut Down on Your Drinking* (NIH pamphlet 96-3770). Rockville, MD: Author. (301) 443-3860. www.niaaa.nih.gov.

National Institute of Mental Health (1994). *Eating Disorders* (NIMH brochure 94-3477). Bethesda, MD: Author. www.nimh.nih.gov/publist/puborder.htm.

Nelson, T. S., and T. S. Trepper, eds. (1993). *101 Interventions in Family Therapy*. New York: Haworth Press.

Nelson, T. S., and T. S. Trepper, eds. (1998). *101 More Interventions in Family Therapy*. New York: Haworth Press.

Novaco, R. (1975). *Anger Control: The Development and Evaluation of an Experimental Treatment*. Lexington, MA: D. C. Heath/Lexington Books.

Nuland, S. B. (1993). *How We Die*. New York: Vintage Books.

O'Leary, K. D., R. F. Heyman, and A. E. Jongsma (1998). *The Couples Psychotherapy Treatment Planner*. New York: John Wiley & Sons.

Olson, D. H. (1986). "Circumplex Model VII: Validation Studies and FACES-III. *Family Process,* 25: 337–351.

Orvin, G. (1995). *Understanding the Adolescent*. Washington, DC: American Psychiatric Association Press.

Patterson, G. R., and M. Forgatch (1987). *Parents and Adolescents: Living Together*. Vol 1: *The Basics*. Vol. 2: *Family Problem Solving*. Eugene, OR: Castalia.

Phelan, T. W. (1996). *1-2-3 Magic: Effective Discipline for Children 2–12*. Minneapolis, MN: Child Management.

Piercy, F. P., D. H. Sprenkle, J. L. Wetchler, and associates (1996). *The Family Therapy Sourcebook*. 2d ed. New York: Guilford Press.

Pipher, M. B. (1995). *Reviving Ophelia*. New York: Ballantine Books.

Pittman, F. (1990). *Private Lies: Infidelity and the Betrayal of Intimacy*. New York: W. W. Norton.

Prochaska, J. O., W. F. Velicer, J. S. Rossi, M. G. Goldstein, B. H. Marcus, W. Rakowski, C. Fiore, L. L. Harlow, C. A. Redding, D. Rosenbloom, and S. R. Rossi (1994). "Stages of Change and Decisional Balance for 12 Problem Behaviors." *Health Psychology,* 13: 39–46.

Resick, P. A., S. A. Falsetti, H. S. Resnick, and D. G. Kilpatrick (1991). *Modified Posttraumatic Symptom Scale*. Charleston, SC: Medical University of South Carolina.

Ricci, I. (1997). *Mom's House, Dad's House: A Complete Guide for Parents Who Are Separated, Divorced, or Remarried*. New York: Fireside.

Robin, A. L., T. Koepke, and A. Moye (1990). "Multidimensional Assessment of Parent-Adolescent Relations." *Psychological Assessment,* 2: 451–459.

Roehling, P. V., and A. L. Robin (1986). "Development and Validation of the Family Beliefs Inventory: A Measure of Unrealistic Beliefs Among Parents and Adolescents." *Journal of Consulting and Clinical Psychology,* 54: 693–697.

Rosellini, G., and M. Worden (1986). *Of Course You're Angry*. San Francisco: Harper Hazelden.

Rubin, T. I. (1969). *The Angry Book.* New York: Macmillan.

Ruch, L. O., J. W. Gartell, S. R. Amedeo, and B. I. Coyne (1991). "The Sexual Assault Symptom Scale: Measuring Self-Reported Sexual Assault Trauma in the Emergency Room." *Psychological Assessment:* 1, 3–8.

Runkle, A. (1998). *In Good Conscience: A Practical, Emotional and Spiritual Guide to Deciding Whether to Have an Abortion.* San Francisco, CA: Jossey-Bass.

Salovey, P. (1991). *The Psychology of Jealousy and Envy.* New York: Guilford Press.

Sanders, C. M. (1992). *How to Survive the Loss of a Child.* Rocklin, CA: Prima Publishing.

Satir, V. (1988). *The New People Making.* Palo Alto, CA: Science and Behavior Books.

Satir, V., and M. Baldwin (1983). *Satir Step-by-Step.* Palo Alto, CA: Science and Behavior Books.

Schumm, W. R., A. P. Jurich, and S. R. Bollman (1986). "Characteristics of the Kansas Family Life Satisfaction Scale in a Regional Sample." *Psychological Reports,* 58: 975–980.

Seligman, M. E. P. (1998). *Learned Optimism.* New York: Pocket Books.

Slaby, A., and F. Garfinkel (1994). *No One Saw My Pain: Why Teens Kill Themselves.* New York: W. W. Norton.

Smedes, L. (1991). *Forgive and Forget: Healing the Hurts We Don't Deserve.* San Francisco: Harper.

Sobell, M. B., and L. C. Sobell (1978). *Behavioral Treatment of Alcohol Problems.* New York: Plenum Press.

Spring, J. A. (1996). *After the Affair: Healing the Pain and Rebuilding Trust When a Partner Has Been Unfaithful.* New York: HarperCollins.

Spielberger, C. D. (1983). *Manual for the State-Trait Anxiety Inventory (STAI Form Y).* Palo Alto, CA: Consulting Psychologists Press.

Straus, M. A., and R. J. Gelles (1990). *Physical Violence in American Families: Risk Factors and Adaptations to Violence in 8,145 Families.* New Brunswick, NJ: Transaction.

Stuart, R. B. (1980). *Helping Couples Change: A Social Learning Approach to Marital Therapy.* New York: Guilford Press.

Stuart, R. B. (1995). *Family of Origin Inventory.* New York: Guilford Press.

Susek, R., and D. J. Kennedy (1999). *Firestorm: Preventing and Overcoming Church Conflicts.* New York: Baker Book House.

U.S. Department of Agriculture. *Family Economics Review.* Washington, DC: U.S. Government Printing Office.

Viorst, J. (1997). *Necessary Losses.* New York: Simon & Schuster.

Volkan, V. V., and E. Zintl (1993). *Life after Loss.* New York: Collier Books.

Walker, R. (1996). *The Family Guide to Sex and Relationships.* New York: Macmillian.

Weeks, D. (1994). *The Eight Essential Steps to Conflict Resolution.* East Rutherford, NJ: Putnum Publication Group.

Wegscheider-Cruse, S. (1989). *Another Chance: Hope and Health for the Alcoholic Family.* 2d ed. Palo Alto, CA: Science and Behavior Books.

Weisenberger, P. (1993). *Anger Workout Book.* New York: Quill.

Wholey, D. (1992). *When the Worst That Can Happen Already Has.* New York: Berkley Books.

Wilson, R. (1986). *Don't Panic: Taking Control of Anxiety Attacks.* New York: Rawson.

Wright, L. M., W. L. Watson, and J. M. Bell (1996). *Beliefs: The Heart of Healing in Families and Illness.* New York: Basic Books.

York, P., D. York, and T. Wachtel (1983). *Tough Love.* New York: Bantam Books.

Young, K. S. (1998). *Caught in the Net: How to Recognize the Signs of Internet Addiction—and a Winning Strategy for Recovery.* Somerset, NJ: John Wiley & Sons.

Zakich, R. (1995). The UnGame—Family Version. Las Vegas, NV: Taicor, Inc.

Zimmerman, M. (1997). *Should I Keep My Baby.* Minneapolis, MN: Bethany House.

ABOUT THE DISK*

TheraScribe® 3.0 and 3.5 Library Module Installation

The enclosed disk contains files to upgrade your TheraScribe® 3.0 or 3.5 program to include the behavioral definitions, goals, objectives, and interventions from *The Family Therapy Treatment Planner.*

Note: You must have TheraScribe® 3.0 or 3.5 for Windows installed on your computer in order to use *The Family Therapy Treatment Planner* library module.

To install the library module, please follow these steps:

1. Place the library module disk in your floppy drive.
2. Log in to TheraScribe® 3.0 or 3.5 as the Administrator using the name "Admin" and your administrator password.
3. On the Main Menu, press the "GoTo" button, and choose the Options menu item.
4. Press the "Import Library" button.
5. On the Import Library Module screen, choose your floppy disk drive a:\ from the list and press "Go." Note: It may take a few minutes to import the data from the floppy disk to your computer's hard disk.
6. When the installation is complete, the library module data will be available in your TheraScribe® 3.0 or 3.5 program.

Note: If you have a network version of TheraScribe® 3.0 or 3.5 installed, you should import the library module one time only. After importing the data, the library module data will be available to all network users.

User Assistance

If you need assistance using this TheraScribe® 3.0 or 3.5 add-on module, contact Wiley Technical Support at:

Phone: 212-850-6753
Fax: 212-850-6800 (Attention: Wiley Technical Support)
E-mail: techhelp@wiley.com

---

*Note: This section applies only to the book with disk edition, ISBN 0-471-34769-8.

For information on how to install disk, refer to the **About the Disk** section on page 319.

CUSTOMER NOTE:* IF THIS BOOK IS ACCOMPANIED BY SOFTWARE, PLEASE READ THE FOLLOWING BEFORE OPENING THE PACKAGE.

This software contains files to help you utilize the models described in the accompanying book. By opening the package, you are agreeing to be bound by the following agreement:

This software product is protected by copyright and all rights are reserved by the author, John Wiley & Sons, Inc., or their licensors. You are licensed to use this software on a single computer. Copying the software to another medium or format for use on a single computer does not violate the U.S. Copyright Law. Copying the software for any other purpose is a violation of the U.S. Copyright Law.

This software product is sold as is without warranty of any kind, either express or implied, including but not limited to the implied warranty of merchantability and fitness for a particular purpose. Neither Wiley nor its dealers or distributors assumes any liability for any alleged or actual damages arising from the use of or the inability to use this software. (Some states do not allow the exclusion of implied warranties, so the exclusion may not apply to you.)

WILEY

Publishers Since 1807

*Note: This section applies only to the book with disk edition, ISBN 0-471-34769-8.